A guide to the abbeys of Scotland

By the same author

A guide to the cathedrals of Britain (1980)
A guide to the abbeys of England and Wales (1985)

A guide to the abbeys of Scotland

with priories and collegiate churches

Anthony New

Constable London

First published in Great Britain 1988
by Constable and Company Limited
10 Orange Street London WC2H 7EG
Copyright ©1988 by Anthony New
Photoset by Rowland Phototypesetting Limited
Bury St Edmunds, Suffolk
Printed in Great Britain by
The Bath Press Limited, Bath

British Library CIP data
New, Anthony S. B.
A guide to the abbeys of Scotland.
1. Abbeys – Scotland – Guide-books
2. Scotland – Description and travel –
1981 – – Guide-books
I. Title
914.11′04858   DA875

ISBN 0 09 467190 7

Contents

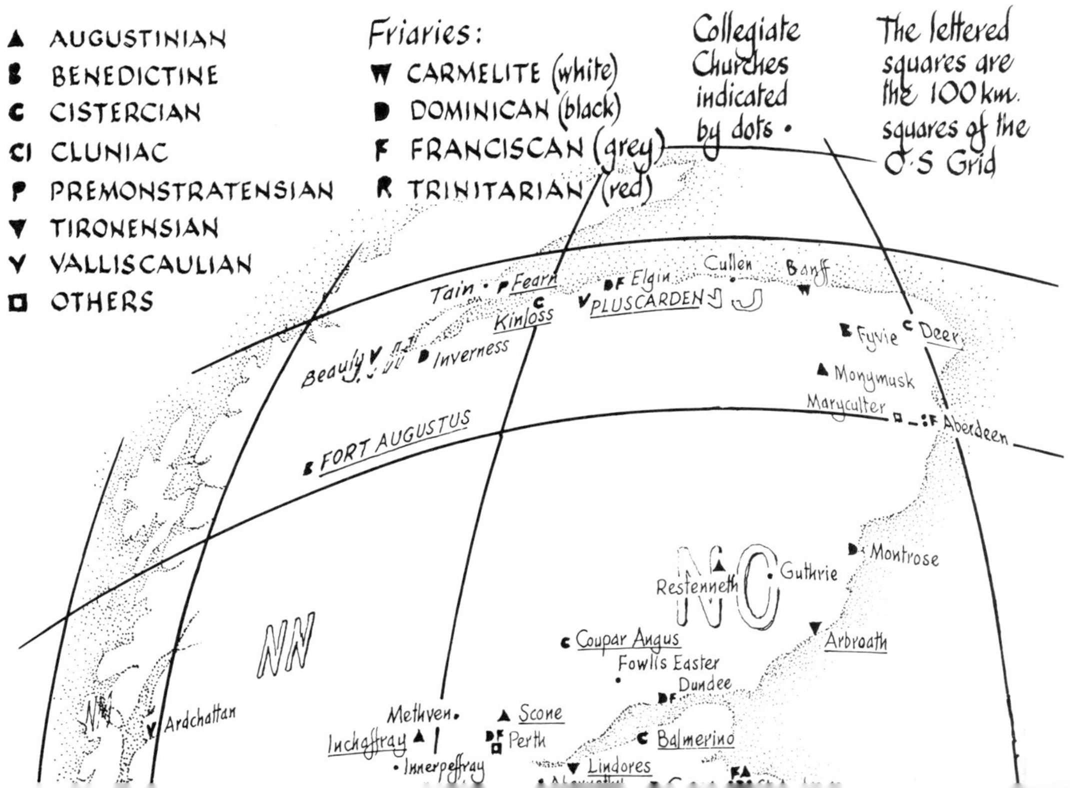

The lettered squares are the 100 km. squares of the O.S Grid

Collegiate Churches indicated by dots.

Friaries:
- ▼ CARMELITE (white)
- ◗ DOMINICAN (black)
- F FRANCISCAN (grey)
- R TRINITARIAN (red)

- ▲ AUGUSTINIAN
- ■ BENEDICTINE
- C CISTERCIAN
- CI CLUNIAC
- P PREMONSTRATENSIAN
- ▼ TIRONENSIAN
- Y VALLISCAULIAN
- □ OTHERS

NN

Ardchattan

Beauly ▼ Pᵐ ◗ Inverness

FORT AUGUSTUS

Methven ▲ Ardchattan
Inchaffray ▲ I
Innerpeffray

▲ Scone
◗ Perth

Coupar Angus
Fowlis Easter
Dundee

Lindores
Balmerino

Tain • Fearn ▲
KINLOSS

DF Elgin Cullen Banff
PLUSCARDEN

■ Fyvie C Deer

Monymusk
Marycultar

■ Aberdeen

Restennet
C Guthrie

• Montrose

Arbroath

FA

NO

NJ

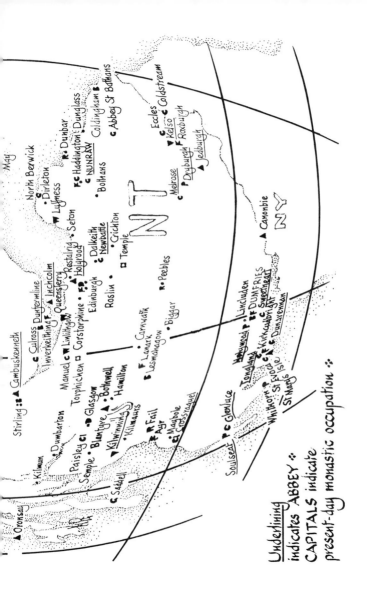

May

North Berwick
Dirleton
Lyghness
R. Dunbar
F,c Haddington : Dunglass
Seton
NUNRAW
Bothans
Coldingham B
Abbey St Bothans

Eccles
c Coldstream
V Kelso F Roxburgh
P Dryburgh F
Jedburgh

c Melrose

Stirling :B ▲ Cambuskenneth

c Culross Dunfermline
Inverkeithing F ▲ Inchcolm
Manuel w Linlithgow Queensferry
Torphichen □ Corstorphine F,P
Restalrig
Holyrood
Edinburgh Newbattle
Roslin
□ Temple

Dalkeith
Crichton

N
T

Kilmun
Dumbarton
Paisley C,I Glasgow
Semple ● Blantyre ● Bothwell
Kilwinning S Hamilton
Kilmaurs
R Fail
Ayr
Maybole
El Crossraguel
Sadell

R. Peebles
Biggar
F Lanark Carnwath
B Lesmahagow

Lincluden
Tongland F DUMFRIES
Whithorn P c Kirkcudbright
St Ninians Isle
Dundrennan
St Marys
Soulseat P c Glenluce

Canonbie

NY

Illustrations

All photographs are by the author

Maps and diagrams

(Those abbeys, friaries, priories and collegiate churches whose plans are unknown appear alphabetically in the main text)

Map of the abbeys, friaries, priories and collegiate churches of Scotland **6**

Introduction

Though this volume supplements the *Guide to the Abbeys of England and Wales* (Constable 1985), its scope is a good deal wider. That came about because the wealth of abbeys in Scotland proved too much for the size of the first book; transferred to this volume however they still left space for similar descriptions of the lesser and associated communities – priories, friaries and collegiate churches. Scottish cathedrals are all described in the *Guide to the Cathedrals of Britain* (Constable 1980), but I felt it would be useful to repeat here in full the four which qualify for both books: the abbey of Iona, the priories of St Andrews and Whithorn, and the collegiate church of St Giles in Edinburgh.

In selecting sites and buildings for inclusion my principal mentor has been Dr D. E. Easson's pioneer work *Medieval Religious Houses, Scotland* (1957). He sifted the evidence for and against the very existence of hundreds of establishments and discarded a large proportion as 'not proven'. Of those whose foundation is in no doubt, I have myself rejected many more on the grounds that they have left no traces and cannot therefore be of much interest to the traveller. They are however listed in an appendix and I would be pleased to transfer any of them to the main list (in the event of there being a future edition) if incontrovertible evidence turns up in the form of minor remains or of the survival of street or similar names.

Monastic history

The documentation of Scottish monasteries is much less complete, and their histories are rather less uniform than those of English, or even Welsh, ones. To begin in the mists of the fourth, fifth and sixth centuries, there were the Celtic clergy, essentially monastic in their organisation unlike other Western churches at that period, and to them we owe foundations like Iona and Abernethy. Then there were the Culdees, about whose exact status and origins much learned argument has raged. For our purposes they can be thought of as Celtic monks who in the twelfth and thirteenth centuries were gradually assimilated by the regular 'foreign' orders.

At this point it may be helpful to explain briefly the purposes and origins of monastic life, which may be regarded as having formally begun under the influence of St Benedict towards the end of the fifth century. His Rule, composed for his own community of Subiaco in Italy, has formed the basis for all others. Wars and strife throughout the so-called Dark Ages smothered the spread of his teachings and discouraged the revivals promoted from time to time by his successors though an exception was the abbey of Cluny (Burgundy), founded in 910 by William, duke of Aquitaine, which prospered under a succession of notable abbots and had powerful influences in many parts of Western Europe. Many orders found it difficult to dissociate prosperity from a decline in observance of their original ideals, and there arose new, stricter ones such as the Carthusian whose monks lived in separate cells within a main enclosure and took their name (anglicised as Charterhouse) from La Grande Chartreuse in Dauphiné, and the Cistercian, founded in 1098 at Cîteaux in Burgundy.

The Cistercian order owed its spread to St Bernard, who went to Cîteaux in 1113 and two years later became abbot of its daughter house Clairvaux. By the time he died in 1153 there were 330 Cistercian houses, mostly in Europe but some in the Near East, all loosely linked in allegiance to Cîteaux. A century later there were some 700. Their monks were distinguished by wearing white habits instead of black.

St Augustine introduced the Rule of St Benedict into Britain in 597, but centuries were to pass before its influence spread into the Celtic area. Eventually it was mostly bands from England who 'colonised' Scotland as forerunners of the same orders who had

crossed into England from the Continent in the wake of the
Normans. Thus the Benedictines of Dunfermline came from
Canterbury, the Augustinians at Scone from Nostell priory in
Yorkshire, the Cistercians of Melrose from Rievaulx and the
Premonstratensians of Dryburgh from Alnwick. Of several
Tironensian houses the earliest, soon removed to Kelso, was at
Selkirk with monks probably sent direct from Tiron in France. The
Valliscaulian order, which bypassed England altogether, came from
Val des Choux in Burgundy and founded three priories about 1230
(one of them, Pluscarden, only became an abbey in modern times
under the Benedictines). There was one Charterhouse, at Perth,
one Gilbertine house briefly at Dalmilling, Ayrshire, and two or
three of Cluniacs from Reading and Wenlock.

The orders of canons, as distinct from monks, aimed to combine
the idea of community life with that of serving cathedrals and parish
churches, rather in the way that Benedictines do today; but
eventually when most monks became priests the distinction became
blurred. The first fully recognised order of canons was the
Augustinian, founded on the Rule of St Augustine of Hippo (not
the English Augustine), which came into prominence about the
time of the Norman Conquest. These were the Black or Austin
Canons. Augustinian houses were independent of each other, and
the priories seem often not to have aspired to become abbeys.

In a similar relationship to the Augustinian canons as the
Cistercian monks were to the Benedictine were the White or
Premonstratensian canons, named after St Norbert's abbey of
Prémontré near Laon in Picardy.

St Andrews and Whithorn became cathedral priories, served
respectively by Augustinian and Premonstratensian canons.

Nunneries, the few that there were in Scotland, were mostly
Cistercian, the earliest being probably that at Berwick-on-Tweed.
The Benedictine, Augustinian, Dominican and Franciscan nuns
seem to have been represented by one or at the most two
authenticated houses.

In these early times Scotland could hardly be called a single
united country. Not only were the local lords (who in many
instances founded the abbeys and priories) the effective rulers
rather than the king, but also the arrangement of archdioceses
meant that quite large areas came under either York or Nidaros

(Trondheim) in Norway. What might be termed the frontier with
England was seldom a very definite line, but for the present purpose
the long-standing existing boundary is taken – excluding as a result
Berwick-on-Tweed which as well as its nunnery had several
important friaries.

The various orders of friars, the wandering preachers, began to
appear in Scotland in the 1230s – the Blackfriars or Dominicans, the
Greyfriars or Franciscans, and the Red Friars or Trinitarians (who
were really canons). The White Friars or Carmelites arrived in
Berwick in 1270 and in Aberdeen shortly afterwards, but the
Augustinian or Austin Friars never really got further than Berwick.
Whereas monks usually sought solitude, the friars were to be found
at the centres of population, and built large churches which have
now mostly been swept away. Of the Franciscans there were two
kinds, the Friars Minor Conventual and the Observants; the latter
arrived from Holland as late as 1447.

The military orders, the Knights Templars and Knights
Hospitallers, were little represented in Scotland – in fact by a total
of three houses only although they owned other property in many
places.

Scottish collegiate churches, each with its own 'college' of secular
clergy, began to be set up about the middle of the fourteenth
century. Unlike England, the country had no surviving (or revived)
tradition of such colleges unless the Culdees are so regarded.
Indeed the first had been based a century earlier on the previously
Culdee church of St Mary on the Rock at St Andrews. That church
and a handful of others (some of them surprisingly small) were
subsequently designated chapels royal. The usual pattern for
collegiate establishments was for a provost, about six or eight
prebendaries, canons or chaplains, a number of singing boys and
perhaps some bedesmen. Some had a dean and vice-dean instead of
a provost, and two (King's College, Aberdeen and St Salvator's
College, St Andrews) were the nuclei of important academic
foundations. In many cases town churches acquired collegiate status
through civic influence, that being only a short step from the
possession of a number of chantry chapels each with its own priest.
To English eyes it seems extraordinary that such collegiate churches
were still being set up well into the 1540s when the Reformation
further south was a *fait accompli*.

It is something of a paradox in Scottish monastic history that the processes of decline were accompanied in this way by at least local indifferences to it, and neither the mob violence generated by John Knox and his followers nor the wanton destruction wrought by English soldiery under the Earl of Hertford brought about a dissolution as immediate and clear-cut as Henry VIII's. Nevertheless decline and decay were inescapable but they were spread over many decades and were largely brought about by a slow insidious infiltration of lay control into the monastic estates. Noblemen, who in England would have been rewarded openly by the king with one or more monastic estates already 'dissolved', became in Scotland 'commendators' or lay abbots and slowly bled the revenues that passed into their control – to the extent that one by one the abbeys and priories became extinct. The monks died out because eventually there were none to replace them, and because their buildings were ruined or put to other uses. In fact all remaining monasteries were formally annexed to the Crown in 1587, but that in itself did not prevent monks staying on *sine die* in some houses.

The friaries fared worst from the Reformers through being in towns where they were prey to the full fury of anti-Catholic mobs. The collegiate buildings on the other hand mostly continued to serve the Reformed Church, which cared little for their contents or antiquity and in the course of the next century or two rebuilt many of them in a box-like manner. Those that passed to farm uses are, by the irony of fate, often better preserved.

Whereas in England a large proportion of monastic buildings were converted, some with considerable ingenuity, into mansions, that happened to a much less extent north of the Border. Newbattle was an exception. More typical were Dryburgh and Lindores which descended to farm use, Kilwinning and Fearn where part at least of the site remained in church hands, or Arbroath and Kinloss where the abbot's or commendator's house was kept up and the remainder fell to ruin. A certain respectability was attached to the sites, and it was common for local lairds to appropriate chapels or other compartments, even unroofed, as mausolea for themselves and their descendants. Nearly everywhere the processes of decay were hastened by townspeople using the buildings as quarries for squared stone, and such stones can frequently be detected all round the district, in buildings now of some antiquity themselves. Naturally that happened less in the more isolated cases: Dryburgh and Crossraguel are relatively complete, and Inchcolm remarkably so.

The eighteenth-century cult of admiring ruins for their own sake, with their quota of owls and ivy and musings on the transitoriness of life, spread into Scotland to some degree. It was Sir Walter Scott whose *Lay of the Last Minstrel* contained the well-known lines

> If thou wouldst view fair Melrose aright
> Go visit it by the pale moonlight

and it was in his time that the magnificent S doorway of Dryburgh was dismantled and installed in a mansion some seven miles away. But as the nineteenth century progressed, so a proper understanding of the value of these remains grew. Archaeologists learned to investigate, architects learned to conserve rather than 'restore', and statutory authorities learned to preserve, all trying to avoid the kinds of destruction that had gone before. But it was a slow and often painful process: Trinity College, Edinburgh, was swept away for Waverley Station in 1848, and the Greyfriars church in Aberdeen was deliberately destroyed as late as 1903. By the time protection, or in many cases actual care, by the State (initially in the persons of the Commissioners of Woods and Forests) was provided, an immense amount had been irretrievably lost. What remains, though a mere fraction of the original, is still an enormously rich heritage.

In the fastnesses of the Highlands and Western Isles Roman Catholicism never fully died out. But it was not till after the repeal of the Penal Laws that it could be properly re-established and this form of worship made legal again. In comparison with England, however, there are few present-day monastic communities of any size. The principal are Fort Augustus where abbey and boys' school occupy the miraculously converted old fortress amongst some of the most magnificent scenery in the country, Pluscarden whose long-derelict medieval buildings are busy again with monks, and Nunraw, the totally modern Cistercian foundation high on the Lammermuir Hills. Perhaps there should be added Iona, where the Church of Scotland has revived something very much akin to the monastic way of life.

Monastic layouts

The layout of medieval abbeys and priories became so standardised
that even from ruined fragments it is usually quite easy to identify
the principal parts which remain and the likely positions of those
which have disappeared. The hub of the plan is the cloister, the four
covered walks forming a square around the cloister garth or court
which often contained a well. The positions of all the other
buildings depended on water – the leat or lead (usually an artificial
diverted channel) which supplied the kitchen and washplace, and
the drain that took wastes first from the kitchen and then from the
reredorter or latrines. In the bigger monasteries the system of water
supply and disposal became extremely complex, sometimes
involving dams and long aqueducts, branch cannels and sluices, and
services to outlying buildings, as well as the maintenance of the
stews or fishponds on which the community depended for much of
its food.

So if these watercourses were to the S of the cloister the kitchen
and reredorter were built there; the exact position of the latter
might be determined by the position and direction of flow of a
natural stream – which ideally would be from W to E. In between
would stand the refectory or dining hall. The church would then be
planned to the N of the cloister.

Where, less commonly, the church is S of the cloister it is usually
because the water was to the N of the site, as at Balmerino. That
was less satisfactory because it overshadowed the cloister badly,
especially in more northern latitudes. Either way, the chapter
house, the general meeting room of the monastery, opened off the
E walk. Over that at first-floor level ran the dorter or monks'
dormitory, which was connected to the church by a night stair, to
the cloister at its further corner by a day stair, and to the reredorter
at its far end. If the monastery prospered and the chapter house was
rebuilt to a bigger scale, it was placed clear of the main E range,
leaving the original chapter house as a vestibule over which the
dorter could still pass, as probably happened at Dunfermline.
Usually the dorter was longer than one side of the cloister, so that
beneath its end part was space variously used for a parlour,
common room or novices' room – or for similar purposes. In this
region there was also a calefactory or warming room (the only
heated room apart from the kitchen), placed so that some of its

warmth would reach the refectory. Outside the refectory would be a washing trough and probably some provision for towels. A slype or covered passage led from the cloister to the outer court. Usually there was another space between the chapter house and the church, which became used as a sacristy, treasury or library; book cupboards were sometimes also formed nearby in the cloister.

The church was usually approached from the corners of the cloister by two processional doorways. Its size varied enormously – from the great length of St Andrews with its full nave and quire aisles and transept aisle too, to the modest and plain cruciform structures that sufficed for such isolated communities as Fearn and Saddell. There was a firm division between the lay, western, and monastic, eastern, parts in the form of a pulpitum or screen – not by any means always coinciding with any architectural division between nave and quire. This was particularly important in Cistercian churches, where the lay brothers occupied the W end, and it was retained (as at Melrose) even after they had died out.

The tendency for churches to be extended westwards in the later Middle Ages to accommodate numerous additional chapels and shrines was much less marked than in England, and even in the Border abbeys such as Melrose and Jedburgh such enlargements were quite modest. Conversely, reductions in numbers of brethren prompted some communities to economise by making their churches smaller; Crossraguel and Inchcolm, weakened by English raids, are examples.

The W range of cloister buildings was put to various uses. In Cistercian houses it was used by the lay brothers or *conversi*. They were workers rather than monks. As they did most of the building work, they were the first to be established and thus their quarters are often the oldest buildings on a Cistercian site. Their dormitory also connected with the church, but at its W end. Beneath were store rooms, and at the further end the lay brothers' own kitchen, refectory and common room. Their reredorter or *necessarium* was placed where best it could be, close to the dorter and to drainage. There are no instances in Scotland of the 'lane' and parallel W range occasionally incorporated into Cistercian plans to insulate the calm of the cloister from the bustle of the lay brothers, though Melrose went a stage further and provided them with their own complete cloister. Lay brothers died out in the fourteenth and fifteenth

centuries, and their buildings were either taken down or put to
other uses.

A further Cistercian peculiarity is the change to a north-south
orientation of the refectory sometimes adopted in bigger houses on
rebuilding. Melrose is an instance.

Though in every order the Rule enjoined the abbot or prior to
sleep with his brethren, in fact it became common in later years for
him to have his own quarters and even in many cases (as at
Arbroath and Crossraguel) his own house with a high degree of
personal comfort, not to say ostentation. This arrangement was to
suit the Scottish system of lay abbots or commendators very well
and so has left a bigger proportion of survivals than in England.

The larger monasteries also had a separate infirmary building,
though few in Scotland remain recognisable. Like the abbot's or
prior's house, its siting was dictated by water supply and drainage as
well as convenience of access, and no particular standard
relationship existed. The same applied to many other buildings
within the precinct: guest house, corrodiars' (pensioners') houses,
almonry, brewhouse, stables and stores of many kinds. The precinct
itself usually had a not inconsiderable wall, sometimes with turrets
at intervals and with one or more gatehouses allowing separate
entry for foot traffic and wheeled vehicles and controlled by a porter
with his own lodging. A small prison was often provided too, for the
sake of good order and discipline, as at Pluscarden.

Further afield, sometimes at great distances, were other buildings
associated with the monastery – daughter houses in the form of
priories or cells, granges (working farms), teind (tithe) barns, mills
etc. Parish churches were frequently served by canons from an
abbey or priory, and there was very often a *capella ante portas* or
chapel outside the gates where pilgrims could pray before entering.
Pilgrims coming to shrines in the monastery church were a principal
source of revenue, but most income was derived from commercial
enterprise in farms, forests and orchards.

So far as medieval architectural styles are concerned, the reader
is referred to the numerous books on Romanesque and Gothic
building, which do however seldom give very much information on
Scotland. Until the later fourteenth century the course of
development ran virtually parallel to that in England, though
possibly lagging a decade or two in the adoption of changes in

fashion, and certainly seldom displaying the excesses of ornament indulged in by, for example, the masons of the Midlands limestone belt. Nor was there in Scotland any true equivalent of Saxon although a number of interesting examples do survive of pre-Norman work of robust character which suggests a good deal more concern for defence than beauty.

The Normans carried their own round-arched style right up to the north. Early Gothic with its pointed arches and greater interest in elegance and ornament followed in its wake, and the so-called Decorated which was marked by a multiplication of shafts in the openings, cusping in tracery, and a modest blossoming of naturalistic ornament. Coarse stones – sandstone and granite – inhibited in many areas the development of schools of masons and carvers as skilled as those with access to kinder materials, but it would be unfair to judge too harshly when so much has been destroyed by time and weather and in the name of religion.

From the latter part of the fourteenth century Scotland's worsening relations with England and stronger ties with the Continent had a marked influence, and the distinctive Flamboyant style was brought over from France. Really only a development of Decorated, and tame indeed by comparison with the contemporary excesses of the Ile de France and the Loire valley, it is characterised by flame-like or flowing tracery patterns, often of considerable complexity and in complete contrast to the Perpendicular that spread throughout England at the same time. Nevertheless forms of Perpendicular are to be found, as at Melrose. Another feature of late medieval work in Scotland is the reappearance of the round arch in doorways. Sometimes these have been mistaken for Norman, but the mouldings are quite different even in the simplest examples.

Little need be said in the present context about the Classical revival of the seventeenth and eighteenth centuries, except that it produced innumerable somewhat barn-like preaching churches throughout the country, a few of which, such as Fearn and Kilwinning, were incorporated into monastic sites. The nineteenth-century Gothic revival is however a different matter, for its influence can be seen in so many rebuildings and more or less well-meant 'restorations'. The earlier, often shallow and mechanically finished work of architects like William Burn gave way to the more thoughtful rebuildings by Sir Robert Rowand Anderson and later to the idiosyncrasies and whimsies of Sir Robert Lorimer – the latter a strangely false interpretation of Scots character having little in common with the robust honesty of real Gothic.

As for more recent work, the use of traditional materials has to give way to the realisms of economy. If glass fibre has to be used for essential repairs like the vaults of Kirkwall cathedral and Haddington church, it is infinitely better than that the buildings should suffer from want of repair and deprive their users and their admirers of a vital part of their heritage. On a brand new site at Nunraw the Cistercians are building an abbey in a totally 'modern' idiom, maintaining their traditional rejection of unnecessary ornament, while on long-hallowed Iona plans exist for extending the abbey buildings in a manner very much closer to the true vernacular of the Isles.

The drawn plans

An understanding of monastic remains is almost always aided by a plan, and one of the aims of this book is to provide one, wherever possible, which shows what *was* in a clear relationship to what *is*; for this reason I have used different conventions from those in my *Cathedrals* book in this series.

So far as possible, monastic (or collegiate) walls, of whatever period, still visible are shown in full thick line; interrupted ('dotted') thick lines indicate walls proved by excavation but no longer uncovered. Later walls, i.e. post-Dissolution of whatever period, are in thinner line, and where they themselves have disappeared these thinner lines are dotted. Distinct script and block lettering will also help to separate original and modern features (in the interesting case of Fort Augustus abbey it is the modern walls, conversely, which are monastic). Very fine interrupted lines indicate conjectures (or in some cases earlier buildings lying beneath). Areas now roofed or vaulted (whatever their age) are shaded in half-tone; these, together with the arrow indicating the usual point of entry, will be found of considerable help in the often baffling task of getting one's bearings on arrival at a site. Existing roads and paths of significance are lightly dotted. All plans are to a scale of 1:2500.

Visits

In every case I have given a six-figure standard Ordnance Survey grid reference, which locates each building or site to within 100 metres. These relate best to the 1 : 50,000 O.S. maps, or to the 1 inch to 1 mile edition that preceded them, but can of course be used with those of larger or smaller scales.

I have also indicated ownerships, whether buildings are open to the public, and if so at what times. However, conditions may well have changed, perhaps even before the book is in print. If a church key is kept in a different place, local enquiry will usually produce it, though sometimes at the expense of a good deal of time. If 'official' opening hours have changed, however, there is usually little one can do – especially at isolated sites, the custodian of which may live some distance away.

Ownerships can be broadly classified as State, Church and private. 'State' may mean the Crown Estates Commissioners (i.e., strictly speaking, royal ownership) or the Secretary of State for Scotland, but the latter is in some cases the guardian and not the legal owner. Newbattle is an exception in having been bequeathed to the Scottish nation; it is administered as an educational college. There are also instances of National Trust and local authority ownership. Usually, fixed visiting hours are set (with or without an admission fee), but some smaller ruins are accessible at all times without hindrance. Where 'standard' hours are quoted for sites in Secretary of State guardianship they are 9.30 a.m. (but 2 p.m. Sundays) to 7 p.m. (but to 4 p.m. from October to March).

'Church' may mean Church of Scotland (Presbyterian), or Episcopal, or Roman Catholic. In the course of history the majority of medieval churches in more or less uninterrupted use have passed to the Church of Scotland. Those of the Episcopalians ('piskies') are mostly nineteenth-century, though there is the occasional exception as at Queensferry where they rescued the friary church from ruin. The 'working' monasteries are of course Roman Catholic, and although their churches are open all day the remainder is seldom accessible.

The size and hence the upkeep of monastic and collegiate churches in use being greater on the average than most, some help is always welcomed – in lieu of the admission charge one would expect to pay to see a ruin.

Private owners can impose what restrictions they like (though the giving of grants for repairs is usually accompanied by conditions for public access which have to be complied with) and I owe it to them not to imply otherwise. It is only common courtesy to seek permission before going on to such land, though of course one may have to set foot on it for that very purpose; better still is to write in advance, but either way a warm welcome may well ensue once one has made one's interests clear. It is perfectly understandable that unidentified strangers may be suspected of poaching, letting dogs loose on farms or roaming with metal detectors and it need hardly be said that ideas of that kind are better dispelled before they even arise.

Ownership being sometimes in the names of trusts or companies rather than individuals – a kind of information rather outside the scope of the book – I have mostly limited myself to giving family names.

Much of the information can be examined in fuller detail in numerous other publications, notably the inventories of the Royal Commission on Historic Monuments (Scotland) and the guidebooks of the Department of the Environment available at many of the State-administered sites. In every case I have checked these on site so as to bring them up to date, for it is surprising to what extent surroundings change, new discoveries are made, churches are re-ordered and even ruins are re-roofed. I am greatly indebted to church ministers and custodians, abbots and property owners, not only for their trouble in checking many of my descriptions, but also for their courtesy in allowing access, and these few lines fall far short of an adequate expression of my gratitude to them all – particularly those who have set me off in the direction of things I might otherwise have missed.

Where there are gaps in the plans – and there are many – it is simply because information is not available. In towns particularly, exploration of known sites is often precluded by later buildings or roads – which sometimes totally obscure them. There is nevertheless a fascination in trying to relate the past to the present, whether the past is buried beneath traffic or represented by a few jagged stones in an isolated field. In searching out information amongst the records and reports of archaeologists, especially those of the last century, it is not always evident which wall-lines were

positively identified and which were the results of conjecture or
zealous imagination. I have perhaps tended to give the benefit of
doubt in one or two such cases, both for the sake of the heightened
interest of more complete plans and because one can seldom go
very far wrong in locating the principal parts of a layout as
standardised as that of a medieval monastery, so that their
guesswork is likely to have been somewhere near the truth.

A further difficulty is the over-enthusiasm of 'restorers', who with
more money than sensitiveness have sometimes muddled the
evidence. Obvious examples are the adding of the false cloister at
Kelso and Burn's meddlings with St Giles', Edinburgh and with
Dunfermline, all of which tend to become inseparable in the
public's mind from the genuine history of the buildings.

Summary

The follow table summarises the main points of interest to visitors under various headings, the symbol ○ meaning 'good' and ● 'poor'.

architecture   ○ moderately important ○○ of particular importance (including post-monastic)
fittings and monuments   ○ good ○○ exceptional
setting   ● poor ○ attractive ○○ specially fine
guide   ○ leaflet available at site ○○ more lavish illustrated book available at site
restrictions   ● limited times (or parts) of access ●● no public access ●●● exterior not visible to public
accessibility   ● physically difficult
extent   ○ considerable remains ○○ unusually complete ○○○ 'live' community ● little to be seen above ground ●● exact site uncertain

	archi-tecture	fittings and monu-ments	setting	guide	restric-tions	accessi-bility	extent
Abbey St Bathans Priory			○	○			
Aberdeen: Blackfriars							●●
Aberdeen: Greyfriars	○		○		●		
Aberdeen: King's College	○	○○	○	○○			○○
Aberdeen: St Nicholas	○○	○○	○	○			○○
Aberdeen: Whitefriars							●●
Abernethy Priory	○						
Arbroath Abbey	○		○	○○			○○
Ardchattan Priory	○	○	○○		●		○
Ayr: Greyfriars	○	○	○		●		○
Balmerino Abbey	○		○				○
Banff: Whitefriars							●●
Beauly Priory	○	○	○	○			○
Biggar Collegiate Church	○						○
Blantyre Priory			○○			●	●
Bothans Collegiate Church	○		○○		●		○

	archi-tecture	fittings and monu-ments	setting	guide	restric-tions	accessi-bility	extent
Bothwell Collegiate Church	○	○		○○			○
Cambuskenneth Abbey	○		○	○			○
Canonbie Priory							●
Carnwath Collegiate Church				○			○
Coldingham Priory	○○			○○			○
Coldstream Priory			○				●●
Corstorphine Collegiate Church	○	○		○			○
Coupar Angus Abbey							●
Crail Collegiate Church	○	○	○		●		○
Crichton Collegiate Church	○		○○	○			○
Crossraguel Abbey	○		○○	○○			○○
Cullen Collegiate Church	○	○○	○	○○			○
Culross Abbey	○		○○				○
Cupar: Blackfriars							●●
Dalkeith Collegiate Church	○				●		○
Deer Abbey	○		○○	○			○
Dirleton Collegiate Chapel	○		○○	○			○
Dryburgh Abbey	○○		○○	○○			○○
Dumbarton Collegiate Church							
Dumfries: Greyfriars							●●
Dumfries Priory	○	○			●		○○○
Dunbar Collegiate Church	○	○	○				
Dunbar: Red Friars							
Dundee: Greyfriars				○○			●●
Dundrennan Abbey	○○		○	○			○○

	architecture	fittings and monuments	setting	guide	restrictions	accessibility	extent
Dunfermline Abbey	○○	○		○○			○○
Dunglass Collegiate Church	○		○○	○			○
Eccles Priory			○				
Edinburgh: Blackfriars							●●
Edinburgh: Greyfriars	○	○○	○	○			
Edinburgh: St Giles	○○	○○	○	○○			○○
Edinburgh: Trinity College	○		●		●●		○
Elgin: Blackfriars							●●
Elgin: Greyfriars		○			●		○
Fail: Red Friars							●
Fearn Abbey	○						○
Fort Augustus Abbey	○○	○	○○	○○	●		○○○
Fowlis Easter Collegiate Church	○○	○○		○			○○
Fyvie Priory							●●
Glasgow: Blackfriars			●				●●
Glasgow: Tron Kirk	○						
Glenluce Abbey	○		○	○			○○
Guthrie Collegiate Church			○				○
Haddington Collegiate Church	○○	○	○	○			○○
Haddington: Greyfriars							●●
Haddington Priory							●●
Hamilton Collegiate Church	○	○		○			
Holyrood Abbey	○○		○	○○			○
Holywood Abbey							●●
Inchaffray Abbey			○				
Inchcolm Abbey	○○	○	○○	○○		●	○○
Inchmahome Priory	○	○	○○	○		●	○○

	archi- tecture	fittings and monu- ments	setting	guide	restric- tions	accessi- bility	extent
Innerpeffray Collegiate Church	o	o	o				oo
Inverkeithing: Greyfriars	o				●		
Inverness: Blackfriars			●				●
Iona Abbey	oo	o	oo	oo		●	oo
Iona Priory	o		o			●	oo
Jedburgh Abbey	oo		o	oo			oo
Kelso Abbey	oo		o				o
Kilmaurs Collegiate Church	o	o		oo			o
Kilmun Collegiate Church			o	o			
Kilwinning Abbey	o		●				o
Kinloss Abbey							
Kirkcudbright: Greyfriars		o		o			o
Lanark: Greyfriars							●●
Lesmahagow Priory				o			
Lincluden Collegiate Church	o			o			o
Lindores Abbey							
Linlithgow: Whitefriars							●●
Loch Leven Priory			o		●●●	●	
Luffness: Whitefriars							
Manuel Priory							
Maryculter Preceptory							
May Priory			o		●	●	●
Maybole Collegiate Church	o				●		o
Melrose Abbey	oo			oo			oo
Methven Collegiate Church				oo			
Montrose: Blackfriars							●●
Monymusk Priory	o		o				o

	archi-tecture	fittings and monu-ments	setting	guide	restric-tions	accessi-bility	extent
Newbattle Abbey	○	○	○		●		
North Berwick Priory			○				
Nunraw Abbey	○				●		○○○
Nunraw Old Abbey	○		○		●		○○
Oronsay Priory	○		○			●	○○
Paisley Abbey	○○	○		○○			○○
Peebles Collegiate Church							
Peebles: Red Friars	○						
Perth: Blackfriars							●●
Perth: Charterhouse							●●
Perth: Greyfriars							●●
Pittenweem Priory	○			○	●		
Pluscarden Abbey	○○	○	○○	○○	●		○○○
Queensferry: Whitefriars	○		○	○			○
Restalrig Collegiate Church	○			○○			
Restennet Priory	○		○○				○
Rosslyn Collegiate Chapel	○○	○	○	○○			○○
Roxburgh: Greyfriars							●●
Saddell Abbey		○	○○			●	
St Andrews: Blackfriars	○						●
St Andrews: Greyfriars							●●
St Andrews Priory	○○	○	○○	○○			○○
St Andrews: St Leonard's College	○		○	○○			○○
St Andrews: St Mary on the Rock			○				
St Andrews: St Salvator's College	○○	○		○○			○○
St Evoca Priory							●●
St Mary's Isle Priory							●●

	archi-tecture	fittings and monu-ments	setting	guide	restric-tions	accessi-bility	extent
St Monans: Blackfriars	o		oo				oo
Scone Abbey			o				••
Semple Collegiate Church	o					•	o
Seton Collegiate Church	o	o	oo	o			oo
Soulseat Abbey			o				••
Stirling: Blackfriars							••
Stirling: Chapel Royal	o		o	oo			
Stirling: Holy Rude	oo	o	o	oo			oo
Strathmiglo Collegiate Church					•		•
Sweetheart Abbey	oo		o	oo			oo
Tain Collegiate Church	o			o			oo
Temple Preceptory	o		oo				o
Tongland Abbey	o		o				•
Torphichen Preceptory	o	o	o	o			o
Tullibardine Collegiate Church	o		o				oo
Whithorn Priory	o		o	oo			o

Abbey St Bathans Priory, Borders   NT 758623
in village, 4½ miles SW of A1 at Grantshouse

Cistercian nunnery of St Mary the Virgin, founded late in 12th c.,
  probably by Ada, Countess of Dunbar, a cell to that at
  Berwick-on-Tweed. Secularised to David, Lord Lindsay 1622.

Church of Scotland. Church open during normal hours.

Not to be confused with Bothans (Gifford or Yester), 15 miles
nearer Edinburgh; also not to be regarded as an abbey, which it
never was. A small establishment of which little is known, it was
burned in the English invasions of 1543–5 and given by the last
prioress to Alexander, Lord Hume in 1565. The church passed to
parish use, and in the 18th c. was shortened to about two-thirds of
its already modest length. Only its E wall and part of its N wall are
ancient, probably c.1200. The tower and porch were added in 1858.
Foundations found in Chapel Field nearby in the middle of the
19th c. were ascribed to the original chapel of St Bathan, a cousin of
St Columba said to have died in 600.

Catching the eye just inside the porch is a stone to 'Mr George
Home Minister of the Gospel at Abay St Bathens 1705'. In his day
the church would not have had its present low pitch-pine
hammer-beam roof, patterned glass or varnished pews. The space
beneath the tower now forms a raised transept off the short wide
interior; a blocked doorway also on the N side may once have led to
a small cloister. The recess in the E wall was made in 1858 to
accommodate the worn but recognisable effigy of a prioress found
embedded in another wall.

   Outside, the identities of medieval and 19th-c. masonry are now
hard to tell apart, though it is obvious that the porch and little tower
are Victorian, along with most of the windows. But the narrow
plate-traceried E window of two lights and a quatrefoil is of c.1200.
The churchyard has several quaint 17th- and 18th-c. headstones.
The trout farm at Abbey St Bathans House to the E is a successor to
the priory fishponds, fed by the Whiteadder.

Aberdeen: Blackfriars, Grampian   NJ 939063
in city centre

Dominican friary of St John the Baptist founded *c*.1240 by
   Alexander II. Destroyed by reformers 1560, granted to George,
   Earl Marischal, and given to Marischal College.

No remains.

The buildings stood on Schoolhill to the NW of St Nicholas' church,
and have left no trace beyond the name Blackfriars Street.

Aberdeen: Greyfriars, Grampian   NJ 941063
in city centre

Franciscan friary of St Mary founded 1469 by Richard Vaus and
   others; surrendered to town council 1559.

Church of Scotland. Church open (apart from services) 8 to 9 p.m.
   on Wednesdays and occasionally at other times.

A flourishing establishment in the centre of New Aberdeen, its
church was rebuilt on a larger scale by Bishop Gavin Dunbar in
1518–32. After the friars went, the buildings were put to use as the
nucleus of a specifically Protestant second university founded in
1593 by the 5th Earl Marischal. The church stood neglected for a
time but served as the college chapel from 1624 up to the time of its
demolition in 1903. Three sides of the present quadrangle of what
became known as Marischal College are of 1837–44 and were
designed by Archibald Simpson. The fourth, fronting Broad Street,
together with the church at the side, was rebuilt in 1901–06 under
A. Marshall Mackenzie and is or was the second largest granite
building in the world (second to the Escorial in Spain), as well as
being one of the most ornate, in a highly individual emphatically
Perpendicular style.
   The friary church adjoined the quadrangle of Marischal College,
which was united with King's College in 1860 to form a single
university. The new one, retaining the name Greyfriars, boasts a
splendid tower that punctuates the street corner and groups
splendidly with the college façade.

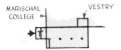

Inside, there are wide arches on simple round columns with
moulded capitals, a clerestory of two two-light windows, a plain
white ceiling on arched trusses, and a big stone sanctuary arch but
no tower arch. The floor slopes.

A lobby screen at the W end was made up with panels from a
door of 1674. Also from the old church is the seven-light window
glass by C. E. Kempe. The chancel panelling with names, initials
and dates (1699 etc.) came from the West Kirk of St Nicholas; some
more is incorporated into the gallery front.

Aberdeen: King's College, Grampian   NJ 940081
in Old Aberdeen, 300 yards W of A92

Secular College of St Mary in the Nativity founded by William
    Elphinstone, Bishop of Aberdeen, 1495.

Owned by the University of Aberdeen. Chapel open every weekday
    9 a.m. to 5 p.m. without charge.

St Andrews and Glasgow Universities were founded in 1413 and
1451 respectively and served the southern and lowland parts of the
country. Aberdeen's King's College (as it at once became known,
after James IV), modelled on Paris and Orleans and founded under
a papal bull by its own bishop, was to teach theology, law, medicine
and the 'liberal arts' to students from the North. The Reformation
nearly brought its undoing and it was in the ensuing turmoil that the
rival Marischal College came into being in 1593 in New Aberdeen.

The first buildings stood round a quadrangle much like the
present nucleus, with the chapel on the N, the hall on the E,
masters' and students' rooms on the S, and principal's rooms on the
W – the last being separated from the chapel by the famous tower
with its 'crown' steeple. Continual rebuilding and extension have
left little that is ancient except the chapel and two other towers that

were parts of a semi-defensive system. The two universities were united into one in 1860.

The chapel was built in 1500–05, and is as notable for the finest group of pre-Reformation fittings in Scotland as for its tower and open spire; the latter actually only dates from 1633 when it had to be rebuilt after storm damage.

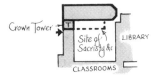

The usual entrance is beneath the W range beside the tower, and then through the S doorway from the quadrangle. This leads into the ante-chapel, which serves as a war memorial. It and the main chapel are under a single roof with boarded ceiling and gilded applied ribs in a low curve, and above the panelling the walls are of white plaster throughout. The screen, now carrying the organ but then a Rood, was originally further E. Its loft was reached through a doorway, now blocked, high in the S wall which led from the former library which stood against the side of the chapel.

Against the E side of the screen and forming part of it, and then continuing for nearly two bays against the side walls, are the fifty-two choir stalls, made at the time the chapel was built and regarded as the finest medieval woodwork in Scotland. Embellished with linenfold panelling, graceful pinnacled canopies, delicate tracery of Flamboyant character, and bands of naturalistic carving, they are attributed to a group of Flemish and local craftsmen who may have worked also at the church of St Nicholas in Aberdeen. Many of the tip-up seats or misericords have carvings beneath. The single ranges of stalls continuing the lines of the back rows on both sides are more recent work, in harmony with the old.

The window glass, nearly all ranging over the last century or so, is of considerable interest and importance, especially in its coverage of the work of Douglas Strachan during the period 1903–38. The first on the N side, a memorial of 1912, shows scenes from the

Aberdeen: King's College Chapel from SE

founder's life, and the second, of 1904, the Presentation in the Temple. The third window, with Old and New Testament scenes, is by Clayton and Bell, 1880.

Just beyond stands the canopied 16th-c. pulpit, on legs. Now much restored, it was originally in St Machar's cathedral and bears the arms of Bishop Steward. In the centre of the chancel is the defaced plain black marble tomb of the college's founder Bishop Elphinstone (d.1514). The brass nearby commemorating the first principal, Hector Boece, is modern.

The next window beyond the pulpit was adapted by the architect Marshall Mackenzie from a Burne-Jones design and depicts Old Testament prophets (1897). Round the apse all three are Strachan windows, and all memorials: the NW Majestas of 1938, the centre Crucifixion 1934, and the SE Creation cycle 1938. Beneath the centre window a big black marble medieval altar slab has been set on modern legs; it had been re-used as the grave cover of sub-principal Peter Udney (d.1601), for not only does it still bear its consecration crosses but also Udney's coat of arms is carved on it.

The eastern window of the S wall was Strachan's first (1903) and has as its theme the coming of the Child Jesus. Stylistically much in advance of its time, its many figures include classical philosophers and sibyls. Bishop Forbes's stall beside it bears a Greek inscription and the date 1627, while over the doorway beside it (formerly leading to the sacristy) is a German carving of the Virgin and Child.

The **ante-chapel** is panelled all round as a memorial to both world wars, over 500 names being inscribed. There is also an alcove with a memorial book, and the N window on the theme of victory over evil is by Strachan (1920). The big W window with mostly Biblical subjects is another by Clayton and Bell (1876), while the small one high on the S side is by William Wilson (1963). The little intricately carved pulpit now displayed high on the W wall originally stood on the rood screen; below it can be seen a holy water stoup. There are also three big 17th-c. paintings, now hung much too high to be appreciated. They are all of Old Testament subjects and were formerly in the Great Hall.

As for the **exterior**, attention always focuses on the crown steeple. The crown itself is of course the topmost embellishment; the name does not refer to the daring system of flying buttresses that support it. It is considered to be an imperial rather than a royal crown, really a symbol of universal rule rather than national but one which appealed to the then king, James IV. Of the chapel itself the S front was obscured in the original design by a two-storeyed sacristy, treasury and library building which was burned down and removed late in the 18th c. Although the whole S front was then refaced with granite and buttressed, its windows remained as they had always been, to clear the adjoining roof. On the buttresses are the prominent arms of various dignitaries and benefactors as well as a big sundial. The leaded flèche or spire on the main ridge is original; the royal cypher 'CR' on each of its six sides refers to a releading in 1655.

It is worth going to the SE corner of the quadrangle, not only because it provides such a good view of the steeple but also because the one remaining defensive round tower can be seen just the other side of the opening which leads beside the library. It dates from 1525. At the NE corner of the quadrangle, facing the chapel apse, is the so-called Cromwell's tower, actually built by General Monk in 1651 to house additional students. The N side of the chapel largely retains its original stone facing of two kinds, still with five incised consecration crosses. Its windows vary a lot in size and design and yet harmonise with one another, their sturdy central mullions and loopy tracery being typical of Scottish late medieval work.

An inscription on the W front, now gilded, confirms that the actual building of the college was begun on 2 April 1500 through the support of King James IV. Three carved coats of arms on the buttresses are (from left to right) of James's Queen, Margaret Tudor, James himself, and his illegitimate son Archbishop Alexander Stewart. They look down on the bronze Elphinstone monument (1926), intended by its sculptor Henry Wilson as a re-creation of the original desecrated tomb within the chapel but because of its size finally put here. Close by is the head of an hexagonal well, as old as the chapel but long lost till the lawns were laid out in 1937.

Aberdeen: St Nicholas' Church: S doorway of West Kirk, by James Gibbs, 1752

Aberdeen: St Nicholas, Grampian   NJ 940062
in city centre, between Union Street and School Hill

College founded 1540 in existing parish church of St Nicholas by
   William Gordon, Bishop of Aberdeen.

Church of Scotland. Open Mondays, Thursdays and Fridays 12
   noon to 4 p.m., Saturdays 10 a.m. to 12 noon; may be accessible
   at other times on application to church office adjoining N side.

The biggest church of the city, and indeed the largest parish church
in Scotland, it had the same misfortune as many other major town
churches of Scotland, that of being split into two parts after the
Reformation. With the change of religion and the new emphasis on
preaching, it was found impossible for a single minister to be heard
and seen throughout a building of such size and shape. The crossing
and transepts belonging now to neither East nor West Kirk, but to
the city, are basically 12th-c. The present West Kirk is of 1752, by
James Gibbs, and the East Kirk of 1834–7, by Archibald Simpson.
The central tower and spire were rebuilt in 1874 under William
Smith after a fire which also severely damaged the East Kirk. St
Mary's chapel in the crypt of the East Kirk is 15th-c. A small vestry
block was added on the N side of the West Kirk in 1937. The two
congregations were united in 1980 and use the two ends of the
building alternately.
   The S aisle of the East Kirk is known as Trinity aisle. Trinity
church took its name from a chapel on the site of a Trinitarian friary
to the SE of the Green, which became a parish church in 1834. It
was sold in 1846 but a new Trinity church was built in Marischal
Street in 1877. The congregation was united with that of the North
Church in 1928 and later with the East Kirk.

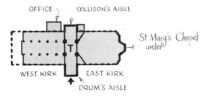

The usual entry is into the **S transept** known as Drum's aisle, which forms part of the big vestibule separating the two churches and giving access to both. Though mostly rebuilt in the 19th c. along with the round-headed N and S arches of the crossing, it stands on a 12th-c. foundation and retains some window openings of that character including a blocked one high in the E wall. The faceted roof with white plastered panels is 19th-c.

The separate piscinae in the E wall indicate former altar positions. Several monuments are of particular interest. That to Robert Gordon, founder of the well-known boys' school, faces visitors on entering. Further along, a very worn stone commemorates Thomas Leith, a former provost of the college. The best one, however, has been pushed into the SE corner – well-preserved praying effigies usually attributed to Sir Alexander Irvyn of Drum (d.1457) and his wife, with a small brass to him above, considered to be the earliest in Scotland (indeed the only medieval one to survive) though the date was never filled in. Over the arch to the S nave aisle (i.e. into the West Kirk) is a large but uninspired tablet to Elizabeth Forbes (d.1761), and on the centre one to the nave itself (this arch and the one opposite were filled in in 1596) a stone coat of arms and a plaque of 1887 recording the carillon in the steeple. This carillon contains forty-eight bells and is the largest in Britain.

The crossing arches, rebuilt following the 1874 disaster, respect the original Romanesque design, with springing foliage caps of rather primitive type. The **N transept**, called Collison's aisle, has rather more 12th-c. masonry surviving including several round-headed windows. That over the arch to the N chancel aisle (i.e. the East Kirk) is wider than the others and shafted. On the W wall the three little heraldic tablets are to provosts of the college: Andrew Cullen (early 16th c.), Thomas Menzies (mid-16th c.) and Sir John Rutherford (late 15th c.). The effigy under a canopy in the N wall is said to be Provost Robert Davidson (killed at the battle of Harlaw, 1411) and shows him as a knight in armour with a lion at his feet; another recess at the N end of the E wall probably led to a chapel. A loose stone is part of a memorial to Provost Robert Blinshell (d. 1482). Above that is an interesting benefaction or 'mortification' board covering the period 1616–1792. A lectern nearby incorporates panels from choir stalls of 1507, and there are two old carved benches, one of which belonged to the guild of Baxters or bakers.

The **West Kirk** has a totally different atmosphere – very little changed from the 18th c. James Gibbs's pure Classical design (he was a native of Aberdeen) has much in common with his All Saints', Derby, now the cathedral. The coved nave ceiling, ornamented merely with double ribs at each bay division, rests on severe stone Roman Doric arcades with tall pilasters facing the nave and shorter ones to the actual arches. The aisles have groined plaster vaults without ornament. Dark box pews with narrow walkways cover as much of the floor as possible, and at each corner a stone and wood stair with 'dancing' treads (at radiating angles in French style) leads to galleries on all four sides which look inwards to a giant polygonal pulpit with towering canopy. Facing this pulpit and the holy table is a so-called Act of Parliament clock dating from 1752. The galleries are quite plain with panelled fronts, but on the E one stands a 'templum' on four Corinthian columns marking the civic pew; this inspired Sir Ninian Comper (another Aberdeen-born architect) in his designs for baldacchini or altar canopies in other churches. Places in the gallery are also reserved for members of seven trade guilds and of Robert Gordon's College; a carved panel of 1946 commemorative of the school is just to the left of the pulpit. Over the central area but above gallery level hang three great twelve-branched brass candelabra, and at the W end is a fine window of 1884 by Burlison and Grylls.

Now a circuit of the West Kirk, starting at the E end of the S aisle. On the aisle window-sills are medieval effigies, attributed as follows: on the second, Margaret Setoun, 15th c.; on the second from the W end, Gilbert Menzies, d.1452; and at the end Gilbert Menzies' wife Margery. The last two were brought from the ruined church of Maryculter. At the SW corner are many more stone fragments – among them some of great antiquity – as well as a showcase of pewter and other ware. Over the stair is another window by Burlison and Grylls showing the Wedding at Cana.

In the W lobby hang four big needlework panels made c.1650 by Mary Jamieson, daughter of George Jamieson who was the earliest known portrait artist in Scotland. They represent (from S to N) Susannah and the Elders, Esther and Ahaseurus, Jephthah and his daughter, and the finding of Moses – the last picture including, rather oddly, the Bridge of Dee. On the opposite side are three interesting memorials: a brass of 1622 to Dr Duncan Liddell, a tablet to John Cushnie (d.1801) (a most unusual composition with sail and anchor by the sculptor Richard Westmacott) and another to Ann Allardyce (d.1787) by the equally well-known John Bacon. Nearby stands a big octagonal table made in 1874 of wood salvaged from the fire. Discreetly tucked into the SW corner of the main area of box pews is the Cowan chapel, formed in 1935 in memory of a former minister.

Over the NW stair is a window by Geoffrey Webb devoted to the miracles of St Nicholas. The N side being filled with pews, with no actual gangway, it is necessary to thread one's way amongst them to reach the vestibule again. On the last but one sill is the supposed effigy of Provost John Collison (late 15th c.), and near the doorway a splendid but worn black marble ledger stone to a member of the Burnet family (d.1657).

Across the transept is a doorway to the **East Kirk** – an interior with another character altogether, that of the early Gothic Revival. Typical of its period and even more suited to a large preaching house than that of the heavy-columned West Kirk is the exceptionally wide single span roof, with white ribs and ochre yellow panels. The trusses are ornamented with curved brackets and pendants above and behind the galleries which with their flat panelled fronts are supported quite independently. The sanctuary in its traditional position in the apse has oak furniture of 1936, incorporating early 16th-c. carved panels from choir stalls. The central window above is by Marjorie Kemp and the side ones by Gordon Webster, 1961. In the S aisle the easternmost window (Jesus and the children) is by Douglas Strachan, another native of the city. The semi-Classical white marble font close to it came from Trinity church when that was made redundant; so did the mahogany furniture of the War Memorial chapel in the NE corner. The pelican lectern is of bell-metal and oak rescued from the old church.

St Mary's chapel in the crypt, a beautiful survival from the 15th-c. church, can be reached by going outside and down the steps beside the apse and is a T-shaped set of compartments with rib vaults – its antiquity disguised externally by being refaced with granite. Restored in 1898, it is largely used as a sales area for fund-raising and is thus open during most shopping hours; the N part however forms a baptistry, and the S is screened off as a vestry. There are windows by three well-known designers: Christopher Whall (E window), Marjorie Kemp (baptistry) and Douglas Strachan (vestry). The sanctuary woodwork – panelling, lectern, sedilia and chair, stall and canopy – incorporates many carved panels which were not only kept at the 1837 rebuilding but also survived the fire.

Outside, the church and indeed the city centre is dominated by the great tower and pinnacled spire of 1874. Surrounding trees and buildings make it virtually impossible to obtain a good comprehensive view of it together with both the West and East Kirks, but a place to appreciate their contrasting styles is a little way along the path towards Union Street. The West Kirk, now of five bays, was 17 feet longer and had nine bays before Gibbs's rebuilding, the well close to the W entrance being previously inside. The East Kirk, also now of five bays plus the apse, had seven until the 1830s.

The strict Classical detailing of Gibbs's streaky grey stonework is characteristic. The interrupted 'rustication' of the S doorway (alternation of plain ashlar with moulded architrave blocks) comes straight from his pattern books on architecture and is almost exactly repeated at Derby; it was no doubt this kind of repetition that enabled him, so it is said, to donate his design without charge. The S transept was refaced in granite and partly rebuilt at the same time as the East Kirk.

On the N side, the transept has been much less interfered with though its main feature, the great N window, was inserted in 1519–20 into walling which is still basically 12th-c.; there are still traces of an early doorway beside it. Close to the transept, adjoining the West Kirk, is the little vestry and office of 1937.

The **churchyard** contains the profusion of table-tombs, headstones, obelisks and other memorials that are usual in a city centre. Architecturally the most interesting are the big ones built into the W wall of the churchyard close to the church itself. North of the church are two rather curiously painted pale blue: to William Guild (d.1659) with a later inscription on pink granite, and to George Davidson (d.1663). Going S from these, the following are also worth noticing: Duncan Wilson (d.1675), a big heraldic tablet with repainted lettering; William Rickart (d.1699), a large Corinthian aedicule painted a pinkish colour; William Fordyce (d.1831), a recess with urn; and James Mowat (d.1662), a round-headed recess flanked by Classical columns. A group of free-standing monuments at the SW corner is dominated by one to Robert Hamilton (d.1829), a large urn within a templum on four Greek Doric columns. Near the centre is a strange cast iron table-tomb to Archibald Reid (d.1819), an openwork affair with miniature Gothic arcading all round.

The Union Street boundary is embellished by a colonnade erected in 1829 in imitation of that at Hyde Park Corner in Westminster and designed by John Smith.

Aberdeen: Whitefriars, Grampian   NJ 940061
in city centre

Carmelite friary founded *c*.1273; granted to town council 1583.

No remains.

Various benefactions from the foundation date onwards are recorded, and the establishment continued till its buildings were destroyed in 1560. Nothing of them is now left, but the name is preserved in that of Carmelite Street.

Abernethy Priory, Tayside   NO 190165
in village 6 miles SE of Perth on Cupar road A913

Augustinian priory founded 1272 on site of much earlier Culdee
    monastery. Refounded as college of priests early in 14th c.,
    probably by Earl of Angus.

Church of Scotland. Tower in care of Secretary of State for
    Scotland: key available without charge at nearby tearoom or
    house adjoining, 10 a.m. (Sundays 12 noon) to 5 p.m.

Known now for its very ancient slender round tower, this site has a whole series of legends and facts woven into its history; here they must be summarised with very little comment. About 462 King Nectan Morbet is said to have founded a church of St Bridget (yet she did not die till 525). About 590 King Gartuaidh (or another

Abernethy: Church tower from S: probably 9th to 11th cc.

Nectan?) made a foundation for Columban monks, also St Bridget's; they were expelled in 717 by Nectan III. In 865 Abbot Cellach of Iona re-established them and Abernethy may have become a bishopric till 887. Culdees were here by 1100 and probably built the tower. By the end of that century the church had been granted to Arbroath abbey. In 1272 an Augustinian priory was founded instead, possibly as a dependency of Inchaffray abbey. Early in the 14th c. that was supplanted by a college of secular canons, the possessions of which went to the Douglas family after the Reformation. Remains of the collegiate church stood to the N of the tower till 1802; the present church of St Bride is its successor. The tower was handed into State care in 1928 by the Earl of Home.

The remarkable round tower (the only comparable one on the Scottish mainland is at Brechin cathedral) is 74 feet high and tapers from 7½ to 5 feet in diameter. The bottom 10 feet or so is in a hard grey stone; the elevated doorway in it is probably no earlier than the 11th c., though the stonework may be as old as the bishopric, 9th-c. The upper part, of softer, yellower stone, is judged to be 11th- or 12th-c. Various Pictish stone fragments have been collected against the base, one of them with an anvil and hammer and other ritual symbols. There is also a joug or penal fetter. The clock face is of 1868.

Inside is an iron stair inserted in 1982, ingeniously designed so as to take no support at all from the walls – the holes in which are a legacy from its 19th-c. wooden predecessor. The bell at the top is of 1782.

Arbroath Abbey, Tayside   NO 643413
in town centre

Tironensian abbey of St Thomas the Martyr founded 1178 by King William the Lion and colonised from Kelso. Became mitred in 1396. Secularised 1606 to James, Marquess of Hamilton.

Owned by Crown Estates Commissioners. Open during standard hours (admission charge).

The dedication, unusual in Scotland, and some features of the buildings underline its connections with Canterbury cathedral, itself begun to be rebuilt in 1174. For example, the change from Romanesque to Gothic which they exhibit is further advanced than might be expected. The twin W towers (there was a central one too) are also a rarity. The church, commenced as usual at the E end, was not finished till 1233. A sacristy was attached to the S quire aisle in the 15th c. So far as their scanty remains reveal, the claustral buildings were contemporary with the church; the abbot's house, which survives, was however much enlarged c.1500. There are also very substantial remains of the main gatehouse, of c.1300. The Declaration of Arbroath, the vow of Scottish independence sent to the Pope in 1320, was probably written in the abbey, and in 1951 the Stone of Scone, removed from Westminster abbey, was set before the high altar here.

Following its extinction, the abbey's stone was quarried away for use elsewhere. Much of the site became occupied by other buildings, not removed till the 1920s. Only the abbot's house survived whole, through being a dwelling and then a factory; it became a museum in 1934.

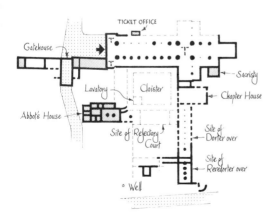

Arbroath Abbey Church: W front

First the dramatic red **W front**, with its twin tower bases (the S one partly hidden by the later gatehouse range, but in any case less complete), deeply recessed central doorway, and the lower half of a great round window. Below the window are three little pointed gables over openings to an upper passage or tribune which connected the towers. **Inside**, this passage has six elegant arches terminating the nave but at a lower level than the main triforium, the design of which happens to be preserved through having been continued uninterrupted across the inside faces of the towers; each bay has a round arch enclosing two pointed ones. The clerestory seems to have been similar, and the main arches pointed and quite richly moulded. The NW tower (rebuilt higher than the other after storm damage in 1272) still has pairs of big lancet windows in its outer walls. The gabled N doorway (close to the ticket office) should be looked at from outside. It is of c.1200.

Though little is left in the nave but some column bases, the S aisle wall stands nearly entire, with its windows and even the base of its vault. The N transept site is bounded by the churchyard retaining wall, but the S is remarkably complete, even to the round window in its topmost gable which forms a land- and a sea-mark. One of the main lancets is shorter to allow for the dorter roof. Within this transept is some of the wall-arcading that is a special feature of Arbroath (the 'syncopated' kind of double arcading, like Lincoln and Ely, that once adorned the towers can no longer be properly seen). Here the third tier screens an upper passage.

The **E wall** retains three lower lancets (much restored) and the base of an upper row. Below is more wall-arcading (also somewhat renewed) and on the S wall the mutilated remains of sedilia. Rough masonry marks the high altar. The two-storeyed early 15th-c. **sacristy** stands high like a tower; the upper room above its high vault, with a spiral stair accessible only from doorways (inside and outside) much above ground level, must have been a treasury. Beneath the stair is a small cell, perhaps a strong room but used in later times to house lunatics. Another wall-arcade (on three sides only) and the once fine aisle doorway should be noted.

Of the **cloister** buildings, reached through the S aisle, little is left. On the E side are the slype, the outline of the chapter house and its curious upstanding corner lump (familiarly called the Pint Stoup), and the long dorter undercroft marked out by neat edging. To the

W of the last is the kitchen court, and at the end the base of the reredorter, with a drain curving to the SE. Between the kitchen court and main cloister the refectory is clear, with the kitchen at its W end and past that the **abbot's house**, built *c*.1500 on and around an original (*c*.1300) vaulted extension of the S range. This fine ground-floor compartment with round columns and a fireplace is entered separately, the main house having its doorway on the N face, leading by a stair to the first floor.

Both the house and the exhibits it now contains are of considerable interest. Perhaps the most important are in the E room on the first floor: a headless effigy believed to be of the founder William the Lion (13th c.) and found close to the high altar, another of St Thomas à Becket (15th c.) and part of the 15th-c. tomb chest of Abbot Paniter. The lancet windows nearby are of the same date as the floor below, but the fireplace is 15th-c.; thus this storey was only partially rebuilt. In the centre room are traces of wall paintings.

The furthest (W) room on the second floor provides a good view of the **gatehouse** range, the nearer half of which can be visited next; it has an impressive vaulted undercroft from the garderobe at the E end of which it is possible (though difficult) to see an intact portion of the 'syncopated' arcading, on the face of the SW tower. Go back to the cloisters and through the church again to look at the outer face of the gatehouse range. Though mainly of *c*.1300, it was altered and strengthened *c*.1500, the tower at the W end being added and the stepped gables built on. The only comparable gatehouse in Scotland is at St Andrews. From here the precinct wall continues with interruptions for some distance to the N. Follow Abbey Street to the S, however, passing the abbot's house on the left; from this direction is a good general view of the ruin.

Ardchattan Priory, Strathclyde   NM 971349
on N shore of Loch Etive, 8 miles NE of Oban

Valliscaulian priory of St Mary and St John the Baptist founded
    1230 or 1231 by Duncan McCowll (MacDougal). Secularised
    1602 to Alexander Campbell.

Owned by Campbell-Preston family, but ruined parts in care of
    Secretary of State for Scotland. Ruins (only) accessible at all
    times (admission charge).

The cruciform church and cloister buildings were erected in the
middle of the 13th c., and in 1308 were the meeting place of a
parliament under Robert Bruce, the last at which Gaelic was
spoken. In the 15th and early 16th c. a larger quire was built, with a
N sacristy, and parts of the crossing, nave and N transept were
rebuilt. The refectory was rebuilt too, and this with other parts of
the S range was converted to domestic use after the Reformation,
while the church quire and transepts were retained for parish use.
Damage was done, chiefly to the house, in 1654 by Cromwellian
troops. After the erection of a new parish church in 1732 the old one
fell to ruin and much of its stonework was used elsewhere. The
house was much altered in 1847–55 under the architect Charles
Wilson, but still has the monastic refectory as its nucleus.
Outbuildings on its N side cover the site of the nave and its former
N aisle and of the cloister, and incorporate various fragments.

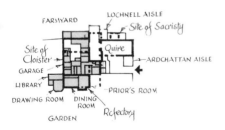

The iron entrance gates at the E end lead to an enclosed area S of
the roofless **quire**, which is to the right. Numerous slate tomb slabs
lie in the grass. The enclosure projecting from the quire is the
Campbell of Ardchattan aisle and dates from 1614. The quire walls,
of slaty stone interspersed with bigger stones, belong to the
rebuilding of *c*.1500 and on the N side still stand up to 25 feet high.
Many more slate slabs are in the floor and two tombs of particular

interest on the N side are protected by wooden covers which may be lifted. The western one is of Duncan McIntyre (d.1695), while the other commemorates two successive priors, MacDougal brothers of 1500–02 and their family. It portrays a skeleton flanked by figures of the two priors, and their mother flanked by their father and another brother. The actual tomb does not belong to the lid and may be that of Alan the brother. On the left three late medieval stones have been leant against the wall, while in the centre of the quire, now looking rather like a headstone, is a piece of a standing cross dated 1500 with carvings of a galley and two animals. An aumbry and triple-arched recess with piscina and credence survive close to the site of the altar, but seem not to be in their original state.

An arch leads into the **sacristy** area, now enclosed by 17th- and 18th-c. walls on different alignments from the original; a good heraldic tablet probably to a Campbell (d.1682) is on the W side.

The arch into the **nave** is double, i.e. two separate semicircular arches in two separate walls, one 13th-c. and the other facing the rebuilt quire probably early 16th-c.; the older one was no doubt intended to be removed. The nave is cut across by the outer wall of the house, incorporating some of the walling that formed the pulpitum, and had quite a small central opening. The N transept contains more memorials, mostly floor slabs, and leads to the **Lochnell aisle** which is of 1620 but was enlarged in 1720. It is so full of table-tombs that it can only just be entered. All have fine lettering and heraldry on the cover slabs. One particularly noticeable for its size is of Alexander Campbell, 6th Laird of Lochnell (d.1714). Against the N wall of this enclosure is a splendid early Christian slate slab with a wheel cross and interlaced and figure ornament.

Back in the **N transept**, a round arched window in the W wall should be noted; though almost certainly 15th-c., it has nail-head ornament of 13th-c. character in an uninterrupted border. Looking next across to the S transept, two domestic sash windows can be seen, inserted into the 13th- and 15th-c. wall. The nearer of these occupies the position of the opening in the pulpitum at the start of the nave. In the further corner of the S transept excavations down to the original floor level have exposed the bases of the round columns of a two-bay E arcade which it is presumed was repeated on the N.

Ardchattan Priory: early Christian cross in Lochnell aisle

At the S end of the dormered part of the **house** is a 19th-c. bellcot, over the site of the chapter house and dorter. Close below is a small garden gate through which visitors may pass on to the main lawn to see the S side of the refectory, and the 19th-c. wing beyond. The medieval parts are much altered, with many inserted imitation Gothic windows. Not accessible to visitors, but of particular interest, are the quite elaborate vaulted refectory pulpit (within the projecting bay towards the right of the elevation) and the once open scissor-braced collar-beam roof much of which survived both the fire of 1654 and the subsequent insertion of attic rooms. The smaller projection at the left end where it adjoins the Victorian addition probably contained a circular stair leading to the undercroft.

The W face of the rear outbuildings of the house, now containing garage doors and a modern arch with bellcot, is really the W wall of the cloister (which had no W range of buildings so far as is known), continuous with the W wall of the church. Just to the left of the arch, close to the return wall of the farmyard, a consecration cross can just be seen; this was at the NW corner of the aisle. Another, also formerly external, is on the left just inside the first doorway on the left within the yard, in what is now a store. As can be seen from the plan, this wall, which was the outer wall of the N aisle, is still fairly complete right up to the transept.

Ayr: Greyfriars, Strathclyde   NS 349219
in town centre between High Street and river

Franciscan friary founded 1472; granted to burgh 1567; parish church built on site 1654–5.

Church of Scotland. Key available from caretaker in bungalow behind parish hall to SE.

In common with Aberdeen, Edinburgh and one or two others, the Greyfriars church here has entirely disappeared but its site and name are perpetuated in a parish church. £100 towards its erection cost of £1,708 was provided by Cromwell when he commandeered the former parish church of St John and included its site in the fort he was constructing. Of that church only the tower survives.

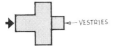

What is now called the Auld Kirk is a typically T-shaped building
standing in a well-treed churchyard with a view of the Auld Brig.
The addition of vestries has made it into the form of a Greek cross.
Inside and out it is remarkable for the many big stone dormer
windows, in debased 17th-c. Gothic – each two-light and uncusped
except for what might be called a bifoil in the head. Much of the
coloured glass is 19th-c. The principal feature of the interior is the
three guild lofts or galleries, appertaining to the merchants, the

Ayr: Auld Kirk (on Greyfriars site) from SE: 1654

traders and the sailors. The pulpit incorporates panelling from the 17th-c. one.

Outside, the date 1654 can be found on the kneeler stone on the right of the main W gable; below it is inscribed 'Renovated 1958'. A tablet at the corner of the S transept refers to the Greyfriars monastery.

At the **churchyard** gateway (which bears the date 1656) are two iron coffin covers or mort-safes, placed at one time over buried coffins to prevent pillaging. A plan indicates the positions in the churchyard of the graves of persons connected with Robert Burns; most are fairly easily found but none are of particular artistic merit and it is unnecessary to catalogue them here. As is common with town churchyards there are numerous memorials around the outer wall, though again none of special merit. The only one perhaps worth seeking out is against the N side of the nave – a Corinthian aedicule containing the sadly worn figure of William Adair (d.1684).

Balmerino Abbey: chapter house

Balmerino Abbey, Fife   NO 358246
in village, 4 miles SW of Dundee and 2 miles N of Glenrothes road
A914

Cistercian abbey of St Mary and St Edward founded 1227 by
    Ermengarde, widow of William the Lion, and Alexander II their
    son, a daughter house of Melrose. Secularised 1603 to Sir James
    Elphinstone, Lord Balmerino.

Owned by National Trust for Scotland and Earl of Dundee.
    Accessible (except roofed parts) at all times without charge.

What little evidence remains accords with a mid-13th-c. date both
for the church and for most of the monastic buildings. However the
chapter house, which with its adjoining compartments survived
through conversion into a house, shows 15th- and 16th-c. work. The
abbey was sacked by the English in 1537 and by reformers in 1547
and 1559. Parts now lie under farm buildings, but the remainder was
excavated in 1896.

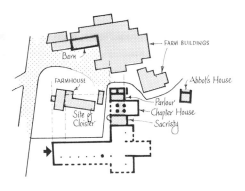

An iron gate and log steps lead to the W end of the church,
practically disappeared except for bits of the N aisle wall with bases
of attached columns. The farmhouse garden behind this wall is on
the cloister site. The N transept wall-base survives too, and beyond

it a more substantial part of the E monastic range. First is the sacristy, still vaulted; then the chapter house vestibule, its 15th-c. foliage-capped column and vaulting being later additions; then a parlour, and at the end two cells (possibly a prison and a treasury) reached by traps from the dorter above. The dorter ran back across the W half of the chapter house as far as the church transept.

On the E side is the watercourse which served the reredorter and, further round, the N wall of the chapter house, showing clearly the inserted 16th-c. domestic windows. Several carved stones are preserved inside.

Over to the E an overgrown vault is all that remains of the abbot's house, while close to the site of the quire is a chestnut tree reputed to have been planted by the monks. Lastly, a 15th-c. monastic barn (attached to a group of modern ones) stands across the farmyard from the house; remains of a dovecot are on its W gable.

Banff: Whitefriars, Grampian   NJ 686645
in town centre

Carmelite friary founded 1321 by Robert I; granted to King's
   College, Aberdeen 1574.

Site in multiple ownership.

Only the name survives, in Carmelite Street. The houses on its S
side are said to stand within what were the friary precincts.

Beauly Priory, Highland   NH 527465
in town on A862, 10 miles W of Inverness

Valliscaulian priory of St Mary and St John the Baptist founded *c.*
   1230, probably by John Byset and Alexander II. Became
   Cistercian *c.* 1510 and then dependent on Kinloss abbey.
   Secularised 1634 and granted to Bishop of Ross.

Crown property, in care of Secretary of State for Scotland. Open
   during standard hours (admission charge).

Beauly, like Beaulieu in Hampshire, means 'beautiful place'. The

buildings that remain, little more than nave and quire, correspond
in style with the recorded foundation date, with the principal
exception of a fairly extensive reconstruction of the W parts *c.*1540.
The Holy Cross chapel, N of the nave, was early 15th-c. but has
virtually disappeared, as also have all the conventual buildings;
Cromwell is believed to have taken their stone to build his fort at
Inverness. The N transept was restored in 1901 under Thomas Ross
as the Kintail or Mackenzie burial aisle, but the remainder is
roofless.

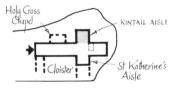

The W front with its three lancets, niche above the almost
round-arched doorway, and high gable is an impressive introduction
to the church. Though closely resembling the 13th-c. style, it was
the work of Prior Robert Reid who was in charge of the monastery
in the second quarter of the 16th c., as is confirmed by his shield on
the niche. **Nave** and quire are long and narrow, and the existence of
transepts is not very evident. The break between Reid's work and
that of the 13th c. occurs between the two lancet windows at the
western end of the S side and the three very elegant and unusual
triangular openings beyond – all quite high up because the cloister
was on the S side. A doorway led to its NW corner. Somewhat
beyond that, an aumbry and piscina show where a nave altar stood,
just in front of the screen or pulpitum which separated the quire;
there is evidence that this screen was originally further E, between
the two two-light windows on the N side. The doorway in this wall
led to the vanished chapel of the Holy Cross.

Both **transepts** were walled off in the later Middle Ages, leaving
in each case a tomb arch with a doorway alongside; on the S side the
transept arch still exists. The N transept, which is vaulted in two
bays, cannot be entered but the five-legged tomb of Kenneth
Mackenzie, Lord of Kintail (d.1491) can be quite well seen through

Beauly Priory: church nave and S transept

the opening. The further one, similar in style, is of a later Kenneth Mackenzie for whom the 'aisle' was restored in 1901.

A number of ledger stones mark burials in the nave and **quire**. Two in the latter are medieval with cross designs, and another bears the effigy of a Lord Fraser in knight's attire; they are not easy to identify. A railed enclosure contains more tombs. Much more important and attractive is the wall-arcading framing the side windows of the quire – Y-traceried two-light openings with blank arches or corbels in between. On the N side this is less elaborated than the S. The E window, to judge from the tracery fragments attached to the jambs and the arch springings, was an elaborate 15th-c. insertion. Beneath in the S wall is a broken double piscina.

The tomb at the S transept entrance, answering that on the N, is of Prior Mackenzie. As it contains some Renaissance details it must have been remade some years after his death in 1479. From the transept a 13th-c. doorway leads into what was the E walk of the **cloister**; the stonework around this is curiously twisted as a result of foundation movement which must have occurred before it was completed. The cloister buildings have almost totally gone as a result of Cromwell's activities, apart from the roof lines and stubs of return wall on this and the opposite sides which mark the beginnings of the E and W ranges. The blank lower portion of the nave wall indicates where the N walk ran. A circuit of the outside is worth while, though no other buildings survive. On the further side of the substantially buttressed quire is the restored N transept, of which the upper parts and the stair turret are 15th-c. Beyond that is the site of the Holy Cross chapel, its piscina now exposed in an outside wall.

Biggar Collegiate Church, Strathclyde   NT 040379
in town on Edinburgh–Dumfries road A702

College of St Mary founded 1545 by Malcolm Lord Fleming in
    existing parish church of St Nicholas.

Church of Scotland parish church. Open during normal hours.

The last collegiate church founded in Scotland before the Reformation, it seems to have been largely rebuilt then, probably partly using older foundations. A substantial 'restoration' was done in 1870–71 and a less drastic one in 1934–5.

The much-modernised interior is dominated by the four robust crossing arches on semi-octagonal piers. The roofs are all timber-panelled, and the window glass a mixture of 19th- and 20th-c. Two on the N side of the nave are by William Wilson, c.1950, and those around the polygonal E apse are all 19th-c. To the N of the chancel in the usual position is a 16th-c. sacristy, and in its S wall a piscina. The very small circular font on the S side of the crossing appears to be 18th- or early 19th-c. A medieval cross-slab is in the S porch.

The little belfry turret on the tower top was added in 1870. Stones in the churchyard commemorate three generations of Gladstones including the great-grandfather of the statesman W. E. Gladstone.

Blantyre Priory, Strathclyde   NS 686594
1½ miles N of High Blantyre and 300 yards E of B758

Augustinian priory founded before 1289 by Alexander II, a
    dependency of Jedburgh. Secularised to Walter Stewart, later
    Lord Blantyre, 1599.

Accessible at all times without charge.

Approachable across fields from the public road, its site is on the precipitous bank of the Clyde immediately opposite Bothwell castle. Low broken wall bases amongst undergrowth are no longer decipherable, and even the 'one small elegant window' recorded in 1900 has disappeared.

Bothans Collegiate Church, Lothian   NT 544671
4½ miles SSE of Haddington and 1 mile SE of Gifford village on
B6355 and B6369, in grounds of Yester House

Collegiate church of St Cuthbert. College founded 1421 by Sir
    William Hay and others.

Owned by Hay family. Accessible with permission from Lady Hay
    at Forbes Lodge, Gifford.

The existence of three different names is a cause of confusion. To begin with, there is no connection with Abbey St Bathans except that both may be derived from the same saint, a cousin of St Columba. Originally called Bothans, the place later became known as Yester, meaning a valley (= Welsh *ystrad* and Scots *strath*). Yester castle was built in the 13th c. by Hugo Gifford. The name Bothans was resumed when the college was founded, but at the Reformation the church became merely parochial and the parish was thereafter called Yester again. Though the village of Gifford only grew up in the late 17th c., it quickly became the centre of population, and the parish has in consequence tended, incorrectly, to take its name, especially since a new church was built there in 1710. The old church had by then become no more than the chapel of Yester House, a mansion which had been begun by the Hays (Earls of Tweeddale) about 1700 and later gained a splendid series of rooms designed by the Adam brothers. The house itself has passed into other hands but the chapel remains Hay property. It is remarkable for the rococo Gothic façade added by the Adams in 1753.

Subject to permission as above, the approach is via the fine avenue of limes leading S from the village centre and through the entrance gates of Yester House (marked 'Strictly Private'). The driveway (which is in fact a public right of way as far as the bridge) forks; the left branch should be taken, to the service yard beside the great house. The chapel, approachable only on foot, stands beside the stream called Gifford Water, beyond the house and to its left and almost hidden even in winter by dense trees.

It was intended to be cruciform, i.e. with simple nave, chancel and transepts. The nave may never have been built, so what is seen first is the W face of the transepts with a blocking wall between. But this is no ordinary blocking wall. It is a fantasy of Gothic elements made up into a form which – summer or winter – appears highly theatrical against its wooded backcloth. A main pointed arch supports a strangely cusped and crocketed gable, far higher than the needs of the stone roof behind, and crowned with a giant vegetated finial. Within the arch are, first, a bull's-eye window with swirling wooden tracery, then a coat of arms flanked by tiny niches, and at the base an ogee-headed doorway with a curiously flattened hood-mould stretching up to meet the heraldry above. In the parapets, particularly those of the transepts with their fretted pattern and the very unmedieval corbel heads beneath, there is rather more sense of the Classical – though not the least hint of the refinement of the house itself.

Inside, there are 15th-c. pointed tunnel vaults throughout, but the chancel arch is thought to be of 1688, when also the vault of the chancel was plastered – which it is no longer. The transept arches are lower and segmental. The only monument of consequence is in the S transept, a pilastered tablet to Sir William Hay (d.1614). The 17th-c. canopied pulpit in Gifford church is believed to have been here until parochial status was transferred.

On the outside of the E window the date 1635 can be seen in the tracery – an instance of Gothic survival alongside the Gothic revival work at the opposite end. A carving of a shepherd and sheep at the S end of the E gable is however medieval.

Bothwell Collegiate Church, Strathclyde   NS 705586
in village on B7071, 2 miles NW of Hamilton

College founded 1398 in existing parish church of St Bride by
    Archibald 'the Grim', 3rd Earl of Douglas.

Church of Scotland. Key available from adjacent lodge.

The chancel of the 12th-c. church was rebuilt *c.*1400 following the establishment of the college but some time after the Reformation it was partitioned off from the nave by forming a laird's loft, a gallery used by the Douglas family and entered from the chancel. Little is known of the earlier nave, but it was much altered in 1719 and in 1833 completely rebuilt under David Hamilton with reversed orientation: the pulpit at the W end, galleries on the other three sides and a tall tower against the W end of the ancient chancel, which was then abandoned till 1898 when it was restored as the 'Old Church' under Sir Robert Rowand Anderson. Finally in 1933 the 'Old' and 'New' churches were united by forming arches beneath the tower and the adjoining vestibules, which latter became transepts. The galleries were removed, the nave floor lowered and gently ramped, and the W vestry made into a porch. The architect for these extensive changes was Jeffrey Waddell.

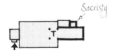

Bothans Chapel in grounds of Yester House, Gifford: façade by Robert Adam, 1753

The W **porch**, built in the 19th c. as a clergy vestry, contains a collection of carved stones, many of them relics of the 12th-c. church, with a handboard explaining them. Arches inserted in 1933 frame the view into the body of the church, which is subtly improved by the slightly sloping floor – leading the eye through the base of the tower to the beautiful Burne-Jones E window.

In the **nave** another handboard describes more stones displayed around its perimeter, many of them in variously shaped niches under the side windows. Amongst them are two medieval cross-slabs at the W end, and a memorial inscription to a priest of the medieval college, Thomas Trayl (d. 1409). The three big W windows are by Cottier & Co., the outer ones being of 1897 (though memorials to persons who had died earlier in the century) and the centre one of 1880 based on drawings by Sir John Millais; the upper glass was only added to the last at the 1933 restoration when removal of the plaster ceiling exposed the tracery. The side windows contain remarkably attractive plain glass with floral borders. In the E wall are the three arches formed in 1933 when the church was unified. Above them can be seen remains of the doorway arches of 1833 which led to the galleries. The octagonal canopied pulpit is of 1890.

The **N transept** is the baptistry and contains the organ at upper level. The very small font is of Caen stone, and the splendid window is a memorial to the Gilchrist family by Douglas Strachan (1936). Nearby is a collection of communion and other old plate in a glass cabinet.

Next the medieval **chancel**, reached beneath another high arch of 1933, following similar contours to the pointed ribs of the tunnel vault but of slightly odd shape owing to the inaccurate alignment of nave and chancel. Of innumerable monuments on the walls much the most prominent is to William, Duke of Hamilton (d.1694). Flanked by 'barley-sugar' columns and weeping standing cherubs, the central descriptive tablet supports a big urn. Of Caen stone and black and white marble, it was made in Paris and stood in the old collegiate church of Hamilton until its demolition. The sacristy doorway alongside is segmental-headed with tall capitals – but badly decayed. The sacristy itself has a rib vault with central boss, and an ancient aumbry and piscina.

The Nativity E window of 1899 is the last and one of the finest of

Sir Edward Burne-Jones's works. Its composition and rich colouring are almost identical with his E window of Hawarden church in Clwyd. The stone hood mould over the window terminates with shields of the Douglas family. The obelisk-shaped monuments on either side are to the first and second Earls of Forfar, the latter killed at the battle of Sheriffmuir, 1715; the protective ironwork is noteworthy. The easternmost window in the S wall is also by Burne-Jones, made by the William Morris studio after his death, and commemorates a member of the same family. The sedilia arches were renewed at the 1898 restoration; by them is an ogee-headed piscina. Also on the S wall an early 19th-c. memorial to the Roberton family will be noticed, and a large wall-tablet to Walter Campbell (d.1735).

The **S transept** (War Memorial chapel) is dominated by the great S window illustrating the life of St Bride, by Gordon Webster (c.1955). The communion table here is of 1890.

Externally it is by no means obvious that the W porch was a vestry, or that the main entrance from 1833 till 1933 was into what is now the S transept. This transept and the 137-foot tower successfully punctuate the junction between 19th-c. and medieval work. The 1898 restoration of the latter involved renewal of window tracery and of most of the priest's doorway, but the richness of their mouldings and of the niched buttresses and interlocking stone roof slabs contrasts strongly with the more mechanical stonework of the western parts. As on the inside, the stops of the stone hood over the E window show Douglas shields, commemorating the college's foundation by Archibald the Grim. Beneath is the curious Gothic Revival tomb of John Pollok, d.1855. Also of interest are two 19th-c. iron standard lanterns, originally inside. The sacristy has a stone roof similar to the chancel. The free-standing granite, terracotta and mosaic memorial in the centre of the main approach to the church is to the poetess Joanna Baillie (d.1851) and was erected in 1899.

Cambuskenneth Abbey, Central   NS 809939
1 mile E of Stirling and ½ mile S of Alloa road A907

Arrouasian (Augustinian) abbey of the Blessed Virgin Mary
   founded 1147 by David I and colonised from Arrouaise. Became
   mitred 1406. Secularised 1604 to John, Earl of Mar.

Owned by Secretary of State for Scotland. Open during standard
   hours (admission charge).

What is left of the buildings is mostly attributable to the early 13th
c., though the bell-tower (the only detached medieval one in
Scotland) is of c.1300 and later.
   The abbey was sacked in 1559 and was quickly quarried away
excepting the tower. The site became a cemetery, owned from 1709
till 1908 by Stirling town council.

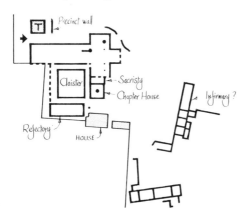

The **tower**, c.1300 in its two lower stages and c.1400 in its belfry, is
well preserved but much of the stone detail – windows, battlements
etc. – was renewed in the 19th c. It may be entered and climbed.
The ground-stage vault is also of c.1400 and is curious in being
supported on a complete added lining to the outer walls. The
first-floor room is a showplace for large stones (mostly grave slabs),
as well as an ancient boat, while in the top room are smaller worked

stones, part of an effigy, and a marvellously intricate piece of late medieval canopy work. From the roof the abbey's general layout is seen and can easily be related to the plan, though not much survives above foundations.

Of the **W front** only the weather-worn 13th-c. doorway is left. The graveyard walls can be seen to rest on some of the old foundations; the nave arcade columns have disappeared, but from the railed path across the nave four half-columns in the S wall (there was no S aisle) are clearly visible. The **cloister** behind is clearly defined, with the refectory closing its further side. Steps lead from that at a former external doorway on its S side, while half-way along the N side is the stone drain outlet from the washplace. The chapter house has the base of its central column. The slype alongside (separated from the S transept by the sacristy) leads out towards the field by the river where various foundations have been uncovered

Cambuskenneth Abbey: church foundations seen from tower, looking SE

but not positively identified; the higher mass at the far SE may be part of the abbot's house.

Now back across towards the **church**, entered from the cloister by a doorway in the transept. Just outside, in the cloister walk, are several grave slabs, while in the quire before the high altar site is the presumed grave of James III (d.1488) and Queen Margaret, marked by a memorial set up in 1865 by Queen Victoria. On the N side a single column base of the N transept arcade should be noticed, also a curving part of the monks' garden wall beside the transept, the foundation of the pulpitum near the E end of the nave, and finally another piece of boundary wall beside the tower.

Canonbie Priory, Dumfries & Galloway   NY 393760
at S end of village 5 miles N of Longtown and ¾ mile E of Galashiels road A7

Augustinian priory founded before 1220 by Turgot de Rosdale, a
   dependency of Jedburgh. Secularised to Alexander Lord Home
   1606.

Owned by Buccleuch Estates. Site accessible at all times.

Little appears to be known of the history of this priory, which was destroyed by English raiders in 1542 after the battle of Solway Moss. What was left of the buildings had been demolished by 1620. They stood close to the old main road (now bypassed) opposite the farm called Priorslynn, where a small tributary of the Esk tumbles down amongst hillocks. Nothing of them is to be seen there, but in the parish churchyard half a mile away is a memorial to the Rev. James Donaldson (d.1854) which incorporates a semicircular arch (probably of a doorway) with dog-tooth ornament, said to have been brought from the priory. It stands in a railed enclosure near the centre of the top end of the lower part of the churchyard, close to the conspicuous Mein mausoleum.

Carnwath Collegiate Church, Strathclyde   NS 976464
7 miles E of Lanark on Edinburgh road A70

College founded 1424 by Sir Thomas Somerville in existing parish
   church of St Mary.

Church of Scotland, but surviving transept owned by Lee and
   Carnwath Estates. Key available during weekday office hours
   from estate office adjoining churchyard.

Probably originally late 12th-c., the church seems to have been
rebuilt when it became collegiate. Only the N transept, now called
St Mary's aisle, survived after the Reformation; the church itself
was last rebuilt in 1866, almost touching the older building.

A single small compartment with ribbed tunnel vault, the 'aisle' has
been somewhat dressed up in the late 19th c. so as to form an entity
in itself. The blocked arch at its S end is filled with a *repoussé*
bronze memorial of 1899 to the parents and brother of Simon
Macdonald Lockhart, a big inscribed panel flanked by angels and
topped by standing figures. The tomb with two rather damaged
effigies, standing near the entrance, is ascribed to the Somervilles,
*c.*1500. In the floor are ledger stones to their successors the
Lockharts, and on the E wall a plain tablet to Philadelphia Lockhart
(d.1825); above the latter three ancient carved corbels have been
built into the wall.
   The big N end window and two two-light ones in the side walls
contain somewhat faded 19th-c. glass. **Outside**, this N window is
broken into at the base by what is now the only entrance. Over the
blocked arch at the inner end of the transept is a big 18th-c. tablet
cataloguing members of the family of Sir Archibald Denham.
Above that are a circular window with loopy tracery, and a 19th-c.
bellcote.

Coldingham Priory: internal N wall of church: *c*.1200

Coldingham Priory, Borders   NT 904659
in village on A 1107, 10 miles NW of Berwick-on-Tweed

Benedictine priory of St Cuthbert, St Mary and St Ebba founded
   before 1147 at pre-existing church; dependent first on Durham,
   then on Dunfermline. Priory secularised to Alexander Lord
   Home 1606, and church became parochial.

Church of Scotland. Church open during normal hours.

St Ebba is believed to have headed the original monastery of monks
and nuns on St Abb's Head, 2 miles to the N, in the 7th c. That was
destroyed c.683, and again by the Danes c.870; when it was
re-established in Coldingham is unknown. King Eadgar of the Scots
granted a church here to Durham priory in 1098 and attended the
dedication two years later, but it may not itself have become
monastic till the middle of the 12th c. Being close to the English
border it was a victim of the continual military strife raging back and
forth, not to mention an ecclesiastical feud between Dunfermline
abbey and Durham. King John laid it waste in 1216, and in 1419 it
was again partly destroyed. Later in the century James III's attempt
to suppress it and to annex its revenues to his Chapel Royal at St
Andrews led in the end to his assassination following defeat in
battle at Sauchieburn. Thenceforward it was controlled by the
Homes and the Stewarts, but it was not transferred to dependence
on Dunfermline till 1509. Though it suffered from Hertford's army
in 1542, from a Scottish siege in 1544 and from Hertford again in
1545, it could still somehow accommodate Mary Queen of Scots and
her retinue in 1566. However Cromwell's men finally destroyed
most of the buildings in 1648, and thereafter they served as a
quarry. The nave and aisles, transepts and central tower and all the
cloister and domestic buildings virtually disappeared, leaving only
the once-splendid quire – patched up in 1662 as a parish church by
means of a plain rebuilding of its S and W walls. In 1854–5 these
walls were again rebuilt, the corner towers carried up to their
original height, galleries removed and the ground stage of the N and
E walls restored, and a new roof and S porch built. In the course of
that work, the foundations of the 11th-c. apsidal church were
discovered. Excavation of foundations of the cloister buildings
began in the 1960s and is incomplete.

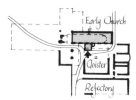

Prominent when approached from the main gates are the rather
squat quire and the isolated semicircular 12th-c. arch which led
from the S nave aisle into the S transept. Entering the church by the
two-storeyed porch of 1854 one is overwhelmed by the richness of
the N wall of the quire, with its end-to-end wall-arcading suddenly
seen at close quarters. The seventeen ground-stage arches (and five
more along the E end) are a spirited restoration of 1854, replacing
work that had been cut away when galleries were put in. The
walkway above has a continuous rhythm of open arches in stepped
triplets, so close together that they read as two low arches, one
high, two low, and so on. Their shafts have beautiful Early English
'waterleaf' capitals, and a clerestory lancet is centred within each of
the high arches. The 19th-c. S wall is quite plain with simple lancet
windows; the W is concealed by the organ. The glass and the flat
wooden ceiling are 19th-c. too.

   Outside, it is well worth making first a circuit of the standing
church, so as to see the external treatment of the two old outer walls
with their pairs of arches still of Romanesque character at the base
of each bay. Apart from iron markers in the grass, no sign of the N
transept or the nave remains, but the position of the crossing is clear
although the present W wall straddles two of its pier bases and the
exposed W end of the 11th-c. church shows rather confusingly in the
middle of the space. Here too are tomb-slabs of two priors,
Aernaldus (d.1208) and Radulphus (d.1209). The standing arch
already mentioned, with prominent nailhead ornament on one
jamb, is only a part of the quite substantial remains of the S
transept, the walls of which stand in parts up to a height of 6 feet or
so. Bases of two other piers are visible, and against the wall are
some interesting old tomb slabs and other fragments of masonry.

   The **cloister** evidently lay S of the early church and was never
rebuilt in the more normal position S of the new nave when the

great enlargement took place in the early 13th c. At least half of its square form is visible in the excavations, with a well in the centre. On its S side, away from the church, a rather higher wall-base, long called Edgar's Walls after King Eadgar, represents the N side of the refectory and shows a series of half-shafts along its inner face. Along the E side of the cloister a series of smaller compartments has been exposed; one of these, with what seems to be a later segmental end, may have been the chapter house and shows another wall shaft which probably supported a transverse arch. Incomplete excavations further S and E suggest, not surprisingly, that many more buildings existed down the slope.

Coldstream Priory, Borders   NT 844397
in town close to A698

Cistercian nunnery founded 1143 by Earl Gospatric. Secularised to
    Sir John Hamilton 1621.

Site mainly owned by Berwickshire District Council. No remains.

The flat triangle called Tweed Green at the junction of Leet Water with the Tweed is traditionally said to have been the nuns' burial ground, though bones and a coffin dug up there in 1835 were attributed to the slain of 1513 from Flodden Field four miles away. Leading away from it are Nuns' Walk clinging to the wall-topped embankment of the Tweed, and Penitents' Walk along the flatter margin of its little tributary which no doubt provided the monastery with water and drainage. Ranking as a priory, it was never of great importance. Following the English raid of 1296 the nuns dispersed in 1315, but presumably they returned, and their buildings were finally burned by the English in 1542 and 1545. The exact site is unknown but may reasonably be assumed to have been near the end of Abbey Road where it emerges on to Tweed Green.

Corstorphine Collegiate Church, Lothian   NT 200728
3 miles W of Edinburgh city centre and 200 yards S of Bathgate
road A8

College founded 1429 by Sir John Forrester alongside pre-existing parish church of St Mary.

Church of Scotland. Key available at the Manse, N end of Manse Road, or as advertised on notice-board.

The chapel of St John the Baptist, founded *c*.1376 by Sir Adam Forrester, (probably the present nave) was extended by his son (to the E it is assumed, i.e. the present chancel) soon after he founded the college. Unusually, it received transepts at the W end of the nave instead of the E, with a low tower against them. In 1593 it became a parish church itself, and about 1644 a N aisle was formed (probably on the site of the original church which was demolished). The W porch was also added. In 1828 the N transept was rebuilt under William Burn and merged into an enlarged N aisle. The interior was 'patched into a kind of meeting house', the chancel becoming a mere vestibule blocked by a gallery stair, and an entrance was formed where the altar had been. A restoration to something resembling the previous arrangement was done in 1903–05 under George Henderson.

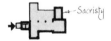

The present entrance is by the W porch of 1646 (in which are several carved stones) through a doorway enlarged from the original W window, and under the barrel-vaulted tower which has a bell of 1728. The arch to the nave is of 1828 and has World War I memorial panels on its jambs. The N arcade, on square piers with chamfered corners, is probably that of 1644, and the enlarged N transept is of 1828. Its large window (Works of Mercy) is by Ballantine and Gardiner, 1904.

The ribbed stone barrel vaults of the N aisle and **nave** were put in in the 1903–05 restoration to replace Burn's plastered ceilings. Six corbels in the nave were carved by Birnie Rhind, using as models the heads in Leonardo's *Last Supper*.

The **chancel** arch is similar to the N arcade but the chancel itself is 15th-c. In its N wall are the arched tombs of two Forresters (another is in the S transept). There is conflicting information on their identities and dates, and the heraldic shields are known to have been somewhat rearranged. The westernmost is attributed to Sir John the founder of the college and one of his two wives, and the second to his son Sir John, also depicted with one of his wives. The big E window (Supper at Emmaus) is by Ballantine & Son, as are all the others in the church not specifically mentioned.

Between the Forrester tombs is the doorway to the **sacristy**, which is also 15th-c. though it has lost its two upper floors, as can be seen from the corbels that supported them. The roof is another tunnel vault. Within the reveals of the window the mensa of the medieval altar is preserved, complete with its five consecration crosses. Also of interest are a piscina, several pieces of 18th-c. pewter, a small 17th-c. chest and some big ancient padlocks.

Beneath the main E window there is a tablet to the first provost of the collegiate church, Nicholas Bannatyne (d. in the 1470s – the date was never completed). In the S wall the easternmost window is by Nathaniel Bryson. The sedilia nearby are rather badly damaged but are interesting for their small-scale imitation vaulting. Beside the S or priest's doorway is an unidentified gravestone with a cross; there are others with inscriptions to Alexander Tod (d.1499) and to the Rev. Robert Heriot (d.1443), a chaplain of Gogar, 2 miles to the W.

The oak pulpit dates from the 1905 restoration but the hourglass behind it is 17th-c. The window at the E end of the S nave wall is another by Bryson. In the **S transept** the big window (Baptism and the Holy Spirit) is by Gordon Webster, 1970. The font here, reputedly pre-Norman but more likely late medieval, was brought from the abandoned church of Gogar. The Forrester tomb nearby has an early 15th-c. knight's effigy, probably of Sir Adam, while on the W wall is a long extract from the book of Ezekiel carved on a ringed stone of 1620 which originally capped the Watson burial vault. The tunnel vault of this transept seems to have had superficial ribs in a lozenge pattern, which have been cut off.

Outside, the stone-slabbed roofs are a prominent feature, though many of them date only from 1903–05. It is odd that a gap is left between the nave and the tower, and that the S transept ridge does not join the nave. The tower carries a modest spire with three somewhat half-hearted bands of ornament, four small lucarnes, and pinnacles at the bottom corners. The most curious feature however is the substitution (perhaps by Burn) of cubical sundials for pinnacles on the tops of the big buttresses. Some of these are in positions of no practical use and one, fixed at a different angle, may have been a much older mass-dial. The main S transept and chancel windows have tracery of Perpendicular design, normal in England but infrequent in Scotland. Above the latter is a niche which traditionally has always held a lamp as a guide to travellers; it is still lit during the hours of darkness.

Coupar Angus Abbey, Tayside   NO 223397
in town alongside Dundee road A923

Cistercian abbey of the Blessed Virgin Mary founded by 1164 by
    Malcolm IV, a daughter house of Melrose. Became mitred 1464.
    Secularised 1606 to James Elphinstone, Lord Coupar.

Owned by the Church of Scotland. Site open to the public at all
    times (church key obtainable at the Abbey Manse, Caddam
    Road).

The abbey church was in partial use by 1186 but was not dedicated
till 1233. Little else seems to be recorded except some repairs soon
after 1500.

    Reformers burned the buildings in 1559; the last monk died in
1607 and an account of 1622 mentions their ruined state. The parish
church, almost certainly on part of the site of the abbey church, was
built in 1618 and reconstructed in 1780 (when a last arch of the
abbey was destroyed) and again in 1859.

What is thought to be part of a gatehouse is the only building
fragment left. It stands next to the road and still has a barrel vault.
Four good 18th-c. headstones stand against the churchyard wall,
and a few moulded stones are built into the nearby octagonal
Watching House of 1822.

    In the church are more relics. The font is built up from pieces of
column shaft and bases. The tomb slab (shattered and mended) of
Abbot Schanwel (d.1506) is in the NW porch; it is unique in
portraying a mitred abbot wearing a combination of eucharistic and

processional vestments. Another stone is attributed to Abbot Alan (d.1335). In the SW porch are six figures from the tomb chest and in the SE corner of the church a knight's effigy, probably one of the Hay family. The framed 'Abbey Plan' (copied in 1900 from an older drawing), although imaginative in its details, shows it within the area of a Roman camp which did indeed extend eastwards from the churchyard.

Crail Collegiate Church, Fife   NO 613079
in village on A917, 8½ miles SE of St Andrews

College founded 1517 by William Myrton in existing parish church
    of St Mary or St Macrubha.

Church of Scotland.

Crail in the Middle Ages was important enough to have a moderately large aisled church, evidently replacing a smaller Romanesque one of which some traces remain. Before becoming collegiate it was held by Haddington nunnery. It was reconsecrated in 1243, a date supported by the surviving arcades and W tower. But the outer walls have been rebuilt (probably in 1828) and the roofs altered so as to be continuous over nave and aisles, thus doing away with the clerestory. In 1877 however the S aisle, at least, was roofless, and at that time a gallery occupied the whole N aisle facing a pulpit and holy table near the centre of a blocked S arcade. Subsequently the arcade was opened up and the aisle re-roofed. The chancel, cut down to less than half its original length, has been made into a vestry and organ gallery.

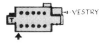

Just inside the S doorway, in the entrance lobby, is a splendid Celtic cross-slab with interlaced work and animal and figure carving. The spacious whitewashed **interior** is attractively unusual for its combination of medieval arcades with blue-panelled ceilings and

windows of Georgian character. The lancet windows of the former
clerestory remain, now opening into the aisles, but two bigger ones
introduced on the S side light the W end and the holy table. The N
aisle windows are square-headed at two levels to suit the gallery
(now removed) but those on the S side are happy insertions of
Georgian-style Y-tracery into pointed arches. The arcades are of
standard plain 13th-c. type with circular columns and moulded caps
and bases, the latter having deep hollows of 'water-holding' type.
The chancel arch, somewhat more elaborate, has springing foliage
in the capitals and quite high bases suggesting that the original
chancel floor was higher.

The pulpit and holy table, now central at the E end, the pews and
other furnishings are modern, but some 16th- and 17th-c. carved
panels are preserved, of the kind which denoted ownership by
means of shields and initials.

The picturesque exterior has a number of points of interest, and
not least the great **tower** of red stone which contains a Dutch bell of
1614. A sturdy stair turret projects on the N side, and the whole
structure gives the impression of having been meant to be higher;
the stone spire was added instead in the 16th c. On the E face the
line of the original nave roof can be traced, quite high up as one
would expect of a 13th-c. clerestory. Moreover the original height
of the **S aisle** roof, lower than the present one, can be clearly seen
on its 13th-c. W wall; the window there however is considered to
have been transferred from elsewhere. Beside it are a consecration
cross and a stone grooved by the sharpening of arrows. The S wall,
neatly ivied, is undoubtedly on medieval foundations but in its
present form is early 19th-c. But the E wall (with an original lancet
window) is 13th-c.

At the E end are several interesting indications of previous forms
of the building. The nave gable for example shows the original roof
line of the **chancel**, probably the 12th-c. one, while in the inner
angles between aisles and chancel (on both sides) the original
12th-c. corners of the nave, antedating the aisles, can be traced. In
fact a large proportion of what is left of the N wall of the chancel is
12th-c. too, though it is concealed by a 20th-c. vestry.

Crail's is a churchyard particularly rich in monuments, lining its
outer wall in the usual manner. The following brief account of the
more prominent goes clockwise, starting at the S end of the W side,

near the main gateway. All were recorded in a 19th-c. monograph, when the inscriptions were more legible than they are now. The first, flanked by twin Doric pilasters, is to John Wood (d.1723). There follow a row of 17th-c. ones, an enclosure containing another of the 17th c., and then a giant of the 18th c. followed by three more 17th-c.

In the NW corner is the oldest, a top-heavy double-spired superstructure on five slender shafts, to James Lumsden (d.1598). The column capitals are copies from a 13th-c. pattern; the centre column looks like an afterthought, necessitated by the sheer weight of masonry above. Further along the N side a big enclosure is labelled 'ERECTED for securing the DEAD/ANN DOM MDCCCXXVI'. There follow a series of minor monuments along the N and E sides. On the S wall is a good 18th-c. double tablet to the Lindsay family, with curved pediment. Then comes a large niche with a gaunt standing statue in armour, now headless and armless. Corinthian pilasters bear emblems of mortality and the frieze has the barely legible inscriptions 'WILLIAM BRVCE OF SYNBASTER' and its anagram 'LOVE CRIST Y[E] LAMBE B[E] WAR[E O]F SIN'; the date is 1630. Further along are two more burial enclosures – one having a pedimented entrance and some small memorials to Lindesays.

At the corner of the wide entrance drive lies a bluish-coloured boulder which, if legend be true, was hurled by the Devil from the Isle of May in a fit of rage.

Crichton Collegiate Church, Lothian   NT 381616
1¾ miles SSW of Pathhead on A68

Collegiate church of St Mary and St Kentigern. College founded
    1449 by William Lord Crichton.

Church of Scotland. Key obtainable at the Manse (Cranstoun
    Cottage, Ford).

Though a church had existed on the site for many centuries, the present one was not begun until the college was founded. Both church and college were due to the first Lord Crichton, Chancellor of Scotland, whose family began the nearby castle. The unfinished state of the church probably resulted from the failure of their fortunes, though it is impossible to be certain whether its nave was ever actually built. The surviving chancel and transepts with crossing-tower continued in use except for a period after the Reformation and were fitted with galleries in 1729. Some repairs were done in 1820–39, but the main restoration, after a long period of neglect, was in 1898 under the architects Hardy and Wight.

Entering through the N porch, built in 1898 on the site of the former sacristy, visitors come into what was the chancel. In the opposite wall are triple sedilia, much mutilated but confirming that the medieval altar stood nearby. There is also an ogee-headed aumbry, on the same side as the doorway. The internal orientation has been reversed so that the holy table, with pulpit and organ, are now in a central position beneath the tower. All three surviving arms of the church look towards them; all have their original plain stone tunnel vaults, and crossing arches with foliage capitals – those of the transepts being quite low.

The window glazing is on the whole undistinguished. The main E window is by Ballantine and Gardiner, while the eastern one on the N side of the former chancel is of c.1940 and the western a war memorial of 1919. The stonework of the E window and the main transept windows was renewed in 1898, and there is some doubt whether the tracery patterns are original. A piscina survives in the S transept, but there are no other ancient features inside.

To the right on leaving the sacristy-porch, the two-light eastern window of the N wall is probably the only one with original tracery. On the other side, the little round-headed priest's doorway is original. Above it are two separate cornices, the lower one approximately marking the line of springing of the vault within, and the upper immediately under the eaves.

The churchyard slopes so much that if the nave was really built the floor at the far end would have had to be raised about 10 feet to avoid a similar gradient. The jagged beginning of the S wall and the odd, nearly detached stair turret on the N offer no definite clues as to whether the walls ever went much further. However the upper walls of the saddleback-roofed tower do show not only the lines of earlier higher transept roofs but also that of a similar one on the nave side. There is also a sanctus bell turret high on the E side of the tower.

Crossraguel Abbey, Strathclyde   NS 276083
on A77 2 miles SW of Maybole

Cluniac priory founded 1216 by Duncan, later Earl of Carrick, a daughter house of Paisley. Became abbey 1286. Secularised 1617 and annexed to bishopric of Dunblane.

In guardianship of Secretary of State for Scotland. Open to public during standard hours (admission charge).

The original 13th-c. church was cruciform and was probably severely damaged in 1306 in the war with England. It and the monastic buildings were rebuilt in the 14th c. and the quire, sacristy and chapter house again in the 15th c. The abbot's house was supplemented with a tower house in the 16th c. and there is an unusual 15th-c. range of corrodiars' or pensioners' houses enclosing an outer court. Also in the 16th c. the gatehouse was built and the church divided into two, the W half becoming a Lady chapel.

Much damage was done by reformers in 1561, but there were still monks at least as late as 1592. The buildings, in open rolling countryside, are remarkably well preserved.

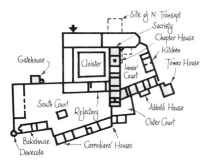

From the ticket office the whole N side of the long narrow church is seen first – its E half being 15th-c. The square marked out in the foreground represents the N transept of the original 13th-c. cruciform church; beyond it, the **nave** N wall is also 13th-c. at its base but the whole upper part is 14th-c. It is entered near its W end through a nice 15th-c. doorway with a niche over and a stoup inside. When the quire was altered in the 16th c. the aisleless nave was divided off by a cross-wall carrying a bellcote and became a Lady chapel. At the same time the lintels across the mostly 14th-c. windows were added to house wooden frames. The S wall is original 13th-c., almost blank except for an opening to the cloister. The two altar sites on either side of the small quire opening are easily traced, as well as the position of the rood loft above (the access to this was on the other side). A grave slab and two ornamental shaft bases by the N altar are relics of the tomb of Egidia, Lady Row (d.1530) and there are numerous earlier grave slabs.

The S side of the **quire** is partly 14th-c. and the remainder in a much greener stone, 15th-c. With the unfortunate exception of the polygonal E end, the walls remain virtually to their full height and there is much paving (though that at the extreme E is renewed) from a further alteration in the 16th c. when the altar was brought forward and another small sacristy formed behind it. The 15th-c. double-drain piscina and four sedilia are specially well preserved. On the S a small stair leads to the vaulted 15th-c. sacristy, standing where the S transept once was (traces of its arch pier are visible in the N wall). There are good carved corbels and a wall seat.

Now back through the quire into the **cloister** with its central well reached by steps. The base of the inner wall survives all round, also many of the roof corbels. Along the E walk the vaulted chapter house (rebuilt with the quire in the 15th c.) is unusually complete. The niche on its E wall indicates the abbot's seat beneath, and two incised floor slabs probably mark abbots' burials. Erosion of the central column gives it a precarious appearance. The 14th-c. rooms that follow were altered in the 15th c. and were: first the treasury (into which a dorter stair was added); next the parlour, forming a barrel-vaulted passage towards the abbot's house; and then the warming room (reached by cross-passages and now a stone store).

Along the S walk, the long room on the left was a common room, with the refectory above reached by a stair at the end. Of the

Crossraguel Abbey: church interior looking E

Crossraguel Abbey: piscina and sedilia: 15th c.

kitchen the serving hatch into the common room survives, but little else. The W range, though walled in, seems never to have been roofed or used, except for a parlour next to the church. Back now into the nave and out by its 14th-c. W doorway. The different mouldings on the buttresses indicate the retention of the 13th-c. angles when the rest was rebuilt. Next, the **gatehouse**, added to give a show of strength in the time of the last abbots. The upper rooms, each with fireplace, window seats and privy, can be visited via the spiral stair; the actual floors and roof are modern. The second-floor window affords a good view of the little circular dovecote and the foundation of the bakehouse beside it.

Diagonally across the big **S court** are the five 15th-c. corrodiars' houses; here lived suitably qualified pensioners, each with two rooms and a privy (the enclosure in the centre of the court still contains running water). In the vaulted room in the NE corner of the court (near the cloister passage) two fine grave slabs are preserved: that with a cross to Sir William Geruan (d.1540, a priest) and the other possibly to members of the Kennedy family.

Next the outer court, reached from the end of the S court, with the 16th-c. tower house ahead and the 14th-c. abbot's house on the left (the projecting bay is a 15th-c. addition) – and then, past another drain with vertical shaft from a privy, through a vaulted passage to the **inner court**. Now the abbot's house, with some partly preserved vaults, stands to the right; the 16th-c. abbot's kitchen is ahead. Going through that, one can then look at the inside of the tower house, two sides of which have fallen away, exposing the three upper-floor levels with their fireplaces and spiral stair. The house was built *c.*1530, possibly not for the abbot but for the young Earl of Cassillis, his nephew.

Lastly one can walk past the outside of the chapter house and sacristy (noting the dorter windows over) and round the E end of the church. The base of the S transept is visible in the angle between the sacristy and quire.

Cullen Collegiate Church, Grampian   NJ 507663
¾ mile SW of town centre and of Elgin-Banff road A98

College founded 1543 in existing parish church of St Mary by
    Alexander Ogilvy and others.

Church of Scotland. If closed, key obtainable at the Manse, Seafield
    Place.

A particularly good example of a small collegiate church continuing in use by the parish up to the present day, and beautifully cared for, it stands right away from the present town and close to Cullen House. As in one or two other instances (Bothans or Yester in Lothian and, further afield, Milton abbey in Dorset) this came about from the local nobleman's wish to see the population more decently housed and at the same time to improve his own privacy.

The earliest part of the present building, the nave and W part of the chancel, antedates the college foundation by three centuries or more. The S transept was added in 1536,and the chancel lengthened in 1543, but the N transept was only built in the late 18th c., and the vestry in 1967. The hand of the restorer has been laid lightly (there

were 'renovations' in 1842 and 1885) so that an atmosphere of
earlier centuries survives in a way seldom met with in Scotland.

The W entrance leads in under a deep gallery on four posts, entered
from outside and added some time around 1800. This gallery
extends to the N transept, on two more posts, so establishing an
endearingly lop-sided appearance – accentuated by the holy table
with its dais and pulpit which are off-centre towards the N. Visually
these are balanced by the laird's loft on the S side of the chancel, a
splendid raised and canopied gallery dated 1602, under which are
four little square enclosed pews called 'pumfils' (a pumfil is a kind of
sheep pen).

All the ceilings are flat plaster, dotted about with skylights and
dormers. The 18th-c. **N transept** has no arch; perhaps its most
interesting feature is the little doorway subtly introduced beside the
pulpit to give access to the new vestry – of which more later. By
contrast, the mosaic behind the pulpit, put in in 1960, is sadly out of
character. The gallery here earned the name Believers' Loft,
because most of the occupants were out of sight of the preacher
when he was round the corner in the chancel. The W gallery was the
Fishermen's Loft and one which formerly occupied the opposite
transept was the Gardeners'.

The **chancel**, extended when the church became collegiate, is
notable for its monuments. On the N wall are a series to Earls of
Seafield: James the 'Chancellor Earl' (d.1730) (a rather flat but big
and delicately wrought white marble tablet), flanked by the 8th and
7th Earls (d.1884 and 1881), each with a medallion head. Last and
much the finest is the canopied tomb of the founder Alexander
Ogilvy (d.1554). An intriguing mixture of late Gothic and early
Renaissance and remarkably well preserved, it contains his
recumbent effigy within a many-cusped ogee arch. Above and
behind the figure is a low-relief carving with emblems of the
Creation, the Trinity and mortality, with a pope-like tiara-capped
figure representing God. Niches along the base of the tomb-chest
contain little figures probably intended as Ogilvy children, while

Cullen: St Mary's Church: detail of monument to John Duf (d.1539)

above the spandrels of the main arch are big roundels of purely Renaissance character with kneeling figures of the couple.

Just beyond is another hybrid of style – a sacrament house or aumbry of uncommon elaboration and state of preservation. It is extraordinary how the flanking shafts, resting on Gothic-style corbels, become Classical architraves in the top part, there framing a pair of angels holding a monstrance aloft. The text on the frieze is from St John. On the E wall is a tablet to a Countess of Seafield (d.1761), with an inscription beneath to her husband who forbade any memorial to himself. The E window is of 1933. The laird's loft can now be seen at close quarters; on the supports are 16th-c. panels of early Renaissance character which formed the ends of family pews in the S transept before it was reseated.

The stonework in the **S transept** or St Anne's aisle bears some interesting inscriptions. Above the W capital of the segmental arch is one to the effect that Elena Hay made the aisle a 'chaplainry', beside the four stepped lancets in the S wall a record of an endowment by her son John Duff, and over the windows a much longer one setting out the terms of Elena Hay's foundation (which preceded the actual college). Several others can be found, as well as many masons' marks. In the E wall is a most unusual memorial by Anthony Stubbins with a pair of stone heads representing the 11th Earl of Seafield (d.1962) and his Countess. Opposite this is the tomb of John Duff (d. 1539). The inscription saying that it was removed from the Isle (aisle) of Cullen and placed 'here' in 1792 refers to a temporary removal to a mausoleum at Duff House, Banffshire. It was brought back in 1967. On the segmental arch runs another inscription to John Hay, 'gudsir' (i.e. grandfather) of Elena Hay. On the front of the tomb, below the horizontal figure, are two unusual and attractive little carvings of knights on horseback, fully caparisoned; in the recess above is a third, bigger one.

On the way out it is worth noticing the 18th-c. collection 'ladles' lying on the organ console and still used for receiving offerings from the pews. The **exterior** is as attractive as the interior. From the S side the roof levels make it evident where the E end was lengthened in the 16th c.; at that time there would have been an altar at the extreme E, by the sacrament house. The two two-light Y-traceried windows reaching above eaves level were probably added or enlarged in 1536 to compensate for the darkening of the nave by the S transept. Like other Scottish work of the period they revert to a 13th-c. style. High on the transept E wall is a blocked doorway that led to the former gallery, in the way that the W gallery is still reached by outside steps on the S side of the nave; the much altered round-headed opening beside these steps is said to prove the 12th-c. origin of the nave. This side of the churchyard contains the oldest and most interesting of the table-tombs, and gives a view of the little square bell-turret. Opposite the W door, set in the churchyard wall, is a quaintly naïve carving of an angel blowing the last trump, with an inscribed scroll and a skeleton. Two other stones fixed to the church walls are worth examination: first, an incised ledger stone on the W wall of the N transept to Alexander Innes (probably early 16th-c.), and secondly a tablet of 1603 on the NE corner of the chancel and transept is the vestry already mentioned, a remarkable instance of a modern addition (it is of 1967) totally in harmony with an historic structure.

Culross Abbey, Fife   NS 989863
in town

Cistercian abbey of St Mary and St Serf founded 1217 by Malcolm,
    Earl of Fife, a daughter house of Kinloss. Secularised 1589 to
    James, Lord Colville.

Church owned by the Church of Scotland; remainder in
    guardianship of Secretary of State for Scotland. Open without
    charge during normal hours.

Occupying a very steeply sloping site, the original buildings of 1217
were greatly altered late in the 14th c., and it seems very likely that
in an effort to rationalise the levels and access some of the earlier
work in the S part of the cloister was buried. The church nave,
really the lay brothers' quire, was abandoned c.1500 and a new W
front formed with tower where the rood screen and pulpitum had
been; a N aisle was begun but apparently never completed.
    The E part of the church became parochial in 1633 and its N
transept was rebuilt. The S transept was rebuilt during an extensive
restoration in 1905. Meanwhile the manse had been built in place of
the N end of the lay brothers' range and the cloister garth is its
garden.

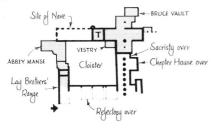

In the **lower part**, one's first encounter is with a massive projection
from the undercroft of the lay brothers' quarters, and a drain
alongside it. Just past it, an iron ladder allows access to the two and
a half remaining bays of their vaulted refectory. Stone steps led on
up to the dorter above.
    Back at the bottom level, an undercroft lies beneath the
refectory, then a privy (with outlet to the drain), then the N side of

Culross Abbey: cloister, looking SE

the undercroft of the monks' refectory with clear remains of
vaulting. The cloister is behind, high above. The line of column
bases running towards the church marks the dorter undercroft and
(at the upper end where it widens) that of the chapter house. At the
lower end, where steps lead down, was the outlet from the
reredorter. All this is late 14th-c.

Now back to the road and up the hill past the Abbey Manse. This
is private, but the outer flank of the lay brothers' parlour and
refectory can be glimpsed in the front garden.

Contrary to first impressions, the embattled **church** tower with its
projecting stair turret was never central. It was only built *c*.1500
after the lay brothers had gone and the nave (their quire) had fallen
into disuse. The two blocked arches on the right in what is now the
manse wall were their night stair doorway and processional

Culross Abbey from SE

entrance. This S wall (N wall of cloister) is original (early 13th-c.) as far as the tower; on it are several much later wall-tablets. The **tower** doorway, a late example of Romanesque, is original too and must have been moved from the previous W front to the site of the original stone rood screen, some of which survives. Above are the arms of Abbot Masoun the tower builder (*c*.1500). Inside, the similarly round-headed arch of the former pulpitum leads into what is now the parochial nave, and its stair now goes to the organ loft. A N aisle from here onwards was projected but never built. The N window of the tower is by Sadie McLellan (1963); opposite are benefaction boards and a medieval stone coffin.

Next the **N transept**. Its arch is late 13th-c., but the arcade and E wall are of 1905 and the remainder of 1642. The NW door was a private entrance for the Bruce family whose 'vault' is attached to the N end. Here stands the big monument to Sir George Bruce (d.1625) with two recumbent effigies. Its little kneeling figures are unusual in Scotland; they originally faced inwards. The big Gothic memorial is to Elizabeth Preston (d.1832), and on the S side are a stone of Edward Bruce (d.1565) and an early 19th-c. brass recording the heart burial of Edward, Lord Bruce (d.1613).

The damaged effigies under a canopy between transept and **chancel** are of John Stewart (d.1445) and his wife. The pulpit with circular canopy is made up of 17th-c. panelling. The main **S transept** is entirely of 1905, but its arch is of *c*.1400, with a smaller arch to the E marking the grave of a de Quincey (*c*.1500).

Finally the **exterior** of the N side. Near the tower stair are two stones with interlaced ornament, one being the base of a Celtic cross-shaft. The N transept and its added mausoleum have typical door and window and crow-stepped gable details of the 17th c. and two separate tablets to George Bruce, 1642. Further round is an unrelated and unfinished 'cloister' of 1905.

Chapel Barn Lodge, at one of the entrances to Abbey House to the NW, contains medieval remains, probably of an abbey gatehouse, but outside only the W gable is original.

Cupar: Blackfriars, Fife   NO 376145
in town centre

Dominican friary of St Katherine founded 1348 by Duncan, Earl of
Fife; incorporated into friary at St Andrews 1519; lands given to
burgh 1572.

Site in multiple ownership.

A small part of the church remained until the 19th c. St Catherine
Street, formed across its site, is named after it.

Dalkeith Collegiate Church, Lothian   NT 333675
in town centre on A68, 6½ miles SE of Edinburgh

Collegiate church of St Nicholas. College founded 1406 by Sir
James de Douglas.

Church of Scotland. Weekday access by arrangement only (see
notice-board at church).

Originally a chapel in Lasswade parish, it was made a parish church
in 1467 and became known as the East Church. The college of
priests was enlarged in 1477 by the 1st Earl of Morton, and he was
probably responsible for rebuilding the E end shortly afterwards.
After the Reformation the sacristy became a family vault of the
Dukes of Buccleuch, who maintained the rest of the church to some
extent. The chancel however was almost wholly neglected and
remains a mere shell, walled off from the rest since 1590. Long
crammed with galleries or 'lofts' used by the Incorporated Crafts of
the Burgh, the nave, aisles and tower were virtually rebuilt in
1851–2 in a rather English manner under David Bryce (restorer of
Rosslyn chapel), retaining very little but the arcades from the old
building.

Sacristy
(BUCCLEUCH VAULT)

The part of the church in use is entered by a S porch, rebuilt, but said to be to the original design; it has a quadripartite vault. The tower arch is of c.1400, and so are the main arcades on octagonal columns. Their mouldings and capitals have been re-formed in plaster, but some medieval corbels remain in the aisles. In the N transept is a very simple piscina. Generally the interior has been made so mechanical and lifeless that one can hardly regret that most of the chancel was left walled off and unrestored – and perhaps hope that as at Bothwell and Haddington it can one day be reunited with the remainder. One or two windows have glass of the present century, and there is a banner of 1665 of the local hammermen's guild.

Externally, Bryce's smoothly tooled stonework is already decaying. It very obviously extends as far as the first bay of the chancel, once a splendid structure but now in a sorry state. It dates from c.1500, and the windows have the kind of simplified Flamboyant tracery typical of that date. Their lower parts are untidily blocked, and their shafts and capitals almost unrecognisably weathered. The bold buttresses between have the remains of niches and there is a worn cornice of foliage carving to disguise the high space above the windows necessitated by the former tunnel-vault. Some big gargoyles remain too.

Even if the church is locked, the interior of the chancel can be quite well seen through the iron gate which occupies the round-headed former priest's doorway. Prominent is the big weather-worn monument to James, 1st Earl of Morton (d.1498), rebuilder of the chancel, and Princess Joanna his wife, daughter of James I. He is shown in 'parliamentary' dress instead of armour, which is very unusual for the period. The doorway beside it leads to the Buccleuch vault, the former sacristy, to which access cannot be had. It has a fireplace and a tunnel vault in the upper storey and a later segmental vault to the lower. On its NW angle, outside, is another niche.

The tower, owing more to the limestone belt of England than to Scottish tradition, has a stone broach spire 85 feet high.

Deer Abbey, Grampian   NJ 968482
¾ mile W of Old Deer on A950

Cistercian abbey of the Blessed Virgin Mary founded 1219 by
   William Comyn, Earl of Buchan, a daughter house of Kinloss.
   Became mitred. Secularised 1587 to Robert Keith, Lord Altrie.

In guardianship of Secretary of State for Scotland. Open during
   standard hours (admission charge).

The famous Book of Deer, containing transcripts of the Gospels as
well as charters and other writings and now in Cambridge
University Library, came from an earlier, Celtic monastery on a
different site. So far as can now be ascertained, the medieval abbey
buildings were almost wholly 13th-c. By the end of the 16th c. they
had been largely quarried away. In 1809 the site was cleared and
laid out, but in 1854 much of what was left was destroyed to make
way for a Ferguson family mausoleum; this in its turn was removed
after the site was made over to the Roman Catholic Church in 1930.

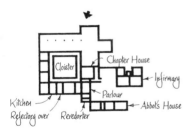

The principal parts remaining above ground are the S range of
claustral buildings. The church, outlined perhaps over-
enthusiastically with rough dwarf walls, is crossed to reach the
cloister. The square chapter house is readily identified; the slype
beyond leads out towards the infirmary, in which are the remains of
the fireplace. Below, across an exceptionally uneven paved court,
stands the abbot's house, in front of which runs the main drain from
the reredorter, protected by massive stones. A stone spout near the
end of the house also discharges into this drain.
   A passage (with the abbot's kitchen on the right) leads right

through the house; the early 15th-c. doorway at its far end has an unusual carved granite keystone. From here the outer wall of the S range can be viewed: the refectory was at upper level with cellars beneath. Its gables are a legacy of the 1809 'restoration'.

Return now across the court and through the slype. On the left is the parlour, over which was the dorter; beyond, at a lower level, are the base of the reredorter and an enclosed soil pit, served by the drain already noted. From the S cloister walk the inside of the refectory can be seen, with three small round-arched windows in its S wall. Beneath are the cellars, and past it the kitchen with stone benching and fireplace. On the W side of the cloister are the remnants of more storerooms. Steps led into the church nave, the W doorway of which was distinctly off-centre.

On the N side of the site, against the high retaining wall, is a collection of carved stones including sedilia arches, a fragment of a knight's effigy, and an extraordinary piscina bowl cut twice out of the same piece of stone – the first attempt the other way up having failed.

Dirleton Collegiate Chapel, Lothian   NT 516840
in village close to A198, 2½ miles WSW of North Berwick

College of priests founded 1444 by Sir Walter Haliburton.

In guardianship of Secretary of State for Scotland. Open during standard hours (admission fee).

Identification of the little chapel in the castle with the college is only surmise, based on knowledge that the establishment was for one priest only and that it was certainly near the castle. If it was actually inside the walls it is by no means the only instance though it may well be the smallest (cf. Warkworth, Northumberland or St George's chapel, Windsor). The most important parts of the castle, now surrounded by a beautifully kept little park, are 13th-c., but the Haliburtons, one of whom founded the college, built or rebuilt most of the E range in the 14th and 15th c. It saw its last fighting against Oliver Cromwell's troops, and its defences were dismantled by General Lambert in 1650.

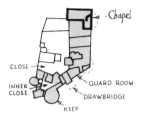

Like most castle chapels, this is an irregularly shaped vaulted compartment fitted in at an upper level amongst rooms used for other purposes, but nevertheless properly orientated with provision for the altar at the E end. Under it, at the extreme NE corner of the building, is the prison, and the approach at lower level along the Haliburton wing is through a dramatic tunnel-vaulted series of storerooms. A little window in the S wall of the chapel looks out along them. Around the altar position are a probable aumbry (N side) and credence and piscina (S), all badly broken. One of the two windows in the N wall has stone seats below, while the two recesses at the W end are thought to be a book cupboard and a holy water stoup.

Dryburgh Abbey, Borders   NT 592317
5 miles E of Melrose and 1½ miles W of Clint Mains on Melrose-Kelso road B6404

Premonstratensian abbey of St Mary founded 1140, a daughter house of Alnwick. Dissolved 1587 and passed to Erskine family 1604.

Owned by Secretary of State for Scotland. Open during standard hours (entrance fee).

Like the other Border abbeys Dryburgh suffered from English invasions, and principally in those of 1322 and 1385. Its general plan and much of the walling that survives is however the original Norman, and little that is now visible is later than the 13th c. when the E half of the church was finished. Its W half was reconstructed after the 1385 raid.

Under the Erskines, the Earls of Mar and the Lords Cardross the buildings passed to domestic use. The Haliburtons, kinsmen of Sir Walter Scott, bought them and lived in the E range of the cloister till 1671. In 1786 they were sold to a later Erskine, the eccentric 11th Earl of Buchan, who treated what by then were largely ruins as a romantic folly. In 1919 they were given to the nation by Lord Glenconner.

The church is approached from the NW. First seen is the rich 15th-c. main W doorway, with two rings of foliage ornament. The low block beyond is a range of cellars added in the 16th c. Go through into the **nave**, represented by little more than the stumps of columns, the foundation of the N aisle wall, and the S aisle wall complete to sill level containing three doorways and a piscina. Some limited evidence of the nave's general design can be gained at the W end where the commencement of the N arcade and the start of the N aisle vault can be seen. The step at the fourth bay is the base of the stone pulpitum marking the W end of the monks' quire.

Of the **crossing** only the NE pier remains to its full height, and here the design of the 13th c. N transept and presbytery can be studied in fairly complete form. The triforium is unusual in presenting no more than a sexfoil opening in each bay; the clerestory alternates wide and narrow pointed arches on its inside face and has a passage. The standard of design and workmanship is high, with a profusion of dog-tooth mouldings. The end wall evidently had three big lancets originally; that of the S transept, which abutted the monastic buildings has five higher ones, with a sill shaped to run over the dormitory roof below.

The survival of the two-bay E aisle of the N transept, and of the similar chapel on the N side of the presbytery is due to the collapse of the central tower having occurred at the opposite corner – and to successive owners having taken over these roofed places as their mausoleum. The first, northernmost one contains the Haig family graves, with the unassuming headstones of Douglas, Earl Haig, d.1928, and his wife Dorothy, d.1939. The quadripartite vaults are of the 13th c. and have carved bosses.

The second, corner bay contains a memorial and the burial place of the Erskines, while that N of the presbytery is of the Haliburtons and Scotts. On the N wall of the latter are a coat of arms of 1682 and a tablet of 1791 recording the Earl of Buchan's grant of the chapel to the Scotts. Another on the E wall commemorates John Haliburton, d.1640; the pink granite tomb in the centre is that of his descendant, the novelist Sir Walter Scott, d.1832.

The line of stone across the **presbytery** is believed to be the base of a stone reredos-screen – in which case the two bays beyond must have formed a separate chapel. On the N wall are a 19th-c. tablet to John Erskine, d.1634, a medieval cross-slab brought from Newstead village, a memorial to James Bain, d.1700, and a stone inscribed 'ELOSE TARSA', which has been variously interpreted. The 18th-c. Earl of Buchan rescued some of these from the floor and set them up. On the E side, past the stair doorway, is a 19th-c. memorial to Hugh de Morville, Constable to David I and reputed founder of the abbey, also an attractive 17th/18th-c. tablet to the Haigs with a nice mixture of upper and lower case lettering, and a medieval cross-slab.

In the chapel at the SE corner of the **S transept** are some stone fragments attributed to the tomb of the last abbot, Lord John Stewart, and on its S wall a cross-slab to Adam Robson, d.1555. From the transept itself steps lead to a barrel-vaulted room at lower level, now known as St Modan's chapel but originally a vestry and library. Being the Earls of Buchan's own burial place it is not open to the public, but some of the memorials can be seen through the grille: two busts on the far wall and a table-tomb in the centre. Modern wooden steps in place of the stone night stair lead to the dormitory on the E side of the cloister. From this level one can look

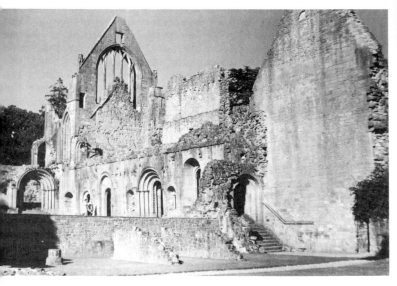

Dryburgh Abbey: church transepts and E side of cloister, looking NE

down into the garth, up at the five-light transept window and (at the
end where the floor has gone) down into the warming house. At one
time there was another floor above this; however the high mass of
wall at the end of the eastward projection, as well as the internal
subdivisions, are relics of the 16th-c. conversion to domestic use. At
the corners of the high wall are spiral stairs of which the right-hand
one provides an interesting vantage point; the attractive wheel
window beyond the cloister marks the end of the refectory in the S
range, and to its left is the late 15th-c. gatehouse built over the old
water channel.

Now return to the church and pass through the Norman opening
from the S aisle into the **cloister**. This splendid shafted doorway of
four orders was reinstated in 1894 after having been appropriated
for a private house! Along the E walk beneath the dormitory are,
first, a book cupboard with grooves for shelves, then another
opening into St Modan's chapel (with another Buchan memorial

visible at the far end), then the parlour, barrel-vaulted and now
containing various carved stones, and then the chapter house with a
doorway very similar to that of the aisle. Its barrel vault and stone
benching should be noted. Below the three E lancet windows is
interlaced round-headed arcading with incised patterns in the heads
of the arches; more important however are the dim remains of
medieval wall-painting on the window reveals and the vault – a
rarity in Scotland. The free-standing stone, almost square and
carved with intertwined creatures and foliage, may have formed
part of a washplace or perhaps originally the base of a standing
cross. In a glass case on the S wall are fragments of a statue thought
to be St Sebastian.

Next on the left along the cloister walk is the day stair to the
dormitory; then at the bottom of the corner steps the entrance to
the warming house. Here the two bigger windows and the fireplace
with leaf corbels on its hood are 14th-c. alterations. The vault still
stood in the 18th c. when the room was used as a cow byre, but only
the springers are now left. Next one can cross the lateral passage or
slype and go directly into the novices' day room, where a full-height
column stands and the fireplace is unaltered (i.e. of c.1200).

Return through the slype and take the path leading W along the
outside of the S range; on the left is the gatehouse and on the right
the refectory undercroft. Go round the end wall of the refectory
(with the wheel window) and back up the narrow steps into the SW
corner of the cloister. On the left at the top is a big arched
washplace; the stone bench is not ancient. At the far end of the W
walk a small doorway leads to the three small barrel-vaulted cellars,
of no special interest but containing a number of stone tracery
fragments from the nave W window. The other two doorways into
the S aisle being blocked, one must return to the nave by the fine
easternmost one.

Go out again by the W door and turn right to commence a
clockwise circuit, passing first the N aisle and transept and noting
again the dog-tooth ornament of the transept windows. The E end
has little left to show, so the E range of the monastic buildings is the
chief interest: first what is now St Modan's chapel, then the parlour
(outside which is a stone coffin), the chapter house with its three
lancets, a stair (now starting about 7 feet above the ground) to the
dormitory above, the two Y-traceried 14th-c. windows of the

warming house, the slype opening, and finally the day room with its two smaller windows.

At the bottom of the grass slope is the old water channel. Follow this past the gatehouse, and look finally at the obelisk beyond, put up by the Earl of Buchan in 1794 and containing quaint statues of James I, James II, and Hugh de Morville, the founder.

Dumbarton Collegiate Church, Strathclyde   NS 399754
in town on B830, close to railway station

College founded 1454 in existing chapel of St Mary by Isabel,
    Duchess of Albany.

Remains accessible at all times.

The church ruin was demolished in 1850 to make space for the railway station, and a single 15th-c. tower arch, sometimes called College Bow, was re-erected in Church Street. In 1907 it was moved again to the forecourt of what are now the Dumbarton District Council offices, still in Church Street.

Dumfries: Greyfriars, Dumfries &Galloway   NX 971763
in town centre on A75

Franciscan friary founded by 1266, possibly by Devorgilla de
    Balliol. Secularised to burgh council 1569.

Site in multiple ownership.

The present tall many-gabled slate-roofed Greyfriars church in the centre of the town, of red sandstone with a high tower and broach spire, dates from 1866 and replaced a church of 1727. The friary however is believed to have been on the other side of Castle Street where a plaque on the William Low supermarket records that in 1306 Robert Bruce slew John Comyn, his rival contender for the crown, and began the struggle for Scottish independence which culminated in the battle of Bannockburn; the high altar of the church is said to have been the scene of the encounter. A small street nearby bears the name Friars Vennel.

Dumfries Priory, Dumfries & Galloway   NX 966757
½ mile SW of town centre

Benedictine nunnery of the Immaculate Conception founded
   c.1880.

Chapel open during normal hours; museum in former school open
   10 a.m. to 1 p.m. (except Sundays) and 2 to 5 p.m. every day
   (admission charge).

Standing high above the town on Corbelly Hill (actually in
Maxwelltown which is in Kirkcudbrightshire), this typical Catholic
revival group of buildings of 1881–4 is the only existing Benedictine
nunnery in Scotland (nearby Lincluden was the only fully
authenticated medieval one). To the big chapel and the L-shaped
monastery range a girls' school was added; that closed in 1982 but
the building was reopened in 1986 as a Christian Heritage museum.
Almost all is of red sandstone, rock-faced but with ashlar quoins,
slate-roofed and lit by Gothic windows.

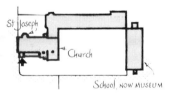

The convent house is of course private. The entrance to the chapel
is by a porch on the opposite side, the three W bays being reserved
for public use, gently but firmly separated by a delicate Gothic
pulpitum of iron and wood. A 14th-c. style arch-braced roof with
ceiled panels extends the whole length, towards the coloured E
window of cinquefoils, which a big pinnacled wood altarpiece partly
conceals. Most of the other windows are plain two-light, with
quatrefoil tracery of Decorated type. However some have glass of
interest: beside the S porch for instance a memorial window of
1971; at the W end a big three-light window of 1929 in memory of a
prioress, flanked by two smaller ones of 1884; and at the W end of
the N wall an Annunciation and Nativity of 1945. Next to this a little

polygonal side chapel of St Joseph protrudes into the front garden court of the monastery.

Alongside the wide main drive are sacristies and small chapels, the end portion of wall, curiously, being harled instead of stone-faced. Behind it, over the sanctuary arch, sits a stone bellcote. Further along, the museum entrance can be found on the further side of the former school block, facing away from the church.

Dunbar Collegiate Church, Lothian   NT 682786
at S end of town centre on A1087

Collegiate church of St Bey; college founded 1342 by Patrick, 9th
    Earl of Dunbar.

Church of Scotland. Key obtainable on request during shop hours at
    9 West Port.

The medieval church (with a tower of 1739) gave way in 1819–21 to
a completely new structure designed by Gillespie Graham, costing
£8,000. Apart from memorials, nothing of the old building was
preserved.

This is not the so-called Abbey church at the end of the High Street, but the one on higher more open ground a little to the S. The spiky Gothic tower is a prominent sea-mark. The four smaller corner turrets were built for stairs to reach galleries over the aisles. Those were removed in 1897 and a polygonal E end added, producing an unusually spacious conventional three-aisled interior with round stone columns and exposed roof timbers.

The principal attraction is the great marble and alabaster arched monument to George Home, Earl of Dunbar (d.1611) at the E end of the N aisle. He kneels in the centre, flanked by knights and surrounded by allegorical figures and heraldry. The stoup nearby is

Dunbar: St Bey's Church from SE: by Gillespie Graham, 1818–21

a very out-of-the-ordinary memorial to the Rev. Robert Buchanan
(d.1901). In the sanctuary the E window is by Edward Frampton,
and the side ones by Ballantine – none of them of outstanding
quality. In one S aisle window is glass of the 1920s by Arthur and
Charles Moore.

Of the great number of memorials in the churchyard the oldest
and most interesting stand along the W wall; particularly noticeable
is a late 17th-c. double-arched one to the Purves family. To the S is
a pretty little Gothic gardener's toolhouse roughly contemporary
with the church.

Dunbar: Red Friars, Lothian NT 678788
in town centre on A1087

Trinitarian priory founded 1218 by Patrick, 5th Earl of Dunbar and
refounded between 1240 and 1248 by Christiana, Countess of
Dunbar. Dissolved 1529, and granted to Peebles Trinitarian
priory. Given to the bailies and community of Dunbar 1567.

Owned by East Lothian District Council. Closely accessible at all
times.

A small establishment with only one friar, it had a modest-sized
church of which the small central tower survived through being
converted in a dovecote after the Reformation. At the time of writing
it was protected by a wire fence in the midst of a redevelopment site
and could not be actually entered.

Nothing but the saddleback-roofed 15th-c. tower remains, set back
from West Port almost opposite the public library. It stood over a
fairly narrow space separating the church nave and quire, the arches
of which have both been blocked, probably at the time when nesting
boxes were inserted. Plain semicircular N and S arches still exist but
are hidden by the small lean-to roofed infillings between the
buttress-like main walls.

Dundee: Greyfriars, Tayside NO 402304
in city centre

Franciscan friary founded in 1289 by Devorgilla de Balliol.
Secularised to magistrates by 1560.

Site owned by City of Dundee District Council. Open during
daylight hours without charge.

Noted as the meeting place in 1309 of an ecclesiastical council that
recognized Robert Bruce, burnt down in 1335 and probably again in
1385, the monastery was eventually sacked by a mob in 1543 and
destroyed altogether when the English burnt Dundee in 1548. Its

land was given to the town by Queen Mary in 1564 as a burial ground because it lay outside the walls – unlike the existing one which she regarded as a danger to health '. . . throu occasioun of ye said buriall pest and uther contagius seikness . . .'

The cemetery, covering several acres now in the heart of the city, continued as such until 1878. It also became a 'howff' or trades' meeting place; though that use ceased on the opening of a Trades Hall in 1778 it retains its popular name The Howff, and it contains one of the finest and biggest groups of tombs and memorials in the country.

The setts or 'cassies' of the paths are comparatively recent, and were salvaged from old street surfacings. They allow an ordered walk, serpentine-fashion, starting at the main gate in Meadowside and turning left, working southwards along the E side, then alternating back and forth from end to end, and finishing up at a gateway in Barrack Street surmounted by the city arms.

Architecturally the best memorials are in the centre and close to the W wall, especially in and around the SW angle. A group of table tombs near the centre of the S side is impressive, and so is the barrel-vaulted Lyall mausoleum at the SW corner, with a very worn late 16th-c. monument at the back. However the special interest lies in the tombstones of ordinary tradesmen of the 17th c. and 18th c., many of them bearing emblems of their crafts and occupations as alternatives to the usual symbols of mortality. An attractive picture book is published by the District Council but unfortunately does not attempt to locate those it describes.

Dundrennan Abbey, Dumfries & Galloway   NX 749475
in village on A711

Cistercian abbey of the Blessed Virgin Mary founded 1142 by David
    I, a daughter house of Rievaulx. Secularised 1606 to John
    Murray, Earl of Annandale, but part of church remained in use
    by parish till 1742.

Owned by Crown Estates Commissioners. Open during standard
    hours (admission charge).

Mid-12th-c. in date, the buildings are mostly Transitional in style with an interesting mixture of round and pointed arches. The chapter house was rebuilt late in the 13th c.

The last abbot died in 1605. The monastic buildings had been largely quarried away by the time the church was abandoned in the 18th c., and it too was then mostly demolished excepting the E parts. In 1838 Lord Selkirk repaired the remains and they passed to State ownership in 1841.

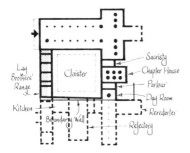

The W wall bears traces of a former porch. There were three separate W doorways; the centre one, which remains, has been partly renewed. Inside the **nave** the column bases are marked out but only one, the first on the S, is an actual survival.

The **N transept** stands relatively complete, with dignified arcades on clustered columns, pointed blind triforium arches in fours, and round-arched clerestory with its own walkway. The three E chapels were vaulted, and in the N one are the remains of a knight's effigy in a recess; a similar recess can be seen in the end wall of the transept. Of the **presbytery** much less is left. Unlike the nave and transepts and crossing, this part was vaulted. On the S side are the usual double piscina and triple sedilia. The **S transept** matches the N in most respects, but its triforium is open and in the S wall are the night stair doorway at high level and that to the sacristy beneath. Another piscina remains in the right-hand chapel.

The S aisle wall, backing the N walk of the cloister, is not entirely authentic following 19th-c. reconstructions. However, the doorway base nearest the transept is certainly original; it leads to the E walk

Dundrennan Abbey Church from SW

of the cloister. Here on the left are first the sacristy-library and then the splendid **chapter house** façade which is late 13th-c. and thus later than the other buildings. The central doorway has an unusual cusped head with foliage ornament while the flanking windows display nail-head enrichments. Above are round panels with fleurs-de-lys and similar carvings; higher up some of the cloister roof corbels survive, and higher still is a remnant of a window of the first-floor dorter. Inside only the column bases remain – but several fine coffin-lids can be seen amongst the old paving in the floor, the last and most ornate being near the SE column, to an Abbot Giles of c.1350. Next to it is an unadorned one to an earlier Abbot Giles, nearer the E end a simple, beautifully lettered but broken one to Abbot Brian (late 14th-c.), and by the NE column one to an Abbot William of the 13th c. Finally in the NE corner is a Tournai marble matrix of a large Flemish brass.

The S range (warming house, refectory and kitchen) extended

Dundrennan Abbey Church: S transept arcade from NW: 15th c.

beyond the present boundary, and only doorways remain. Of the W range, over which was originally the lay brothers' dorter, are vaulted cellars of later medieval date, now containing a collection of fragments of stone mouldings and memorials.

So back to the W end of the nave, where some more memorials can be seen, the best of them under the protection of the blocked N aisle doorway. The strangest is a once recumbent effigy of an unknown 13th-c. abbot with a dagger in his breast, and at his feet the supposed figure of an assassin, himself mortally wounded. Another, flatter, stone (badly broken) is the so-called cellarer's monument to Patrick Douglas (d.1480) and facing it across the recess is a mutilated tablet to Sir William Livingstoun (d.1607).

By returning through the W doorway and taking the path to the left it is possible to see the inner face of the kitchen wall. Any remains of the refectory (projecting at right angles in the Cistercian manner) or of the dorter beyond are still buried in the uneven ground.

Dunfermline Abbey, Fife　　　　　　　　　　　　　NT 090873
in town centre

Priory of the Holy Trinity founded *c*.1070 by Queen Margaret (St Margaret of Scotland); refounded *c*.1128 by David I as Benedictine abbey, a daughter house of Canterbury; became mitred 1244. Sacked 1560; dissolved 1593 and annexed to the Crown.

Owned by Church of Scotland and Crown Estates Commissioners. Nave open during standard hours; parish church open 9.30 a.m. to 4 p.m. (but not 12 noon to 1 p.m., and on Sundays from 2 p.m. only); both without charge.

Beneath the present nave there exist foundations of a church antedating Queen Margaret, and of an apsed eastward extension built for her *c*.1070. It followed Iona about this time as the burial place of Scottish kings. Of the church built between 1128 and 1150 the nave is the only remaining part; it resembles Durham cathedral and follows it chronologically. The quire (now gone) was enlarged in the 13th c. The surviving parts of the monastic buildings –

principally the S range – indicate a 13th-c. date but they were much rebuilt by Robert the Bruce after destruction by the English under Edward I in 1303. The guest wing was converted *c*.1600 by James VI into a royal palace, in which his son Charles I was born. The NW tower of the church was rebuilt and the N porch added in the 15th c.; this tower was again rebuilt *c*.1600.

The nave ('outer kirk') continued in use for many years. The E end fell down in 1672 and the central tower in 1716; in 1818–21 their remnants were demolished and the present parish church built in their place by William Burn. Meanwhile the SW tower was also rebuilt in 1810 after lightning damage.

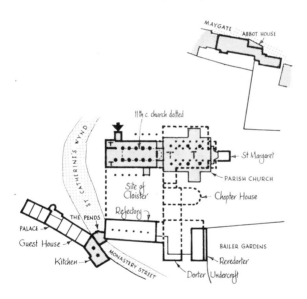

The **nave**, entered by a 12th-c. N doorway with three orders of zigzag, gains grandeur from its virtual lack of furnishings. The marching Romanesque arcades are reminiscent of Durham, especially towards the E where helical and zigzag fluted piers produce curious optical effects of taper. But the refinement of

pairing the bays is lacking – every pier is circular – and the triforium
and clerestory are single austere openings. The flat ceiling, probably
not unlike the original but marred by assertive curved ribs, is 19th-c.
At the W end the S arcade finishes with a smaller arch for the tower;
on the N side the 15th-c. rebuilding of the tower involved the main
arcade too, so the end pier is different; the aisle vault in its two W
bays is also 15th-c. Beneath this tower is a big clumsy memorial to
its architect William Shaw (d.1602).

The **N aisle** still has its shallow wall-arcade with paired shafts, for
the outer wall was spared in the rebuilding. The change to 12th-c.
vaulting in bay 3 is clear. None of the glass is specially attractive,
but some medieval fragments are included in the window of bay 3.
Another inelegant monument, in bay 6, is to Robert Pitcairn
(d.1584). Past this, one more bay of the main arcade tails off into
solid wall, one bay sooner than the crossing-arch where the nave is
blocked off. This is because Burn used the aisle end bays to house
the stairways of the parish church beyond. Across the nave but in
line with the present aisle ends is the base of the pulpitum. Between
it and the crossing-arch lie the foundations of the 11th-c. apse.
Bronze strips and lighter paving mark the plan of the early church,
parts of the foundations (exposed in 1916) being left visible through
grilles.

The internal parish church doors are normally locked, so
inspection of the outer kirk should now be completed by returning
W along the **S aisle** – similar to the N except that the vaults are
17th-c. reconstructions. It is worth looking outside at this point to
see the E doorway to the cloister, unusually perfect Romanesque,
preserved by a mausoleum which stood against it till 1905. Within
the aisle, towards the W end, is a capped-off well. The SW tower is
of 1810 and has a window by Sir Edward Burne-Jones. The main W
window (by Sir Noel Paton) was given by Andrew Carnegie, who
was born in Dunfermline.

The **N porch** has a two-bay vault with very worn bosses; though
probably 15th-c. it has been attributed to Shaw. The outer doorway
is round-headed – often the case with later Scottish Gothic.
Externally the aisle details are mostly 12th-c., but the big flying
buttresses are early 17th-c. Where the ancient work stops and
Burn's starts in only too clear. His **church**, standing on the site of
the monastic E end, can be entered by the N door and has a

spacious interior with clustered columns and plaster vaults. The three main windows are noteworthy: those of the transepts by Gordon Webster (N) and Douglas Strachan (S) and the main E window by Ballantine and Gardiner (1904). The central pulpit is of 1890 and stands over the tomb of Robert the Bruce (d.1329); the brass is of 1889. In the S transept are a cast of his skull taken when the tomb was found in 1818, a marble memorial by J. H. Foley to Maj. Gen. Robert Bruce (d.1867), the tomb-chest of Charles Bruce (d.1864), and a display of plate, tokens etc. Below the N transept window is the front of a magistrates' pew of 1610 which stood in the outer kirk, while just S of the holy table is a modern (1972) royal pew; the lectern is of 1931.

Next go to the S side of the churchyard in order to see the whole S front: 12th-c. nave aisle with big windows, altered little 13th-c. gallery windows over, and 12th-c. clerestory above that; big 17th-c. buttresses; 14th-c. NW and 12th-c. NE doorways to the cloister (which has wholly disappeared); and, to the right, Burn's tall imitation Perpendicular work topped by the extraordinary rectangular central tower displaying in its parapet the enormous words 'KING ROBERT THE BRUCE'. Turning about, one looks down into the 13th-c. **refectory**, through two vanished floors into its undercroft. The purpose of the unusual intermediate floor is not known; it seems to have lacked any direct access to above or below. The pulpit on the further wall is prominent. The traceried windows of the upper hall are 14th-c., the W in particular being amazingly well preserved and closely similar to some in and near Canterbury (with which the abbey had links). The S façade of the refectory can be seen from the furthest corner of the churchyard, also the late 14th-c. 'Pends' or gatehouse over Monastery Street and, immediately below, the end of the dorter undercroft and that of the reredorter with its drain channel. From the public garden below, this channel can be reached and followed to a street gate.

The kitchens were beside the W side of the Pends, whence the route to the refectory hall seems indirect and inefficient. The ruined shell beyond is the **Palace**, begun in the 13th c. as a guest house and adapted and enlarged by James VI as a gift to his bride Princess Anne of Denmark. It can be reached through Pittencrieff Park and has a long undercroft with remains of 13th-c. vaulting in the E part. Above were two more floors; in the middle one the enlargements

from Gothic to bigger mullioned windows are evident. The W part
is largely of *c*.1600; the room where Charles I was born is the upper
one with a fireplace and large bay window.

From this direction the **W front** of the church exhibits its very
dissimilar towers, the N one of *c*.1600 and the S a rebuilding of
1810. The doorway between is 12th-c., the window above 15th-c.

Finally two outlying buildings: in Maygate to the N the 16th-c.
commendator's house called Abbot House, and in St Margaret
Street to the E the remains of the 14th-c. Nethiryet or lower gate.

Dunglass Collegiate Church, Lothian   NT 767719
7 miles SE of Dunbar and ½ mile S of A1

Collegiate church of St Mary founded by Sir Alexander Home
  c.1450.

In guardianship of Secretary of State for Scotland. Open at all times
  without charge. Leaflet available at custodian's cottage nearby.

Some doubt exists about the year of foundation of the college, but
certainly there was a chapel here by 1423, close to a castle of the
Homes which was destroyed by English invaders in 1532 and 1547,
rebuilt, and finally blown up in 1640. The present building, virtually
complete but long disused as a church, is 15th-c. throughout but
shows clearly a change of plan during construction from a simple
nave and chancel to a cruciform shape with central tower. In the
English raid of 1544 the tower was used defensively. By the 18th c.
the church was being used as a barn, and the E window with the wall
below was torn out so as to allow horses and carts in. Dunglass
House, successor to the castle and designed by Richard Crichton, in
the park of which it stands, was demolished in 1947 after a fire,
leaving an elegant stable block as the church's nearest neighbour.

On rising ground amongst mature trees, approached by smooth drives from the N or W, of fine white stone flecked with purple, and with traditional stone-slabbed roofs entire, the church suggests from a distance nothing of the troubles that followed its century or so of collegiate existence. Low and spreading, with a stumpy tower, it is in fact a shell, paved only in the S transept and elsewhere floored with shingle.

The nave, like the chancel and transepts, has a pointed barrel vault. The rows of holes probably housed the ends of wooden joists of upper floors inserted when the church was a barn, though some may have been for the original scaffolding. Over the small crossing-arch is a rectangular opening which gave access to the upper parts of the tower.

From the crossing itself the arches to the transepts can be seen to be similar to that to the nave (except that their inner rings have been taken out), but that to the chancel with its foliage capitals is somewhat earlier; wall foundations found across the transepts, and the rather clumsy junctions between transept walls and crossing piers, all confirm that the original plan was without transepts or central tower. The tower has lost its intermediate floors and is now open to the underside of its roof.

The N transept contains many interesting 16th- and 17th-c. ledger stones; the recessed 15th-c. tomb in its end wall bears the arms of Sir Thomas Home and his wife, grandparents of the founder. A similar tomb in the S transept is unidentified, but nearby are 19th- and 20th-c. tablets to the Hall family. The chancel still has tracery in the side windows, as well as relatively undamaged ogee-arched triple sedilia. Equally interesting are consecration crosses cut into the side walls and picked out in red to make them more conspicuous. Five more of these can be seen in the sacristy, which is also vaulted and has another 15th-c. tomb recess, embellished with angels' heads at the inside ends.

Emerging through the gap beneath the narrow E window, one can look up at the one-time pinnacle bases on the gable ends, and then turn right to pass the priest's doorway (with shield and niche over). The tower must originally have had a wooden spire instead of the present low roof, but the sturdy stone roofs of the remainder are in their original form.

Eccles Priory, Borders   NT 763413
in village 5 miles NE of Kelso on Berwick road A699

Cistercian nunnery of the Blessed Virgin Mary probably founded
    or refounded 1156 by Earl Gospatric and his wife Derdere;
    secularised to Sir George Home 1609.

Owned by Forster family. Accessible with permission from house.

Like its more illustrious neighbours the Border abbeys, the nunnery
suffered severely from the depredations of English soldiery in 1523
and under the Earl of Hertford in 1545. Up to that point its history
seems to have been fairly uneventful, or at any rate undocumented,
and such remains as there are suggest building development
through the 13th c. It is likely that these are parts of the E claustral
range. They now form a barrier between the parish churchyard and
the garden of Eccles House. The parish church, rebuilt in 1774, was
always quite distinct from the nunnery church.

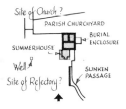

In the SW corner of the churchyard a curious sunken passage leads
along the back of an obviously medieval wall to a gate into the
private garden. This garden may be reached via a driveway
somewhat S of the church and (subject to permission from the
house) across lawns. The wall already seen is reached first and on
this side displays an intriguing series of architectural fragments,
some of them probably not *in situ*.

    Beyond is an 18th-c. summerhouse built against the S wall of the
most substantial part of the ruin – part of the undercroft of the
dorter. The winding stone steps inside would have been the day
stair, leading on to what is now a roof terrace but was the dorter
floor. The summerhouse possibly occupies the site of the chapter

house, in which case the two-bay wall first seen would represent the side of a common room or warming room. The burial enclosure within the churchyard, backing on to the vaulted compartments, has no connection with the priory, but the garden wall returning towards the W could possibly stand on the site of the S wall of the priory church. That would place the existing well somewhere within the cloister garth. The isolated column however is an assemblage of fragments in an arbitrary position.

Edinburgh: Blackfriars, Lothian   NT 262734
in city centre, ½ mile E of castle

Dominican friary founded 1230 by Alexander II; lands granted to
    magistrates and town council 1566.

No remains.

An important establishment having a large cruciform church with a spire, it was built on the site of the King's Manor and continued to enjoy royal use. It housed the Exchequer officials and on occasions important visitors such as Henry VI and Perkin Warbeck. Following fire damage in 1544 it was completely demolished in 1559. The name is perpetuated in Blackfriars Street, but the actual site is largely occupied by the Geography and Oral Medicine departments of the University.

Edinburgh: Greyfriars, Lothian   NT 257733
in city centre, 600 yards SW of castle

Franciscan friary founded 1455 or 1458. Dissolved 1490 and grounds
    secularised to town council 1562.

Church of Scotland. Church open (April to September) 10 a.m. to
    12 noon on Saturdays and till 4 p.m. other weekdays.

The present Greyfriars church, otherwise known as the Tolbooth and Highland Kirk, has no connection whatever with that of the medieval friars except that it stands within what were their precincts. Its resemblance to a genuine friars' church, at least in plan, is partly fortuitous, but does of course result from an emphasis on use for preaching. Its inclusion here can perhaps be excused by the microcosm that it provides of the history of the city and its inhabitants over several centuries.

The friary itself stood under the castle wall just beyond the bottom or N end of what is now a very large churchyard but was then its garden; nothing is left of it. The new Greyfriars church was an entirely new parish church built in 1602–20; its simple six-bay plan did however incorporate stone from the destroyed Cistercian nunnery of Sciennes not far away. In 1638 the National Covenant was signed within its walls (or partly in its churchyard) but in 1650–53 it was used as a barracks; gunpowder which afterwards continued to be stored in the W tower exploded in 1718, virtually destroying it and the two W bays. The remainder was patched, and within three years a separate and supplementary church (New Greyfriars) was built against the W end, repeating back to back without any originality the by then four-bay design of what became Old Greyfriars. The same architect, Alexander McGill, shortly afterwards added a big Classical porch serving both.

Old Greyfriars was completely burned out in 1845 and after much delay rebuilt (with a single-span roof and no arcades) in 1856. In the 1930s the congregations – and the churches – were united. The arcades of Old Greyfriars were put back, the extent of the original six-bay church being marked by an arch and a distinctive ceiling.

The churchyard is noted for its great number of monuments, particularly the 17th-c. ones around its perimeter.

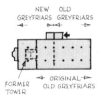

The two-storeyed twin N porch, like the church itself, has been thrown into one, so that one can enter the church by either of two doorways with cherub's-head keystones. Now effectively a hall-church with heavy arcades on octagonal piers, it is clearly subdivided into six bays and two, by the arch across the nave and walls across the aisles. These divisions are of c.1935 when also the four E bays of the arcades were put back; the others, evidently older than the rest, are only as old as 1720. The ceilings also differ: very high wooden panelling gives way at the W end to plastered barrels, though in the aisles the 1720 ceilings have been kept over all four bays so as to mark the extent of 'New Greyfriars'. Descriptions of the banners hung above the arcades (copies of those of the Covenanters) can be found beneath each. The rather strident patterned glass with roundels, around the four E bays and the E end, is of 1857. This was the first Presbyterian church to have stained glass or an organ. The marble font at the E end of the N aisle is 19th-c.

Another font in the **chancel** consists of an antique bowl and stem dug up from a Roman villa and presented by the antiquary William Moir Bryce. The wooden eagle lectern is of 1893 and the communion table and panelling, and probably the pulpit, of 1912.

In the **S aisle** is a memorial to Margaret Lady Yester (d.1647) removed from Lady Yester's Church in Infirmary Street: a tablet with rhyming epitaph and a stone below. There is also yet another font, a small Classical wooden one. The westernmost window of the aisle proper, showing St Helen and St Margaret of Scotland, dates from the 1930s restoration and is by Marjorie Kemp. Nearby is a tablet to Major Thomas Cochrane (d.1730), flanked by banners.

At the **W end** there are galleries to the aisles only, leaving a big clear central space. The large Resurrection window is by Ballantine and Gardiner (1898).

'Old' and 'New' churches are distinguished **externally** by having double lancet windows and big single lancets respectively. The strange 'Dutch' shaped W gable with pedimented top, and the small porch below it are of c.1720, while the E gable is a 1930s reconstruction. Below that is a monument to James Borthwick, surgeon (d.1676), with a scythe and skeleton. There are others fixed to the church walls. As for the **churchyard** a full guide to the monuments and a summary with plan are available and what follows can only be selective of some of the more interesting or dramatic. The start is downhill from the main churchyard gates to Candlemaker Row and the route follows (with small diversions) the perimeter wall, against which such structures were permitted by the

Edinburgh: Greyfriars churchyard: 17th c. monuments against E wall

town council during the 17th and 18th c. Some are still quite
medieval in concept: for example a few yards to the left of the gates
an arched tomb-recess with added Classical details, to James Harlay
(d.1617). Two big ones with Corinthian columns are prominent, to
Sir Robert Dennistoun (d.1626) and Alexander Bethune (d.1672).
Amongst these and standing forward from the wall are later
monuments mostly of the early 19th c., far too numerous to
describe but equally interesting for their architectural and pictorial
qualities. Next of note on the wall are somewhat similar monuments
to John Naismith (d.1613), Richard Dobie (d.1612), and John
Laing (d.1614), the first with a now headless effigy. Some have been
re-used; for example a pilastered memorial to John Morison
(d.1615) bears a tablet to one Robert Kerr, yet the worn tomb
beside it is probably Morison's. George Heriot's (d.1610) is an
elaborate affair with inscriptions at the top, and was once gilded.
Last in this row is one to James Murray (d.1649).

After a series of less theatrical compositions comes a bigger one to Sir Hugh McCulloch (d.1688) and then the well-known Martyrs' Monument commemorating the Covenanters – built in 1706 but the long eulogy added later in the century. Past the bottom corner, along the N side, are two little mausolea, to John Bayne (d.1681) with his figure hidden in the gloom, and to the Trotter family, 1709.

Now following the W wall of the churchyard, another show of 17th-c. prosperity. Starting from the bottom, two with fantastic twisted columns are to Magdalen McMath (d.1674) and a relative, Thomas Bannatyne (d.1635). Four more, to Foulis, Henryson, Byres and Primrose, stand out but their architecture and heraldry need hardly be detailed here. On this side the upper or 'Ovir Kirk Yaird' is separated from the lower by a retaining wall, in which can be seen a carved capital from Trinity College church (see p. 135).

Continuing again up the W side, an enormous monument to Elizabeth Paton (d.1676) can hardly be overlooked; it contains, amongst much else, naïve sculptures of Adam and Eve, Father Time and a quaintly welcoming skeleton. Catherine Tod's (d.1679) nearby also has its skeleton and other fashionable reminders of the transitoriness of life.

At this point an opening leads into the West Yard, containing 19th-c. burials, and a forest of monuments of no great individual interest. Past the entrance however are one of the 17th c. and three of the 18th c. which should not be missed. The oldest, clear of the wall, is a pillar and urn to Alexander Henderson (d.1646). Behind are, first a Corinthian-columned one to William Carstares (d.1727), then the domed mausoleum of William Robertson (d.1793) and at the top corner the mausoleum of the architect William Adam (d.1748) by his son John Adam. Each reflects the most advanced taste of its period.

A locked iron gate leads to the South Yard, known also as the Covenanters' Prison, though the truth of the story that those captured at the battle of Bothwell Bridge in 1679 were held there for five months without shelter is open to considerable doubt. Here the memorials are mostly in the form of enclosures, the earliest being of 1710. Not very much can be seen through the gate, and it must suffice to say that their general character is similar to those in the main churchyard.

Resuming then along the S wall, facing the centre of the church is perhaps the finest monument of all – the domed mausoleum of Sir George Mackenzie (d.1691) based on Bramante's little temple of San Pietro in Montorio, Rome. Further along is the rectangular mausoleum of William Little (d.1680) containing his recumbent effigy. There are many more. The last for particular mention is to John Mylne of a family of master masons and it is strangely inscribed all over to successive descendants – even, for want of space, vertically on the Corinthian columns. Many visit the churchyard to see the 19th-c. grave of John Gray, owner of Greyfriars Bobby, the shepherd dog who for many years kept watch over it until he himself died; it is to the left of the path leading downhill from the main gate towards the Covenanters' memorial.

Edinburgh: St Giles, Lothian   NT 257736
in city centre

Collegiate church of St Giles; college founded 1467.

Church of Scotland. Open during normal hours.

Perhaps the most important of all the Scottish collegiate churches, it had no more than parish church status throughout most of the Middle Ages. It contained a bishop's throne from 1633 to 1639 and again from 1662 to 1690 and was thus a cathedral for only a short time; yet it retains its courtesy title and is still popularly regarded as one.
    The earliest recorded date of a church here is 854. It was refounded in the 12th c., burned down in an English invasion in 1385, and almost at once rebuilt. Collegiate status, granted in the period 1466–9 after petitions to the Pope over a period of nearly 50 years, coincided with the extending of the quire and transepts and prompted the adding of more chapels. The famous 'crown' steeple was completed in 1495.
    St Giles' was at the centre of the religious storms of the 16th and 17th c. and became divided into three and then four separate churches. A destructive 'restoration' was done in 1829–33 under William Burn and a more responsible one in 1872–83 under the guidance of William Chambers. The Thistle chapel was built in 1909–11 under Sir Robert Lorimer.

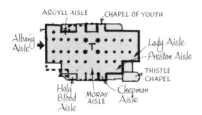

The ornate and totally 19th-c. W entrance is the best starting point.
The **nave** arcades in their present form with octagonal columns and
moulded capitals are by Chambers but the clerestory and plaster
vault are Burn's; earlier roof levels can be traced on the E face of
the tower. In the 16th c. parts of the W end were walled off to form
an annexe to the Tolbooth or court building, and subsequently what
was called the Tolbooth Kirk. The outer arcades with their
clustered columns, and the aisle vaults, are 15th-c. The elaborate W
door lobby with seats and canopies and a royal arms in the centre is
of c.1880 and the main W window (Prophets) is by Daniel Cottier.

War memorials cover the W wall of the **N aisle**, and its W window
is by Sir Edward Burne-Jones, made by William Morris & Co.
(1881). At the time of writing the font stands nearby, an imitation of
Thorvaldsen's Angel with Shell at Copenhagen, carved in Caen
stone by John Rhind. A low iron screen separates off the **Albany
aisle**, founded c.1400 and now reserved for private prayer. Its walls,
too, are lined with war memorials but its chief interest lies in the
modern furniture and decoration – the Cross with four texts in
stone, the big sanctuary lamp ornamented with thistles, the
patterned marble floor with heraldic roundels, and the plain low
chairs around the table.

Continuing along the aisle, there are yet more war memorials, the
first (to the Royal Scots Fusiliers) being in a recess which led to
Haddo's Hole, a small chamber where Sir John Gordon was
imprisoned in 1644. Not only this but also the magnificent
Romanesque 'Marriage porch' were removed in 1797, their place
being taken by the former Session Room to which there is a small
doorway. Next on the left is the former St Eloi's chapel, containing
an ornate 19th-c. memorial in 17th-c. style to the 1st Marquis of
Argyll, executed in 1661. The window behind, by the Glass

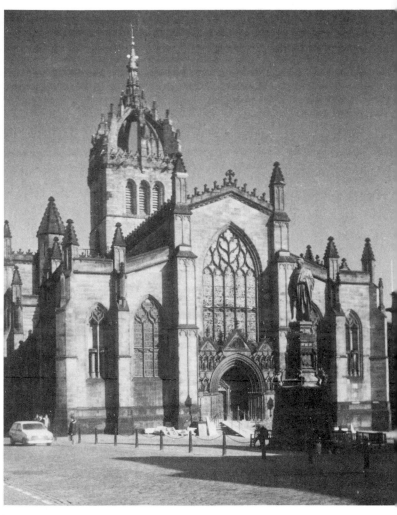

Edinburgh: St Giles' Church from NW

Stainers' Company of Glasgow, shows the arms of the leaders of the Covenanters. The banner on the W wall is of the Edinburgh Auxiliary Air Force Squadron. The Irish marble and mosaic floor and the holy table frontal chest with fine ironwork are all worth noting.

The outer end of the **N transept** was completely rebuilt by Burn to make a ceremonial entrance; its grey Gothic screen of Aberfeldy stone was added by Chambers. The figures represent patron saints of the craft guilds which had altars in the church. Of the memorials in the stair lobby, the bronze bas-relief head of Chambers' architect, William Hay (d.1888), should be noted. Burn gave the transept a plaster vault like the nave. The **crossing** vault is medieval, however, and the big octagonal piers – no higher than those of the arcades – probably encase Romanesque ones.

Now into the **N quire aisle**, with first a look at the 14th-c. quire design which (except in the two E bays) is similar to the nave but lower and with a later, tierceron, vault. The aisles again have quadripartite vaults. The Chapel of Youth on the left is virtually all 19th-c.; its oak screen and Nativity reredos form a memorial to Dr William Chambers, benefactor of the 1870s restoration. The banners include one of Field-Marshal Earl Haig, and the Victorian carved seat with Flamboyant tracery is of interest. The glass here and in all the ensuing windows round to the SE corner is by Ballantine.

On the left of the aisle is a door which is to lead to a new cathedral shop etc. on two floors. The recess beyond is of an unknown person's tomb; the many 19th- and 20th-c. memorials here are of only minor artistic interest, but include those of the women medical pioneers Sophie Jex Blake and Elsie Inglis; on the E wall the royal arms and arms of the Company of Merchants commemorate the Queen's visit in 1953; the big Gothic oak communion table in front formerly stood beneath the crossing. Note the different treatment of the two E bays where the columns are clustered and have heraldic capitals: these, with the whole quire clerestory and vault, are 15th-c.

Beneath the E bay of the S quire arcade is a big statue of John Knox, guarding the new stair to the Lower Aisle where a restaurant was formed in 1982 just below street level. On the E wall of the **S quire aisle** is a war memorial to ministers, on the S a Jacobean style

one to Lord Justice Inglis (d.1891), and a bas-relief bronze bust by
Pilkington Jackson to the Rev. J. Cameron Lees (d.1913). A similar
memorial to Andrew Williamson (d.1926) is just past the
sumptuous wrought iron screen to the ante-chapel of the Thistle
chapel, made by Thomas Hadden. The chapel's designer, Sir
Robert Lorimer (d.1929), is remembered on a tablet round the
corner on the E wall of the Preston aisle, and above it is another
bronze bust, of Dean Stanley of Westminster (d.1881). An older
carved stone set in the wall bears the civic arms of Edinburgh, a
castle. Another rich screen guards the ante-chapel which has giant
bosses on its vault and a roll of knights on the left wall. A fee is
charged for entering the **Thistle chapel** itself, built in 1909–11. In it
an irrepressible flow of magnificent craftsmanship seems somehow
to have overwhelmed other considerations, so that the high
windows and over-bossed vault, and the rich stalls and their
canopies with delicate twisted columns, are quite alien to the
sombre dignity of St Giles' itself. (It is only fair to add that the
intention of the donors, the Earl of Leven and his brothers, was to
restore the Chapel Royal of Holyroodhouse for the same purpose,
to be the chapel of the Order of the Thistle.) There are more details
to admire in the splendid royal arms on the sovereign's stall at the
back, the stall plates on the panels and the crests over them, and the
heraldic windows. Another royal arms set into the plain grey floor is
a memorial to King George VI.

The **Preston aisle**, tierceron-vaulted, is furnished chapel-wise and
contains the sovereign's stall on the S side with seats for the royal
suite, and below for the Lyon Court. It was founded in 1454. From
1643 until 1829 it was used as a separate church. The little chapel
opening off it through a low iron screen is the Chepman aisle (St
John the Evangelist's), founded in 1513. It houses the big canopied
monument (of 1888) to the Marquis of Montrose, executed 1650. A
small but intricate brass by Francis Skidmore on the W wall
commemorates Walter Chepman (d.1532). The heraldic window is
by Ballantine. The framed parchment is the original portion of the
National Covenant (1638) sent to Linlithgow for signatures. A
portion of the **S transept**, once St Anthony's chapel, is taken up
with the organ.

Turn now to the **crossing**, where the principal communion table
now stands with seating facing it from E and W. The N transept

window, well seen from here, is by Douglas Strachan, and the main
E one by Ballantine (1877). The ornate octagonal Caen stone pulpit
is by Sir George Gilbert Scott, the Acts of Mercy scenes being by
John Rhind.

The outer S or **Moray aisle** is temporarily filled with stalls and
there is no altar. It has a canopied hexagonal pulpit commemorating
the 'restoration in 1844 of daily service in this church after an
interval of two hundred years'. The little chapel at its SE corner,
originally the Holy Blood aisle but halved in width in 1829, retains a
14th-c. foliated tomb recess and a brass to the Earl of Murray
(d.1570) set into a more modern memorial. Outside this bay it is
worth exploring along the S wall for the memorials to Margaret
Oliphant (d.1897) and Robert Fergusson, both in bronze by
Pittendrigh MacGillivray; John Blackie (d.1895); and Thomas
Chalmers and Dr John Brown (both d.1882), both portrayed by
Jackson. Here also are a music bell of 1698 on a stand, and a bell
from HMS *Howe* (1942). The giant art nouveau bronze plaque on
the W wall to Robert Louis Stevenson (d.1894) is by Augustus Saint
Gaudens (1902).

Under the nave arcade are ranged several other items of interest
– a square grave-marker stone (formerly outside) with the
inscription 'ik 1572', and a stone inscribed 'john knox 1559' (these
are the dates of John Knox's first and last sermons here); on the
floor a bronze tablet to Jenny Geddes who (so the story goes)
hurled her stool at the Dean; and a vesper bell of 1452.

The outer S arcade ends with two very shallow bays (till 1829 the
Moray aisle continued to the W end); they are used temporarily as a
shop. Both contain memorials (mostly military). The white marble
bust at the W end of the main S aisle is of General Lockhart
(d.1900), by Sir George Frampton.

Apart from the tower, the **exterior** has been so much straightened
out and refaced as to have lost practically all interest. The big
monument outside the W doorway is to the Duke of Buccleuch
(d.1884) by Clark Stanton. On the S side, the little oriel window
formed part of the vanished S porch, while the unsightly blocked
window further round lies behind the organ. The equestrian statue
in the S part of Parliament Square is of Charles II. The Thistle
chapel in the SE corner of the church has its own external entrance
incorporating a 15th-c. round-headed arch from the old S porch.

The octagonal structure near the NE is an 1885 reproduction of the 16th-c. Old Mercat Cross.

Finally the tower, the most distinctive feature of St Giles', late 15th-c. in its upper parts. The 'crown' is by no means unique, though more elaborate than most in having eight flying buttresses.

Edinburgh: Trinity College, Lothian   NT 262737
In city centre, ½ mile ENE of castle

Collegiate church of the Holy Trinity founded before 1460 by
    Queen Mary of Gueldres. Granted to city 1567 and made
    parochial 1580. Demolished 1848 and partly re-erected 1872.

Owned by City of Edinburgh District Council. Accessible only by
    arrangement with City Art Gallery.

Once amongst the finest Gothic buildings of Scotland, it became perhaps the unluckiest of all victims of the railway age when Waverley Station was erected on its site. The dismantled stones were numbered and meant to be erected elsewhere in their entirety, but after a long delay a virtually new church of the same name was built in Jeffrey Street 200 yards away, merely re-using some of the old work in an altered form. The original building, which is quite well documented, had an aisled apse-ended quire of 1460–1530, transepts begun c.1530, central tower with saddleback roof, N sacristy, and S porch. The nave was never built – so in that and other respects it resembled Rosslyn chapel.

Only the quire was re-erected, shorn of its aisles, except on the N where two bays of the arcade opened into a wing which in its turn was demolished in 1964. Long disused as a church, the building serves as an overflow store of the City Art Gallery, and has become known as the 'Apse'.

Hemmed in by other buildings, the church is difficult to find and even more difficult to appreciate owing to its height against the narrow alleys surrounding it. The best view is that of the towering apse from Trunk's Close to the SE, the most dispiriting that from beneath the modern office building on the N (Jeffrey Street) side. There the blocked arcade is exposed, two bays of the three there once were, and above it the lines of the big roof of the now demolished Victorian wing. High on the wall two pieces of capital and two pieces of niche hood have been built in. At the W end the big four-light window with loopy tracery was formerly in the end wall of a transept, while the circular one above was on the W side of a transept – as can be seen from old engravings.

The S wall has to serve for a reproduction of the S side of the original but, the aisles being omitted, the three clerestory and the three aisle windows are all in one plane. High above are two cornices, big gargoyles, and more bits of capital. Numerous other carved stones are collected on the paving below. The E apse is the least changed, but the top of its middle window is altered, and the niches on the buttresses really belonged to those of the aisle.

Internally, there is tierceron vaulting right up to the apse, with carved corbels supporting the vault shafts, and big bosses. The former sacristy doorway, now at the W end of the N wall, has a piscina built rather oddly into its centre, while in the W wall is a 15th-c. fireplace transferred from a house in Sandilands. Some 15th-c. painted panels from an altarpiece formerly in the church are now in the National Gallery of Scotland; they are attributed to Hugo van der Goes.

Elgin: Blackfriars, Grampian   NJ 218630 approx.
200 yards NW of city centre

Dominican friary of St James founded 1234 by Alexander II.

No remains.

The friary stood in the locality still known as Blackfriars, close now to the loop road which skirts the city centre to its N. Little or nothing is known of its history but Blackfriars Road and Friars Road are named after it and the little Episcopal church now stands close to the site.

Elgin: Greyfriars, Grampian   NJ 219627
¼ mile SE of city centre

Franciscan friary founded *c*.1281 by William, Earl of Ross and
refounded 1479 by John Innes; granted to burgh *c*.1559.

Owned by Sisters of Convent of Mercy; chapel open on application
during normal hours.

Originally adjoining the S side of High Street at Little Close, the
friary was rebuilt on the present site in 1406–14. Its ruins stood till
the late 19th c. when all but the church was demolished, some of the
walls being incorporated in a house called Greyfriars, but much of
the stone being used up for garden walls and the like. The house
developed into a convent (founded 1891), and the church ruin was
largely rebuilt under John Kinross in 1896 for use as its chapel,
through a benefaction by the 3rd Marquis of Bute.

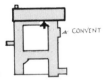

The way in for visitors is not from Greyfriars Street but via the
convent entrance in Abbey Street, whence one is conducted along a
corridor to enter the chapel midway along the S side, at the point
where the pulpitum or double screen divides it. The rich carving on
the screen (the work of Clare Westlake, *c*.1910) continues behind
the stalls in the quire. Running the full length of the building is a
perfectly plain boarded barrel ceiling, resting on wall plates with
carved cresting and vine ornament. The E window (Procession of
the Virgin) is a notable work by Lavers and Westlake, of the time of
the 'restoration'. To its right is a piscina, and another is just W of
the screen on the S side where the altar of St Francis now is.
    On the nave walls five fine ledger stones have been mounted,
mostly bearing heraldry, while at the W end is a big two-
pedimented monument to William King (d.1716) embellished with

three Corinthian columns and flanked by two smaller ones of about the end of that century.

It is permissible to walk right round the outside of the convent, but there is nothing of antiquity and very little in the chapel itself, so thoroughly did the restorers work. The porch is totally modern; so are the stone-slated roofs and a large proportion of the grey stone walling. However the big four-light window of intersecting tracery is medieval in origin and so is the little window on the N side against where the screen has been reinstated.

Fail: Red Friars, Strathclyde   NS 421286
7 miles NE of Ayr and ¼ mile E of Galston road A719

Trinitarian friary of St Mary probably founded *c.*1252, probably by Andrew Bruce. Secularised *c.*1540 and lands acquired by Wallace family.

Site owned by Douglas family. Accessible with permission from owner at cottage called Fail Castle.

Very little is known of the history, but the buildings are said to have been in a poor state in 1459 owing to the decadence of the friars, and to have been destroyed in 1561 by reformers. An old rhyme runs:

> The friars of Fail drank berry-brown ale,
> The best that ever was tasted.
> The monks of Melrose made gude kail,
> On Fridays when they fasted.

(Kail is a soup made with greens.) A single-storey cottage with smallholding occupies the site and has somehow acquired the name Fail Castle though there is not the least sign of fortification or outwardly even of antiquity. But the base of the field wall bounding the rear yard may well be medieval. Nothing else is visible, but minor remains have been found from time to time.

Fearn Abbey, Highland   NH 837773
½ mile SE of Fearn and 4½ miles SE of Tain

Premonstratensian abbey founded *c.*1227 at Old Fearn (9 miles
    WNW of Tain) by Ferquhard Macintaggart, Earl of Ross and
    colonised from Whithorn priory. Moved here 1238. Granted to
    Sir Patrick Murray 1597, but church remained in use by parish.

Church of Scotland. Church open during normal hours.

The evidence suggests a simple 14th-c. cruciform church, with
additions at the sides of the presbytery said to have been completed
as late as 1545. It was used as a parish church till 1742 when the nave
roof fell in at service time, killing forty-four people. The quire was
patched up in a Classical style in 1772 and again altered in the 19th
c. The monastic buildings are known to have been rebuilt in
1338–72; hardly anything of them survives, but the area enclosed by
the churchyard wall on the S is likely to have been the cloister,
which was 15th-c.

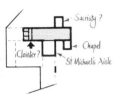

The church now standing is the abbey quire and presbytery, shorn
of its transepts. The main S door leads into a partitioned-off
corridor with vestry etc. on the left and two doors to the church
itself on the right, now barn-like with its modern flat ceiling.
Though patched and altered, much of the walling is 14th-c. The
blocked arch to the former S transept is clear, also those of a
doorway to the sacristy on the N side, and of another doorway
probably reset when the N transept was demolished. The thin
partition closing the W end of the present nave is a convincing
imitation of stone walling.
    Behind the platform at the E end a lower stone floor is visible but
even that is above the original level, as can be seen from the piscina

and triple sedilia. The memorials are to Charles Ross (d. 1731), Sir John Lockhart-Ross (d.1790) (by A. Farquhar with a ship in relief), David Ross (d.1661), and General Sir Charles Ross (d.1814). This end was at one time partitioned off as the 'Ross Vault'.

The **exterior** is of more interest. The W wall may well stand on the line of the medieval pulpitum; its three lancet windows are 19th-c., but above can be seen the remains of a 'Venetian' window of 1772. In the N wall the lancets seem to be 13th-c., but in fact are likely to be 14th-c., the plain style having persisted much longer than further S; a break in the string course half-way along may indicate the start of the N transept, whose blocked doorway has already been seen inside. Next is a small chapel or sacristy, probably 16th-c., with two stone roof ribs still standing and a damaged 18th-c. memorial. The adjoining upper part of the church wall is obviously much later. The E wall is 14th-c. at the base but (as at the W end) the lancets are probably 19th-c. – in this case renewals since they were certainly there before the Venetian window above was blocked. Another small chapel on the S side of the E end, no longer linked with the church, is of *c.*1540 – with a round-headed doorway, two windows once two-light, and a tomb recess containing various carved stones.

The big enclosure on the S side is – or was – the S transept, its walls truncated, capped off, and refaced on the outside. It is called St Michael's aisle. Inside will be found a tomb recess with sadly worn effigy of Abbot M'Faed (d. 1485), a small fireplace, and a very worn 17th-c. tablet. The area to the W was the cloister; close to the church doorway some corbels of its N walk roof survive. The boundary walls to W and S may indicate its extent, the sides of the E or dorter range being marked by the length of wall that turns S and by an isolated short piece parallel to it.

Fort Augustus Abbey, Highland   NH 382092
in village, close to A82

Benedictine priory of St Benedict founded 1876 by Dom Jerome
    Vaughan and Simon, Lord Lovat; became abbey 1883.

Church open to the public during normal hours; frequent guided
visits in summer months to a limited part of monastery, without
charge (between 11 a.m. and 6 p.m.).

The land belonged in the Middle Ages to the Benedictine priory of
Beauly. The abbey buildings' nucleus is the actual fort built in
1729–42 under General Wade, named after Augustus, youngest son
of George II, and captured by 'disaffected clans' in 1746 (its
predecessor of 1716 stood behind the present Lovat Arms Hotel).
In 1867 it was bought by Thomas, Baron Lovat, whose son gave it to
Benedictine monks in succession both to the 11th-c. Scots abbey of
St James at Regensburg, Bavaria (suppressed in 1862), and to the
English Benedictine abbey of Lamspring in Hanover (founded
1643). The transformation to a Victorian Gothic monastery was
largely done under Joseph A. Hansom in 1876–70, but the
slate-spired tower is by Peter Paul Pugin, and so is the cloister of
1880–93. The school in the N wing, originally founded in 1878, was
extended in the 1950s. The church is an amalgam of various dates,
largely on foundations by Pugin. A temporary building opened in
1890 no longer exists. The SW chapel is Pugin's, 1893, the quire and
S transept 1914–16, the SE chapel 1917 and nave 1949–56, all by
Reginald Fairlie, the W porch 1965–6 by Charles Gray, and the E
end by William Allan, 1980.

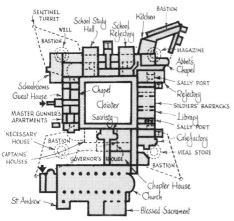

Fort Augustus Abbey: cloister, looking E: by Peter Paul Pugin, 1880–93

A visit is in two parts: first the church and then (accompanied by a
guide) a glimpse of the monastery. The spacious narthex of 1966
leads to Fairlie's nave of the 1950s, with very tall octagonal stone
piers supporting concrete arches across the main span and flat
beams with transverse vaults over the aisles. The 'central' altar and
tester are of 1978. The quire may not be entered but the imitation
Romanesque arcades of 1914–16 (also Fairlie's) – three bays of
heavy columns with cushion caps, simple clerestory and open oak
roof – can be seen well. A big round E arch frames Allan's
polygonal apse with its big orange cross window and clerestory slits.
   Adjoining the N quire aisle (but not accessible to the public) is
the chapter house of 1896. On the S side is the Blessed Sacrament
chapel of 1917, in Geometric Decorated style but with round
arches. The unusual curtained ciborium is of painted deerskin. W of
it is a transept in Romanesque style (the base of a tower of Pugin's
unrealised scheme) and then a side altar with mosaic by Arthur

Fleischmann. Further W is the smaller vaulted chapel of St Andrew and St Margaret (1893), the school War Memorial chapel. The narthex or covered porch of 1966 contains the baptistry, with a curiously domestic bay window and very small font.

Visitors to the monastery assemble at the guest house entrance (at the end of the main front nearest the church). In the Gothic entrance hall is a fascinating model of the fort made by a monk from the original drawings and seeming so small in scale that it is not easy to imagine how the entrance building became the guest house, the left-hand range the school, the furthest one the monastery, and the courtyard the cloister garth. The fourth side was demolished.

The hall, with its bright colour scheme and amusing wooden stair with birds on the newels, gives way to a vaulted corridor with old plans and pictures of the fort on its walls, and a Roman stone carving of three 'mother goddesses' found near Edinburgh. At the further end is a brick-floored former prison converted into a chapel in Early Christian style with paintings copied from some in Roman catacombs. A door behind the altar is popularly supposed to have led to an inner cell where Lord Lovat was held in 1746 after the Jacobite Highlanders had captured the fort; it now goes to the boys' assembly hall.

Lastly the cloister is shown, from the centre of the W walk. The walls around, to a height of about 20 feet, are of the fort, Pugin's tiled cloister walks with their transverse arches and quadripartite vaults having been built on its inside. Ahead is the monastery proper (with square spired tower), to the left the school with clock tower (by Hansom), and to the right the chapter house and church.

The entrance drive affords the only close external view for visitors, who are not normally allowed into the school parts, nor past the church. Between the guest house and church are the shop and other temporary buildings; the polygonal apse behind them belongs to a scriptorium by Pugin.

Fowlis Easter Collegiate Church, Tayside   NO 322334
5 miles WNW of Dundee and 2 miles N of Perth road A85

College probably founded 1453 by Andrew, Lord Gray in existing
    parish church of St Marnan or Marnock.

Church of Scotland. Key available at cottage no. 7 opposite.

The early history is uncertain. Even the chapel said to have been
built in 1142 as a thank-offering for the return of a Mortimer from
the Crusades may not have been the first on the site. In 1177 it was
granted to the Prior of St Andrews. A dedication recorded in 1242 is
likely to have been necessitated by a rebuilding, and certainly it
must have been rebuilt about the time of the college's foundation
(1453) unless, as has been suggested as an alternative, the
foundation was *c.*1530 under Patrick, Lord Gray who seems to have
been responsible for introducing many of the treasures the church
still contains. Remarkably unscathed by the Reformation, it was
repaired in 1842 and again in 1889 under the Dundee architect T. S.
Robertson.

The uninviting N side facing the road gives no hint of the quite
exceptional amount of interest inside. Entry by the S doorway is
into a kind of **ante-chapel**, separated from the remainder by a
19th-c. wooden screen incorporating 15th-c. doors from the former
rood screen, with linenfold and Flamboyant traceried panels. Two
corbels still in place on each of the side walls supported the rood
loft, a third one on the N side having probably been part of the top
step of its stair. The dark open timber roof running the length of the
church has arched trusses, alternately high and low, resting on wall
brackets with shields; these are all of 1889.
    Reverting to the 'ante-chapel', there are holy water stoups just
inside both N and S doorways, and beside the former hang the
parish jougs or penal shackles, an ancient oak collecting ladle, and a
German bronze alms dish of 1487 depicting the Garden of Eden
with Adam and Eve. On the W wall are five pieces of a portrait
painting in a frame, probably 16th-c. Close by is a late medieval
font, disused because its top part has been hacked off. Nevertheless
it shows in its eight deeply carved panels sculpture of rare quality.
They depict scenes from the life of Christ.
    The nave is dominated by an impressively large and detailed late
15th-c. painting of the Crucifixion. In tempera on oak boards, it is

more than 13 feet long and 5 feet high. Whether it was done by a
Scottish artist (or artists) or a Continental is unknown; if the
former, it shows Rhenish and Bohemian influences in the twenty or
so figures, the many horses, and the background depicting the
Jerusalem countryside. Curious inclusions are King Herod with his
crown and sceptre and his jester with fool's cap, and the 'souls' of
the two thieves coming from their mouths like modern cartoon
'balloons'. At the base of the Cross are St John, Mary Cleophas, the
Virgin Mary, Salome and Mary Magdalen, and around it the
Roman soldiers and a centurion pointing to an inscribed scroll. On
the bottom member of the frame runs an inscription, probably
16th-c. but not directly connected with the picture, recording the
erection of the church to St Marnock in 1453 following a pilgrimage
to Rome (by Lord Gray) and a vow.

Further E is a smaller rather damaged painting of Scriptural
subjects: four upright figures at the top, then an obliterated band, a
picture of the Entombment, and at the base some more figures that
may originally have formed part of the Crucifixion picture. The
central figure is thought to represent Lord Gray himself.

The **sanctuary** rail is unusually high, of spiked wrought iron, with
the Beatitudes and Lord's Prayer displayed on boards above either
end. All these are 19th-c. The sacrament house or aumbry in the E
wall is one of the finest of the distinctive Scottish group that includes
also Crichton and Cullen; at the head is a figure of Christ,
surrounded by angels. Behind the holy table, as though it were a
reredos, hangs yet another late medieval painted panel depicting
Christ with five saints on either side. Most of these are identifiable
by their attributes, e.g. St Peter with his key and St Anthony with
his pig. The unusually small circular E window above bears the lion
of the Grays in early 19th-c. floral-patterned glass; the family
continued to use the chancel as a mausoleum until 1888. The giant
seven-sided pulpit is 19th-c. too. The window behind is of 1867;
further along is a more recent one showing St Andrew, by Margaret
Chilton and Marjorie Kemp.

The **exterior**, though plain and simple, has more than at first
meets the eye. To begin with, the stonework is unusually fine ashlar
with wrought faces of very high quality. The S (main) doorway is
round-arched, but has an ogee hood mould, crocketed and with
delicate leaf ornament. The stops on either side are angel heads,

and the finial is a helmet guarded by ape-like creatures. Further along, the priest's doorway is plain round-arched, but the S window of the sanctuary is distinguished by a deeply moulded surround. Continuing round the E end to the N side, the little circular E window shows no sign of ever having been bigger. The N doorway contains a slipped stone which looks oddly like a misshapen keystone in its round arch. At the W end is the best window of all, Decorated in character yet 16th-c., and above that a little turret with a bell dated 1508.

The **churchyard** has relatively few headstones of any interest. In amongst them, however, to the SE of the main doorway, is a medieval standing cross, and close to it lies a 16th-c. hog-backed grave cover bearing a sword and hunting horn.

Fyvie Priory, Grampian   NJ 765377
in village 22 miles NNW of Aberdeen on Banff road A947

Tironensian priory of St Mary and All Saints founded *c.*1285 by
   Reginald le Chen. United with Arbroath abbey 1508 but date of
   dissolution unknown.

Site owned by Fyvie Estate.

The position of the buildings is marked by a prominent but uninscribed granite cross on a cairn in a field of Lewes farm between the parish church and the river Ythan. A mid-14th-c. stone to Prior Cranno is in the parish church. Parts of the aqueduct that served the priory were found when modern water pipes were being laid in 1937.

Glasgow: Blackfriars, Strathclyde   NS 598653
in city centre

Dominican friary of St John the Evangelist founded by 1346 by
   Bishop and Chapter of Glasgow. Given to city 1566.

No remains.

After the Reformation the church on the E side of High Street
stood long enough to be called in 1638 the finest medieval building
in Scotland after Whithorn. Destroyed by lightning fifty years later,
it was rebuilt in 1699 as Blackfriars or College church. That in its
turn gave way in 1876–7 to Midland Railway offices (now
themselves demolished) and was replaced by a church in Wester
Craigs Street which is now derelict. The name alone survives, in
Blackfriars Lane on the W side of High Street.

Glasgow: Tron Kirk, Strathclyde   NS 597653
in city centre

Collegiate church of the Blessed Virgin Mary and St Anne founded
    1525 by James Houston.

Owned by Glasgow District Council. Existing building accessible at
    most times except during theatre performances.

Being begun so late, the church only had a limited period of use
before the Reformation came. It then stood empty till 1592 when it
was taken over by the Presbyterians and used as a parish church –
called the Tron Kirk from the proximity of the Tronc or public
weighing machine. The Hellfire Club was blamed for a fire in 1793
that destroyed all but the steeple, which partly dates from 1637. It
was at once rebuilt. Abandoned again as a church in recent times, it
was converted into a theatre and opened as such in 1982.

The tower, with its open base arched over the pavement of
Trongate, brown colour-washed walls, windows outlined in white,
big blue clock faces, and lead spire over-enthusiastically ringed and
windowed, is a familiar accent in a busy shopping street. It now
marks the entrance to what has become the Tron Theatre, standing
behind and separated by a short area of paving.

Nothing whatever remains of the medieval church. The 18th-c. one that took its place, a typical galleried hall with segmental-fronted entrance bay and once-elegant stairs in the two W corners, is hardly recognisable as a church now that the lower part has been broken up with foyer, dressing-rooms etc.

Glenluce Abbey, Dumfries & Galloway   NX 185587
1 mile NW of village and of A75

Cistercian abbey of the Blessed Virgin Mary founded 1192 by
    Roland, Lord of Galloway, a daughter house of Dundrennan.
    Secularised 1602 to Lawrence Gordon.

In guardianship of Secretary of State for Scotland. Open during
    standard hours (admission charge).

Not much is known of the abbey's building history but most of it
probably dates from the early years, i.e. the early to mid-13th c.,
excepting the chapter house and cloister E range which were largely
rebuilt early in the 16th c.
    The later years of the 16th c. saw much harassment and
spoliation. The S and W ranges were altered by the commendator at
the start of the 17th c. and in 1641 parts of the buildings became a

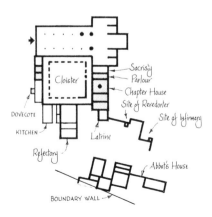

Glenluce Abbey: chapter house doorway: early 16th c.

manse. Forty years later much still stood though the church had
partly gone. Little of the church is left now, but some of the
claustral buildings are still comparatively unharmed.

The approach is from the N, towards the W front of the **church** –
represented by low wall-bases except the S transept which stands
high. The columns have gone but a wall-base in line with the S
arcade indicates the enclosure of the lay brothers' quire. The N
transept has little to show but the grave slab of Robert Lochinvar
(d.1548) with a bold inscription (the others are modern), and a
piscina in the right-hand chapel. In the presbytery the S wall has
evidence of the arch that adjoined its W end; also there is a worn
late 17th-c. wall-tablet to Thomas Hay, a descendant of the last
abbot.

In the S transept both chapels retain their piscinae and parts of
their vaults. One has an aumbry in its N wall and there are bases of
13th-c. clustered piers at the chapel entrances. The central stair
turret high in the gable is an unusual feature; it began at dorter level
on the other side and led to the roof spaces and apparently to a
room over the chapels and transept. Remains of the night stair and
upper doorway to the dorter are easy to trace, as well as a book
recess and the doorway to the sacristy.

Next the **cloister**. Following its E walk first, on the left are
another book cupboard, the sacristy, the inner parlour with a barrel
vault, and the chapter house which is the finest remaining part of
the abbey. All this range was altered very late, c.1520–30, and has
been restored in recent years. The fine doorway with carved capitals
and the reversion to a Geometric style of window are typical of late
medieval Scottish work. The low floor level achieved extra height
whilst not impeding the dorter above. The tall central column and
vault are noteworthy, also the two restored seat tiers and a patch of
old tiles reset in the centre. Outside in the cloister walk are more
tiles and a reconstructed length of outer wall with continuous
windows.

Beneath the barrel-vaulted passage beyond the chapter house
earthenware piping has been exposed; this brought fresh water.
Outside the doorway at the SE corner of the cloister a cobbled path
leads to another room. Adjoining this is a latrine, with a drain

leading from it. A pit further E indicates where the reredorter
stood; from there the drain leads past the remains of the infirmary
and then towards the foundations of the abbot's house on the edge
of the site.

The S range of the cloister was altered early in the 17th c. First on
the left is the washplace. The area with modern tiles was part of the
refectory – a room later divided into two halves and two floors and
added to at one side. The kitchen to the W of it was altered too; it
has a big fireplace at the far end. The W range, originally the lay
brothers', is likewise not in its original state; the tall thin slated
building was probably a dovecote built of stones from the old walls.

The museum behind the ticket office contains a collection of
carved stones and tiles and more specimens of water piping.

Guthrie Collegiate Church, Tayside   NO 567505
in village 6 miles E of Forfar and ½ mile N of Friockheim road A932

College founded *c.* 1479 by Sir David Guthrie in existing parish
    church of St Mary.

Owned by Guthrie family. Open during normal hours without
    charge.

The church, built *c.* 1150 as a prebend of Brechin cathedral, was
granted to Arbroath abbey in 1178 by William the Lion and bought
from it by the college's founder. What is now the chapel of St Mary
was the S transept; the remainder has been demolished and the
present parish church dates from 1826. They stand within a few feet
of one another in the same churchyard.

The chapel or Guthrie aisle, said to be late 15th-c., has certain
details which appear somewhat later, particularly the flat-headed
doorway and window on the W side. The flat ogee-headed entrance
doorway has evidently been transferred from elsewhere into the

Guthrie: St Mary's new and old churches from SW

blocking wall of the former transept arch, which is semicircular. The collar roof is old, but the bosses and painted wood ceiling panels are now in Guthrie castle. Plastered and whitewashed walls and a shingled floor complete the interior structure, but several memorials should be noted – especially one commemorating the restoration by Jane Guthrie in 1881. In the centre stands a round font bowl on a modern stem. Other stone relics include two stoups.

The 'new' church is typical of the 1820s, double-aisled, and tastefully painted throughout with white coved ceiling, cream walls and ochre woodwork. The churchyard contains many old tombstones; the picturesque stone gateway bearing the Guthrie arms is of 1639. A Celtic bell from the church is in the National Museum of Antiquities at Edinburgh.

Haddington Collegiate Church, Lothian   NT 518736
in town close to Bolton road A6137

Collegiate church of St Mary; college founded *c.* 1540 by magistrates and community.

Church of Scotland. Open 10.30 a.m. to 4.30 p.m.

Probably the finest of Scottish burgh kirks, it is 2 feet or so longer than St Giles' in Edinburgh. With some justification there has tended to be transferred to it the title Lamp of the Lothians which actually belonged to the long-vanished Franciscan friary nearby (see p. 157). That having been destroyed in English raids, the burgh built St Mary's to replace it. No dates are known apart from a grant of 1462 from the Prior of St Andrews for building the quire. It suffered in the fighting of the 1540s, the roofs and vaults being destroyed in the Duke of Somerset's siege of 1548.

The burgh then repaired the nave and aisles, under the direction of John Knox who had worshipped in them as a boy, for use by the Reformed Church, and in 1811 they were 'fitted up in a superior manner' under James Burn. This entailed the insertion of galleries in the aisles. To achieve the extra height required he dismantled the arcades and heightened the columns by several feet, raised the outer walls of the aisles, and gave them flattish plaster vaults. New furnishings were put in in the last decades of the 19th c., and the central window traceries of the E end and the S transept were renewed. The quire and transepts remained in a ruined state until 1971–3 when a major restoration was done under Crichton Lang, their vaults being replaced in fibreglass and the stonework extensively renewed.

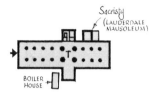

From inside the W doors the first impression is of space and uniformity. Both are newly re-acquired, for until 1971 there was a wall across the W arch of the crossing and the quire could only be seen from outside. Though most of the nave stonework is late 14th-c. its present proportions are due to Burn, who in 1811 inserted additional stones in the height of the columns and rebuilt everything above. Some of the capitals are moulded and some have foliage carving. His plaster vaults replaced an open timber roof over the nave and stone vaults over the aisles. The cut-back edges of the latter are still visible. His galleries have now gone except the W one which was remodelled in 1891 under George Henderson, and is rather like a rood loft with niches along the front; the space beneath is now partitioned off for a foyer and other uses. The regimental colours above the arcades are the Haddingtonshire Militia (1808–18) and the 8th Battalion Royal Scots (1910–21).

In the N aisle the second window from the W is of the 1890s, by Ballantine and Gardiner, and the easternmost of 1945 by William Wilson. Nearby is the Victorian Gothic pulpit on six pink columns, carved by Birnie Rhind (1892). The N transept, used for vestries since its rescue from ruin, has above them an organ gallery of severely plain design. Above that is a new vault made, like all those in the restored E parts, of fibreglass so as to lighten the load on the old walls.

The central circular holy table and dais at the crossing form the focal point of the entire newly restored church, though in medieval times the principal altar would of course have stood much further E. The very simple oak pulpit is of 1984, and the brass eagle lectern on a stone shaft carved in the manner of Rosslyn chapel dates from 1892.

The N quire aisle vault, also reinstated in fibreglass, has no ridge rib, giving it a somewhat disjointed effect. Simple stone benches (concealing the heating pipes) have been put in along the wall, and the entire floor is handsomely repaved with stone slabs. That has had the effect of partly burying the bases of the main arcades, where subsidence had to be checked in the 1920s while the quire was still a shell. The squat proportions of these weather-worn arcades are much less satisfying than those of the nave where Burn's raising of the columns, though perhaps done for the wrong reason, can now be seen to have been enormously beneficial. The weakness of the quire design is accentuated by the position of the clerestory, leaving too much plain walling below.

Beneath the N arcade is the tomb slab of the Rev. John Gray (d.1717) with elegant, almost copper-plate lettering. To the left are plate glass doors to the former sacristy, now the Three Kings chapel, dominated by the giant monument to the 1st Earl and Countess of Lauderdale (he d.1638) and his parents Lord and Lady Thirlestane. Double-arched and with alabaster effigies of all four in lying positions, it is mostly of black and white marble, with plenty of fully coloured heraldry of the Maitland and associated families. Lit only by a high E window, this room has a pointed tunnel vault. It became a mausoleum for the Lauderdales in 1595.

Various ledger stones are set amongst the quire paving, that to John Welsh (d.1819), father-in-law of Thomas Carlyle, being particularly pointed out. The communion table at the E end (now the Lady chapel) is of 1892; built in the wall nearby is a carving of Haddington's goat emblem (probably 17th-c.) found during the restoration.

The S quire aisle being a repetition of the N (its E end is the Columba chapel) one can next go into the S transept, where glass of 1877 by Burne-Jones and William Morris, moved from a redundant church in Torquay, has been put into the main window. The vault here (also a fibreglass reproduction) has tierceron ribs, as were originally intended over the N transept. The principal monument is on the E wall, to William Seton (1682). The window opposite, in memory of Margaret, Lady Scicluna, is by Sax Shaw, c.1975. Round in the S nave aisle is the font, matching the pulpit on the other side. The second window along from the transept is another by Burne-Jones, to the Rev. John Brown (1895) – attractive and unusual with its squared light greenish background. The fourth in the same wall is by Ballantine and Gardiner (1893) and the high end one (above what is now a tea preparation area) a Transfiguration of the 1930s by Heaton, Butler and Bayne.

As a part of the church's ministry to visitors, refreshments are often available at the W end of the S aisle.

The W front, thoroughly worthy of the church, has a big six-light window firmly divided by a wide central mullion in the local manner. Below it are twin round-arched doorways with bands of foliage and, above, a set-back gable with a gallery along the offset. Round on the S side the effects of Burn's changes begin to be seen. The medieval aisle walls were lower, without the openwork parapets and the big pinnacles – all of which give the building a more English appearance. The parapet above the clerestory is not even battlemented, and so retains the boldness of the original; further round, past the transept, is the restored E end with aisles unaltered by Burn for they were then hollow shells. The transept itself, and indeed the whole E end, is of redder stone. Rising above them is the sturdy but graceful central tower with triple belfry windows in each face. The top is evidently incomplete, and it is believed that a 'crown' of the type of St Giles' or Newcastle cathedral was intended. The E window tracery, renewed in 1877, is not to the original pattern but was copied from Iona abbey. The path beneath it passes pleasantly close to the bank of the Tyne, giving a glimpse of the medieval Nungate Bridge downstream.

On the N side of the quire the former sacristy projects. Before it became a mausoleum it had two storeys and a higher roof, as is indicated by lines on the buttresses. For the rest, the N side virtually repeats the S, though it is of interest that the further (NW) corner of the transept had to be completely rebuilt in the 1971–3 restoration, and that the nearest window of the main clerestory has long been blocked, probably to allay fears of structural movement at the tower junction.

Haddington: Greyfriars, Lothian

NT 518739

in town centre

Franciscan friary founded by 1242. Destroyed by English 1356.
   Secularised to burgh 1567.

Site owned by Scottish Episcopal Church. Holy Trinity church open
   during normal hours.

The Franciscan church is said to have been renowned as the 'Lamp
of Lothian' (Lucerna Loudoniae) till its destruction in 1355 in an
English invasion. Its role as the principal church of the town was
then taken by St Mary's. That is the commonly accepted sequence,
but a subsequent burning of the friary by the English in 1544, an
order of 1561 against demolition, and a final decision to demolish in
1572 suggest quite a full recovery after the 14th-c. disaster.
Certainly nothing positive remains today, though the Episcopal
church in Church Street is known to occupy part of the site and is of
some architectural interest.

Holy Trinity church was built in 1769–70 and originally had plain
Classical windows on the S side only, and galleries on the N side and
at the W. In 1843 it was Gothicised, a W porch added, and the W
gallery altered. The altar and pulpit are later 19th-c. The E end was
altered in 1930 to a Byzantine design by B. N. H. Orphoot. The
reredos is also his, and was carved by Pilkington Jackson. It is an
attractive and beautifully kept building set back from the street
behind a lawn. The SE boundary of the churchyard is a heavy but
featureless wall built in two stages which could well have been
connected with the friary.

Haddington Priory, Lothian

NT 533746 (approx.)

1¼ miles E of town and ½ mile S of A1

Cistercian nunnery of the Blessed Virgin Mary founded by 1159 by
   Ada, Countess of Northumberland. Secularised to John Maitland
   1621.

Site uncertain.

One of the largest nunneries in the country (ranking, like the others, no higher than a priory), it has nevertheless so completely disappeared that its exact site is forgotten. Obviously it was fairly close to Abbey Bridge over the Tyne, a three-arched medieval structure, because in 1358 the convent was nearly swept away by a flood, disaster being averted only by one of the nuns threatening to throw a statue of the Virgin Mary into it. It could well have stood on the flat triangular meadow on the right bank below the bridge or at Abbeymill farm on the left bank. Indeed some 70 yards beyond the farm is an old graveyard containing two table-tombs and some old headstones. Like so many other monastic houses it suffered at the hands of English invaders in 1336 and 1544–5; at the latter time it still had about eighteen nuns. A parliament held in it in 1548 sanctioned the sending of the infant Queen Mary to France to prepare to marry the Dauphin.

Hamilton Collegiate Church, Strathclyde   NS 723555
in town, 10 miles SE of Glasgow on A72

College of St Mary founded 1451 in existing parish church by James, Lord Hamilton.

Church of Scotland (present church: key obtainable from church secretary in nearby hall 9.30 to 12.30 weekdays: guided tours at 11 a.m. on Saturdays).

The medieval collegiate church was destroyed by the Duke of Hamilton when he built a new one in 1732 to a design by William Adam on a fresh site in what is now the town centre. A family mausoleum marks where the old building stood in Low Parks beside the Clyde.

The present church has only a tenuous connection with the medieval collegiate foundation, but is of interest as the only one designed by William Adam, father of the famous brothers. His unusual Greek cross plan with central circular body is unchanged, but a glazed lantern has replaced the original dome, thus letting more light into the interior but not improving the outside appearance. A horseshoe-shaped gallery in polished wood extends round three-quarters of the interior, the fourth side against which the pulpit and holy table stand being blocked by the tower. A Majestas window by Gordon Webster (on the SW of the rotunda) is noteworthy.

Outside at the E end stands Netherton Cross, reputed to be of the 6th c., originally on Mote Hill but brought here from North Haugh in 1926. There are also innumerable churchyard tombs and monuments from the 18th c. onwards.

The great monument to William, Duke of Hamilton (d.1694), formerly in the old collegiate church, is now in that of Bothwell (q.v.).

Holyrood Abbey, Lothian   NT 269740
¾ mile E of Edinburgh city centre

Augustinian abbey of the Holy Cross founded 1128 by David I, a
    daughter house of St Andrews; became mitred 1379. Secularised
    to John Bothwell 1606.

Owned by Crown Estates Commissioners. Open (nave and aisles
    only) during standard hours (admission charge); guide
    accompanies through palace.

The first abbey was on the castle rock. Of its Romanesque successor at the opposite end of the old town only the NE doorway of the cloister remains. The nave was rebuilt in the 13th c. with twin W towers, followed by the transepts and quire. In the 15th c. the nave roof was rebuilt and a system of heavy buttresses added. The guest house immediately to the W was increasingly used by royalty and became the nucleus of a permanent residence. Of the other monastic buildings little is known. About 1500 James IV began the NW tower of the palace proper that was to become Holyroodhouse.

His son James V continued the buildings but they were only completed with their balancing SW tower in the reign of Charles II, under the architect Sir William Bruce.

The E end of the church was taken down *c.*1569, and the nave adapted to serve Canongate parish. In 1672, on the building of a new church, it became a Chapel Royal and in 1688 was prepared for use by the Order of the Thistle under a college of Jesuits, but news of William of Orange's landing at Torbay fired a mob to ransack and wreck it. Following a period of neglect, its roof collapsed in 1768. Meanwhile Holyroodhouse had ceased to be a royal residence, a role it did not resume till 1850. Under Prince Albert the approaches were then re-formed and the gardens around the church ruin laid out.

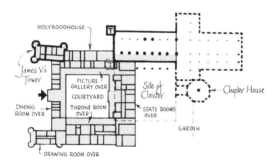

The central entrance past the ticket office leads into Bruce's cloister-like **palace** courtyard – which bears no relationship to the abbey cloister. The guided route takes in the state apartments, rightly laying emphasis on the pictures and furniture and starting on the first floor with the Long Gallery on the N side. Its far windows look out amongst the flying buttresses of the nave. The state rooms on the E front provide the only available close view of the E end of the church and the monastic site – the latter having little to show but a few bits of the chapter house. The circuit is completed with the drawing room and throne room, after which the interior of the NW tower is shown. This is the only part of the palace older than 1672 but is much altered internally since the drama of Rizzio's murder by

Holyrood Abbey Church: early 13th c. W doorway

Darnley in the presence of Mary, Queen of Scots, and in any case
has only a tenuous link with the abbey.

Visitors are free to pass along the N walk of the court and through
its NE corner into the **church**. Its interior is well seen from the W
end. The N arcade is gone, excepting some column bases, but the S
is complete – 13th-c. clustered columns with foliage capitals, and
triforium too (though walled up in the 17th c.) with twin two-light
units in each bay and varied plate tracery in the spandrels. The
clerestory has gone but its height can be judged from the crossing-
arch, which is complete but also walled up and provided with a
reticulated window. Some vault springers are visible too.

The **N aisle** wall has interlaced Transitional wall-arcading, and the
wall shafts, foliage capitals and springers of its vaulting, all early
13th-c. Beneath the NW tower (not normally open) is a white
marble memorial by John Schurman to Robert, Viscount Belhaven
(d.1639); also hidden from the normal visitor is the ornamental
outer side of the 15th-c. Abbot Crauford's doorway inserted in bay
2. The big wordy monument in bay 7 commemorates Bishop
Wishart (d.1671), the smaller one George, Earl of Sutherland
(d.1703). The canopied memorial with crude Classical detail in the
next bay is to Jeane, Countess of Eglinton (d.1562). At the E end a
wrought iron gate allows a view of the 13th-c. foundations
excavated beyond.

Across in the **S aisle** the Royal Vault at the E end contains various
royal remains collected in 1544 after the quire had been violated by
the English army, but again more than once subsequently
disturbed. Behind it, blocked, is the one surviving 12th-c. doorway.
The roof vaulting is complete throughout this aisle. In bay 6, the big
cross-slab with marginal inscription is to Prior Cheyne (d.1455); of
numerous others in the aisle, most are unnamed.

The palace cuts into the aisle, and more severely into the W front,
which is nevertheless the best surviving part of the church,
decidedly French in character. The splendid central doorway of six
orders is sadly defaced; so is the niched tympanum. The angels on
the lintel below and the twin double window above date from a
'restoration' of 1633; the outer tracery has curious fleur-de-lys
heads. The gallery below forms a kind of open-air pulpit. The
shallow 13th-c. wall-arcading continues across the NW tower, being
no doubt originally balanced by the destroyed SW one. The N side

of the church is closed off, so little can be seen except its big 15th-c. buttresses.

The brass eagle lectern given in 1522 is now in the church of St Stephen at St Albans.

Holywood Abbey, Dumfries & Galloway   NX 955796
2½ miles NNW of Dumfries and ½ mile E of A76

Premonstratensian abbey possibly founded between 1121 and 1154 by John Maxwell, Lord of Kirkconnel, a daughter house of Soulseat. Secularised 1609 and granted to Kirkpatrick of Closeburn.

Owned by Church of Scotland and Weatherall family. No remains visible.

Or Dercongal. Its history is thoroughly obscure. The church quire survived as a parish church till 1779 when it was demolished and the materials used for the present building. The abbey stood to the SE of it, partly in what is now churchyard and partly in the field adjoining, where some stonework was dug out in the 1930s. Two bells in the tower are said to have come from the abbey. The tradition of a tunnel connection with Lincluden College 1¼ miles away is due to the existence of stone drainage culverts. Part of the precinct boundary is marked by a line of larches, Scots pines etc. towards Abbey farm.

Inchaffray Abbey, Tayside   NN 954225
6 miles E of Crieff and ¾ mile S of A85

Augustinian priory of St Mary and St John the Evangelist founded 1200 by Gilbert, Earl of Strathearn. Became abbey 1220 or 1221. Secularised 1669 to William Drummond, later Viscount Strathallan.

Owned by Dewhurst family. Accessible at all times.

Though many abbey charters exist, hardly anything of its building history is known, and its chief claim to fame rests on the mass said

by its abbot before the battle of Bannockburn. An isolated mass of
trees and undergrowth approximately represents the cloister and
adjoining ranges; the church lay in what is now a cornfield to the N.
The only substantial masonry left is a vaulted cellar at the N end of
the W cloister range; having a fireplace, flue and upper window, it
must have been converted to a house after the Dissolution, but the
surviving traces of its doorway to the cloister seem to be 13th-c.
Starting from this cellar it is just possible to trace the line of the
cloister N wall (church S wall) eastward, and that of the cloister W
range southward; no doubt more could be discovered by clearance
and excavation.

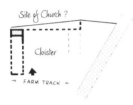

Inchcolm Abbey, Fife   NT 191827
on small island 2 miles SSW of Aberdour

Augustinian priory of St Columba founded *c*.1123 by Alexander I;
   became abbey 1235. Secularised 1609 to Henry Stewart, Lord St
   Colme.

In guardianship of Secretary of State for Scotland. Open during
   standard hours (admission charge): summer boat services from
   Aberdour and/or South Queensferry.

A stone cell close to the island abbey is attributed to a mysterious St
Colm, understandably confused with St Columba by King
Alexander, whose rescue by the resident hermit inspired his
foundation of the monastery – now the best preserved in Scotland.
The complexity of development of the little buildings was due in
large measure to frequent raids by English warships and pirates.
The 12th-c. church was extended eastwards in the 13th c., a tower
added over its chancel, and the chapter house built. In the 14th c.

permanent monastic ranges were erected, with the very unusual
arrangement of guest hall, kitchen, refectory and dorter all on top
of the cloister walks, and warming house over the chapter house.
Moreover the original nave and chancel were divided horizontally
to complete the cloister square below and to provide rooms for the
abbot above. The gatehouse-reredorter wing was extended
southward towards the beach and fortifications against pirates were
built. In the 15th c. the SE or infirmary wing was added, and at the
same time the church was made bigger again and assumed a simple
cruciform shape separated from the original by an open court; also
the cloister was given a new N walk clear of the original church.

The English sacked the abbey in 1542 and 1547. In 1548 the
French occupied it. The last mass was said in 1560, the abbot's
house became the commendator's, and the church stone went to
rebuild the Edinburgh Tolbooth. In later years the island served as
naval quarantine station, fort, and even (in the 1790s) Russian naval
hospital. The abbey was passed to the Commissioners of Works by
the Earl of Moray in 1924, and subsequently restored and cleared of
post-1560 additions.

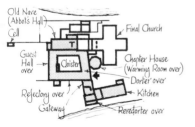

From the landing stage the rebuilt pyramidal roof of the 13th-c.
chapter house is prominent. To its left are the gatehouse, with
dorter end over, and the ruined 15th-c. infirmary wing right beside
the sea. Of the two doorways ahead, the right-hand one leads into
the 14th-c. cloister, an evocative wide barrel-vaulted passage,
extraordinarily well preserved. On the inner wall angle is a cresset
stone, and to the left a little washing trough. Turn right, however,
and right again into the 13th-c. **chapter house**, vaulted too. The

Inchcolm Abbey from SE

triple arcade on the E wall marks the abbot's seat, higher than the
canons' on the other walls. The central foliage boss has a hole for
raising a lamp from above, and the doorway a round arch and
graceful shafts.

Back in the cloister, the E walk next leads to a doorway to the
court separating the original church from the later one. But
continue along the N walk, added in the 15th c. and now reduced to
foundation level. Other doorways on the right lead to the tower and
into the lower part of the original nave, vaulted over in the 14th c.
for storage purposes when the abbot's room was formed above. Still
following the cloister, off the W walk a stair leads up to the
impressive little **refectory**, with pointed barrel vault, pulpit
platform, and on the S side a second stair down to the S walk. The
W part, with big fireplace, was screened off as a kitchen, which also
served the very similar guest hall over the N walk. A lobby at the far
end of this leads into the abbot's room in the upper part of the old

level with the double-arched top of the 13th-c. stone rood
en. Through that is a second room (within the **tower**) and then
another smaller one with a garderobe.

Here one can survey the cruciform E end which formed the final
church but of which little survives. A narrow stone stair and steep
wooden steps lead past chequered stone dove-holes to the tower
roof, which allows an even better view of the whole abbey.

Down now to the N cloister walk, across the cloister and out by its
far right (SW) doorway to look at the austere S front and the W side
of the gatehouse and infirmary range. In the opposite direction, in
the further top corner of the garden, is the tiny original hermit's
cell; its vault is probably medieval.

Continue round the main exterior. On the N side is the shell of a
16th-c. domestic building. Alongside, from the open court between
the churches, can be seen the triple arch of the pulpitum, which in
the 13th c. separated the tower space or retro-quire from the quire
itself. Close to the chapter house is the night stair, leading to the
dorter over the E walk of the cloister. Opening off it, added in a
most unusual position high over the chapter house, is the 14th-c.
warming room. The rooms beyond the dorter at this level –
reredorter and infirmary – are ruined, and there was never a way
through to the refectory.

Back then in the **church**, a wooden enclosure near the night stair
protects a unique wall painting of seven standing clergy (headless
but otherwise amazingly little damaged), believed to have adorned
the tomb of John de Leycester, Bishop of Dunkeld (d.1214 but
reinterred 1266). It can be seen on request. The E end of the church
has been seen from above, but the 13th-c. stone mensa on the high
altar site should be noted, also the remains of two altars and
piscinae in the S transept, and the start of its vault above.

Finally complete the outside circuit past the chapter house to the
gatehouse, barrel-vaulted too. A steep stair here makes it possible
to see the cellars and drains below the infirmary.

Inchmahome Priory, Central   NN 574005
on island in Lake of Menteith, 6 miles SW of Callander and ½ mile
S of Glasgow road A81

Augustinian priory of St Colman founded 1238 by Walter Comyn, Earl of Menteith; secularised to Earl of Mar 1604.

In guardianship of Secretary of State for Scotland. Open during standard hours or as advertised at jetty (ferry normally suspended during winter months). Admission charge covers motor-boat access.

The name means the 'island of St Colman' (or Colmoc or Macholmoe). Known also as the Isle of Rest, it is the largest of three in the lake – which is the only one in Scotland not called a loch. The buildings, fairly complete in extent though much ruined, are in their earliest parts 13th-c.; alterations subsequent to that period included the NW tower and W doorway, and the re-siting of the S wall of the nave and of some of the claustral buildings. As at Inchcolm the W and E ranges extend over the respective cloister walks, an unusual arrangement that has no obvious connection with islands.

For a short period at the start of the 16th c. the priory had a direct association with the Chapel Royal at Stirling. Robert Bruce visited it in 1306, 1308 and 1310, and David II was married here. A link with Mary, Queen of Scots, who was sent here for safety for a few weeks when not yet five, has become much exaggerated; what is known as Queen Mary's Bower is really only part of the monastic garden. From the end of the 17th c. the island was owned by the Marquises, later Dukes, of Montrose – one of whom handed the ruin into State care in 1926.

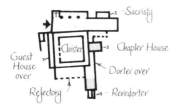

During opening hours a continuous boat service plies from the jetty at Port of Menteith, and when at the priory visitors need have no fear of being stranded. The ruins are only a short way from the

Inchmahome Priory: church interior, looking E

landing stage, amongst the mature trees which cover the island and
make it one of the most picturesque monastic sites in the country.

The **W front** has a fine many-shafted doorway thought to have
been intended for another building, possibly even the cathedral of
Dunblane. The extra width needed to accommodate it with its twin
blank arches on either side may have been the cause of the nave S
wall being built so markedly out of parallel, and of the consequent
out-of-square layout of the cloister. Of the richly moulded N arcade
the two W arches stand complete but the other two have fallen,
leaving only the base of the clustered pier between. The tower is
much later in date, rather clumsily added within the N aisle so that it
is hard to see what the builders intended to do where it adjoins the
arcade. On its E wall is the line of the aisle roof which, with most of
the outer wall, has disappeared.

The **quire**, at a substantially higher level than the nave, is
dominated by the handsome E gable with five lancet windows, but
its other walls are virtually complete too. It contains numerous

19th- and 20th-c. burials and monuments, mostly of the Graham or Grahame family. A doorway on the N side led to the sacristy, but there only the wall-base is left. Most of the memorials in the quire have been put into the chapter house, but a 13th-c. one remains under a heavy wooden cover. In the S wall a simple aumbry, piscina and triple sedilia remain without too much damage. A doorway leads out into a grassed area with corbels in the outer wall face, indicating a former covered way that led to the night stair and the first-floor dorter. A second doorway at the start of the nave opens into the **cloister**, the walls of which are marked out though little is to be seen of the arcades. The blank S wall of the nave shows traces of the high windows that pierced it above the level of the cloister roof.

The chapter house is apparently practically complete with its barrel vault but this is partly due to its conversion in 1644 into a mausoleum for Lord Kilpont. The effigies now laid out on the floor are medieval. The single knight with a shield is a Stewart of c.1300, while the knight and lady (formerly on a tomb-chest) are Walter Stewart, Earl of Menteith (d.1295) and his Countess. Against the W wall is a very large 14th-c. slab with the bas-relief effigy of Sir John Drummond; at its head are figures, possibly of St Michael and St Colman. Various other stone fragments include roof bosses and some cross-slabs of Celtic type.

The next compartment is the parlour, followed without a division by the warming house or common room, the far end of which is still vaulted and retains its fireplace. The arched structure against the W side is the remains of the day stair to the dorter above. Of the refectory little but the N wall is visible, a few feet high; the S wall has gone altogether but markings in the grass indicate the extent of its predecessor. Reverting to the E range, the reredorter is relatively complete: its upper storey was approached from the dorter and the lower from outside.

From there it is best to go along the further side of the E range, past the two prominent gables of the chapter house (from here the 17th-c. alteration of the upper part is more obvious), round the outside of the quire and past the sacristy foundation. The stepped plinth of the N aisle is well preserved, with buttress bases not aligned with the arcade piers; each of the four bays contained a chapel, till the tower was inserted into the westernmost. Back past the main front, the W claustral range has nothing left but foundation; its upper floor consisting of the prior's and guests' lodgings extended like the E one over the cloister walk.

Innerpeffray Collegiate Church, Tayside   NS 902184
4 miles SE of Crieff and ¾ mile S of Auchterarder road B8062

College founded between 1506 and 1542 in existing chapel of the
   Blessed Virgin Mary, probably by John, Lord Drummond.

In care of Secretary of State for Scotland. Open without charge
   weekdays except Thursdays 10 a.m. to 12.45 p.m. and 2 to
   4.45 p.m.; Sundays 2 to 4 p.m.

A chapel here was mentioned in a document of 1342. It was rebuilt
early in the 16th c. about or just after the time of founding the
college, but still to a small scale and really little more than a private
chapel. Even smaller is the adjoining 18th-c. building housing the
library founded in 1691 by David, 3rd Lord Maderty; also in State
care, it ranks as the oldest public library in Scotland.

Little more than a long single compartment, the **interior** is virtually
unfurnished except for memorials and a medieval stone altar. The
walls are bare plaster, the open timber roof and the paving a
modern restoration. Corbels midway along the side walls are
believed to have supported a rood loft. There is no E window – only
a niche outside. A little blocked opening on the N of the chancel
was meant to lead to a sacristy, though the continuous plinth
outside raises doubts as to whether it was actually built. The recess
opposite was probably an aumbry, while just inside the main S
doorway is a stoup for holy water. Two consecration crosses can be
seen on the N wall, as well as two funeral hatchments. These and
the monuments commemorate descendants of the founder, the
tablet in the centre of the N wall being to James Drummond
(d.1638) and the tombstone below to Rachel Drummond (d.1788).

The early Gothic Revival table-tomb is that of Clementina, Lady
Perth (d.1822). Above is a table to James Drummond, Lord Perth
(d.1800), and on the opposite wall one to the Hon. James
Drummond (d.1799).

The **laird's loft** at the W end was the original library room, the
books being later transferred to the separate building alongside. It
can be reached by a narrow spiral stair and has a fireplace and a slit
window looking into the very top of the chapel interior. Under it is
an ornamental ceiling painted in tempera.

Outside, the principal interest of course lies in the library, which
is opened during similar hours (an admission charge is made).

Inverkeithing: Greyfriars, Fife   NT 129827
in town, ½ mile E to A90 and 1½ miles N of Forth Road Bridge

Franciscan friary founded probably in 1268 by Philip de Mowbray;
    secularised 1559 to John Swinton.

Owned by Dunfermline District Council. Site accessible at all times.
    Museum on upper floor of guest house open at advertised times
    without charge; lower floor not open to public.

The friary site in the town centre is now a public garden. The only
roofed building to remain is the former guest house which has been
called, with probably little foundation in fact, the Palace of Queen
Annabella (wife of Robert III). Earlier than that, in the reign of
David I, the last assembly of the Culdees is said to have been held
here.

The irregularly two- and three-storey 14th-c. range of buildings
fronting the High Street was altered in the 17th c. and provided with
two open stair flights as well as a circular stair built on to the back. It
was restored in 1935 after falling into a variety of uses and degrees
of neglect, and one of the front stairs was removed. Nothing in them
particularly relates to religious use, and there is no certainty where
the church or other buildings stood, except for a series of vaulted
compartments some distance to the S.

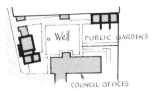

The street front is picturesquely haphazard, with crow-stepped
gables at either end of the higher and longer eastern portion, an
assortment of openings of various dates, and a stone stair to the
museum on the first floor. The museum interior is of no great
interest architecturally, nor does it yet house anything very relevant
to the friary. A bigger archway at pavement level leads into a
transverse passage, with at the end the circular stair, on the right
two small vaulted rooms and on the left a bigger one. Used as a
senior citizens' centre, they are not normally accessible to the
public.

The S front, very similar, faces a formal garden with a well – not
enhanced by the civic offices forming its W boundary, though civic
over-tidiness must in the long run be preferable to decay and
neglect. The squareness of the garden is intended to suggest that it
is the site of a cloister, but that is not proven. The three
barrel-vaulted chambers, part of an undercroft, can be found on the
left at the bottom of the slope beyond.

Inverness: Blackfriars, Highland   NH 664455
in Friars Street ¼ mile N of bridge

Dominican friary of St Bartholomew founded by 1240 by Alexander
  II; dissolved by 1567.

Owned by Inverness District Council. Site accessible at all times
  without charge.

History records a burning in 1372 and restoration by 1389. The
buildings apparently stood till 1653 when the materials were sold to
the Commonwealth commander for the building of Oliver's Fort at
the river mouth. The nearby Old High Church, said to have been

built in its stead by Cromwell, was rebuilt in 1769; its locality is for
some reason known as 'Greyfriars' instead of Blackfriars, so the
adjacent Free Church of Scotland building is called Greyfriars Free
Church. The priory site is still a churchyard, but curiously bridged
over between commercial blocks on either side. It contains a
fragment of vault perched on a single octagonal column, the
relationship of which to the remainder is unknown – as well as an
upright and very weathered medieval stone effigy reputed without
any particular evidence to be of the notorious late 14th-c. 'Wolf of
Badenoch', Alexander Stewart. Close to that, ledger stones to
Bailies and Mackintoshes are built into the wall, and numerous
others of the 17th c. onwards lie flat. Incongruously under the
bridge is a family burial enclosure.

Iona Abbey, Strathclyde   NM 287245
on island of Iona, ¼ mile N of village

Monastery founded 563 by St Columba; refounded late in 11th c.
after Danish and Viking raids; re-established as Benedictine
abbey of St Mary c.1200 by Reginald, son of Somerled, Lord of
the Isles; became mitred 1247; became cathedral c.1507(?).
Secularised 1588 to Hector McLean.

Church of Scotland. Church, museum etc. open during normal
hours.

It is quite likely that St Columba's foundation was not the first on
what is widely regarded as the most holy ground in Scotland. Being
at the mercy of Danes and Vikings it had a chequered history, and
following a refounding late in the 11th c. (probably at the instance
of Queen Margaret) it actually passed under Norwegian rule and
into Trondheim archdiocese, where it remained for a century and a
half. Parts of the existing church date from its first years under the
Benedictines, early in the 13th c., but the majority is 15th-c. During
the first half of the 16th c. when the abbot was Bishop of the Isles, it
probably served as his cathedral. Apart from some repair works
c.1635, the buildings fell into ruin and neglect.
    In 1899 they were given by the Duke of Argyll to Trustees for the
use of the Church of Scotland, and in the following decade or so

extensive restoration and re-roofing of the church was done under
John Honeyman, Thomas Ross and P. Macgregor Chalmers.
Reconstruction of the monastic buildings began in earnest in 1938
for the benefit of the Iona Community, and at the time of writing
there are proposals for extending them.

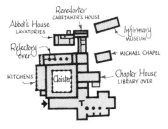

The W entrance leads straight into the aisleless nave of bare
multi-coloured masonry with a plain stone floor and simple flat
20th-c. roof. The N and W walls are largely 12th-c., but the W was
refaced and the S side extended outwards in the 15th c., when the
tower was also built. A stair in the NW corner leads to a tiny
watching chamber. The font, lifelessly carved with Celtic emblems,
is of 1908. More in keeping are the simple seven-fold standard iron
candlesticks, and the octagonal pulpit with linenfold panels standing
against one of the very weather-worn tower piers.

The **N transept**, set aside for private devotion, is separated by a
screen given by the Queen in 1956. The doorway in its W wall goes
to the cloister, and the stair at the N end to the rebuilt dormitory of
1954. The rose window is of 1905. The thick E wall with its two deep
window recesses is considered to be of *c.*1200 and contains a wall
passage above the windows; the Crucifixion painting over the altar
between them is by Roy le Maistre. The carved capitals of the
15th-c. E arch of the crossing should be looked at before moving
into the **quire**. One of them bears a damaged inscription formerly
recording the 15th-c. master mason's name, Donald O'Brolchan.

The whole floor of the E part was originally at the level of the
piano loft with its two 13th-c. arches, and there was a crypt beneath.
The loft was meant as the start of a N quire aisle. By the time the

Iona Abbey: N doorway of quire

sacristy was formed on that N side in the 15th c. (the aisle above it being removed and the arches blocked) the quire floor had been lowered; but its rather fine trefoil-headed doorway is probably 15th-c. too, though copied from 13th-c. types. The glass of the N clerestory is by Douglas Strachan (1939). On the other side, the arcade and aisle are 15th-c. though (as will be seen outside) a big transept of quite different form seems to have been begun in the late 13th c. The pillars have a fascinating set of capitals, some Biblical and some showing everyday happenings such as the scene with a cow. The two banks of stalls are 20th-c. and in the centre of the floor is a fragmentary grave slab. The big communion table is 20th-c., of Iona marble. The effigy resting on four lions (one is medieval) to the left is of John MacFingon, the last abbot (d.1499). Opposite is the earlier figure of Abbot Dominic, behind are a piscina and triple sedilia, and in the floor is the matrix of a big Flemish brass, said to have been of a Maclean. The Flamboyant tracery of the E and S windows is a special feature.

The **S chapel** also retains its piscina. The internal flying buttresses are a device to arrest movement of the arcade, the capitals of which are worth examining again from this angle. The **S transept** is dominated by the tomb-chests of the 8th Duke of Argyll (d.1900) and his wife (d.1925), with effigies by Sir George Frampton. Only the Duchess is buried here. In front of the rail is a showcase with a facsimile of the Book of Kells.

Now across the nave, past the pulpit and into the **cloister**. The sculpture in the centre of the garth is the Descent of the Spirit by Jacob Lipschitz. Almost all the cloister arcading has been rebuilt since 1960 on its original base and the capitals are still in the process of being carved by different sculptors with their own naturalistic designs. Those of the E walk are leaves and flowers. Off to its right is the chapter house, restored in 1940. The further half with seat recesses, separated by two 13th-c. arches with dog-tooth ornament, is the chapter house proper and now has a library above; the upper floor of this E range was the dormitory, and as now rebuilt it has fifteen bedrooms within the roof space.

The doorway near the W end of the N walk led to the refectory on the upper floor. This range was rebuilt in 1948–9. In the corner the trefoil-headed opening leads to the bookshop, and across the garth from here the unusual tracery of the tower belfry can be seen. The

W range, rebuilt in 1965, contains kitchens; towards the end of its arcade are a bay and a half of original stonework, incorporated in the modern rebuilding. The first bay of the S walk also contains 13th-c. stones but built into heavier work of later date; the new part has birds carved on the capitals. Two restored doorways lead the visitor back into the nave. The W doorway is 15th-c. Of the three big stone **crosses** outside, thought to be of *c*.850, that immediately beyond the well is St Matthew's – part of a shaft only. To its left is St Martin's, a single piece of epidiarite with superb jewel-like carving facing the cathedral and a Virgin and Child and Old Testament scenes on the W face. The third and biggest cross, to the right, is St John's: what is seen now is a replica, the original having been too often broken in gales since its restoration in 1927.

Now a circuit anti-clockwise round the **outside**, starting at the S wall of the nave with its great pink blocks of stone and the S transept with its fine main window tracery flanked by modern head stops of a girl and a boy. The clock-face on this side of the tower replaces a medieval one. S of the S chapel a depression and a piece of foundation wall indicate the transept that was begun in the 13th c. and never built. Here the 15th-c. quire clerestory and corbel table are visible, and next the fine tracery of the S and E windows. Round on the N side are the sacristy and the other transept, the E wall of which, like the adjoining N wall of the quire, is of *c*.1200. Then comes the chapter house. The nearer, separate building, which can be entered, is the infirmary chapel, probably 13th-c. and now called the Michael chapel. Its roof and simple dark furniture of West African hardwood are all modern. The other detached building is the infirmary itself, also restored in recent years and now used as a museum. It contains a great number of local carved stones of the 7th to 16th c., a rich field for study. The small part of the main block projecting over the drainage channel was the reredorter, and that round the corner the abbot's house; in their rebuilt form these are staff quarters. Then the restored N and modern W wings lead back to the W front and just to the left of this is a tiny chapel (with seating for four) revered as St Columba's shrine and restored in 1954.

The rocky hillock called Tor Abb just to the W has been identified as the site of St Columba's cell. It provides an excellent view of the buildings, of the ancient cobbled way which led from the village, and of Reilig Odhrain, the burial ground reputed to contain the bones of forty-eight Scottish, four Irish and eight Norwegian kings close to the walls of its little Romanesque chapel of St Oran. In the area S and E of Tor Abb, excavation has revealed traces of timber buildings of the Columban monastery; this was surrounded by an earthwork whose impressive remains are visible W of the road ¼ mile or so to the N.

Iona Priory, Strathclyde   NM 284240
in village on island

Augustinian nunnery of St Mary, possibly originally Benedictine, founded by 1208 by Reginald, son of Somerled, Lord of the Isles. Lands granted to Hector McLean 1574.

Owned by Iona Community. Open during normal hours.

The early history is fairly obscure, but the first main building period was the early 13th c., from which there are substantial remains. Around 1500 the refectory was rebuilt alongside a much enlarged cloister, and some minor changes made in the church, which from the start had a N aisle and chapel.

The buildings passed to farm use and fell gradually to ruin; it is known that the chancel arch and vault collapsed in 1832. Some repair work was done in 1874 under Sir Rowand Anderson and more in the 1920s. In 1899 the priory was made over to the Iona Cathedral Trust, but schemes to restore it to the same extent as the cathedral were abandoned, and it remains a picturesque preserved ruin.

Entry to the SE corner of the site brings the visitor into the E claustral range – largely early 13th-c. and represented (except at its SW corner) only by low wall-bases; its extreme end, presumably containing the reredorter, must now lie beneath the road. The first two entire compartments were the common room and chapter house – the latter being distinguished by its slightly bigger doorway and by the stone wall seats around its perimeter. Next is a rather larger room, possibly a sacristy and library, with no architectural

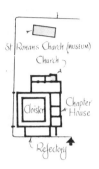

features remaining. The cloister itself, originally a square extending as usual only as far as the length of the church, was enlarged to about double the area c.1500; nothing of the inner arcade is left, the present wall-base being a reconstruction by Rowand Anderson.

The **church**, by far the most substantial and rewarding part of the ruin, is very largely early 13th-c., still late Romanesque at a time when Gothic pointed arches had been long established further south. However the chancel arch is known to have been pointed, and the chancel itself had a ribbed quadripartite vault. The round-arched N arcade on its circular piers with octagonal capitals is weather-worn but nevertheless striking in design and in its degree of preservation – assisted to some extent by the blocking wall built across it c.1500 when a separate chapel was made within the aisle. The lower parts of this wall remain. The variously carved corbels on the other side of the nave supported a gallery put in about the same time. Of the door opening in the S wall, leading into the cloister, enough remains to see that it was very unusually narrow for its height. The W wall with its round-headed windows one above the other is remarkably complete, and so indeed is the clerestory of two openings above the arcade.

The **chancel** is more fragmentary, no attempt having been made to restore the upper parts. The wall-shafts are there however, and the N wall virtually to its full original height. A door opening leads into the N chapel, still vaulted in its E bay and with a robust arch to the aisle, as well as an aumbry and piscina, a curious triangular headed E window evidently built before the vault, and a stone stair

Iona Priory: N arcade of church: 12th c.

leading to a much restored and re-roofed upper room which probably served as a sacristy. Not much remains of the aisle outer wall and only the bases are visible of the cross-wall erected late in the life of the priory to divide off the two W bays, and of the altar platform which stood against it. The fine memorial slab of Prioress Anna MacLean (d.1543), broken when the chancel vault fell, is now in the abbey museum. Some less important stones are ranged along the E side of the church.

At this point it is worth going across to the little detached church of St Ronan – not really part of the nunnery but now used as a museum in connection with it. This was the parish church of the island in the Middle Ages, and did not go to ruin till the 19th c. In 1923 it was restored and given a glass roof so as to display stone crosses and other fragments; the principal one in it is the richly carved 8th-c. St Oran's cross, possibly the earliest major one on Iona.

Next, the W gable of the church should be seen from the outside, followed by the W side of the cloister. Much of the site of the W range of cloister buildings is covered by the road, but parts still stand, including the base of a doorway from near the middle of the W walk. The refectory, S of the cloister and abutting the road, is relatively complete. Probably late 15th-c., its distinctive walling contains big blocks of granite laid in a more or less coursed pattern. The E end appears to have been altered later to provide for a dwelling room with fireplace.

Jedburgh Abbey, Borders   NT 650204
in town centre on A68

Augustinian priory founded c.1138 by David I, a daughter house of St Quentin (Picardy); became abbey c.1154. Secularised to Alexander, Lord Home after 1545.

In guardianship of Secretary of State for Scotland. Open during standard hours (admission charge).

Indications exist of an earlier church on the site of King David's monastery, one of the four great Border abbeys (all of different monastic orders) which owed their importance to him. Its position

laid it open to constant attack and plunder by English armies. The
main building period was c.1140–1220, the presbytery and transepts
being built first, then the W end, and then the nave and aisles
eastwards to meet the presbytery. The permanent monastic
buildings followed. Late in the 15th c. the crossing and transepts
were rebuilt following a series of English raids, the present tower
being completed in 1508.

Following further attacks in 1544–5 the ruined monastic buildings
became a convenient quarry, but parts of the church continued to
be used by the parish up to 1875, when the then owner the Marquis
of Lothian built a new kirk nearby. Ownership passed to the Office
of Works in 1913.

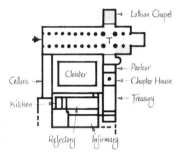

The late 12th-c. **W front**, best seen from Abbey Close before
entering the gates, is a fine instance of the transition from
Romanesque to early Gothic – a rich Norman doorway with triple
gablets over, a big round-headed window flanked by little pointed
arches, and in the restored gable a wheel window dating from the
late 14th or early 15th c. Inside the gates on the right are the ticket
kiosk and a small museum.

The **nave**, though unroofed, is one of the finest examples of
medieval architecture in Scotland. It too exhibits round and pointed
arches – pointed in the main arcades on their clustered piers, round
in the big wide bays of the triforium (each containing twin pointed
arches with central shaft) and pointed again in the clerestory, which
is continuous in its general concept, yet really alternates twin

Jedburgh Abbey Church: interior, looking W

windows with twin blank arches. The roof was of timber only, though the aisles were vaulted. The crossing arches were rebuilt late in the 15th c., but their piers are partly Norman. Along the N aisle are a number of minor 17th- and 18th-c. memorials.

The **N transept** still shows in the start of its E side the almost unique 12th-c. bay design for which Jedburgh is notable; it may have been copied from either Romsey abbey or what is now Oxford cathedral and, like them, has its main arches carried up to a sufficient height to enclose the triforium as well as the openings into the aisles. The rest of this transept was rebuilt in the 15th c. and has been much restored by the Kerrs, Marquises of Lothian, for use as a mausoleum. The central tomb seen through the wicket door is that of the 8th Marquis (d.1870). Beyond it, on the far wall, is the canopied tomb of Archbishop Blacader of Glasgow (d.1508) adapted as a memorial to Andrew Lord Jedburgh (d.1656). On the E wall is a memorial to Christian Hamilton Lady Jedburgh (d. 1688), while the remaining tablets commemorate various members of the Ker family (then with one 'r') from the 16th c. onwards.

The N presbytery chapel was destroyed in the process of adapting the **presbytery** itself as a parish kirk, but its vaulting springers against the main arcade can still be seen. These arcades are also of the Oxford/Romsey type, the method of housing the double twin triforium arches within the heads of the main chevron-ornamented arches being distinctly unusual; the care with which the details at this level are worked out is, however, not matched by the arbitrary relationship of the lower arches to the main circular piers. Much of the clerestory remains too, but this dates from the 13th c. when the original apse was replaced by the existing longer square termination. The conspicuous Gothic Revival canopied tomb at the NE corner is of John Rutherford and dates from 1847.

Turning now to the S side of the presbytery, the bases of the sedilia can still be seen. The late 15th-c. chapel this side is fairly complete, with quadripartite vault, reglazed windows and, on its E wall, some minor memorials. The Norman **S transept**, unlike the N, was never lengthened because of the monastic buildings against it; indeed it was shortened in the 16th c., with the loss of its apse, so necessitating the present spiral stair at the corner to replace one further S which was taken down. All four crossing-piers can be seen to be different; the NE is the least altered from the original

Norman, merely having had its capital raised by a few feet. The others bear names or initials of 15th-c. abbots.

From the S nave aisle a 12th-c. doorway leads to the NE corner of the **cloister**. From there walk S, away from the church, passing on the left the foundations successively of the apsidal Norman chapel opening off the original S transept, the parlour, the day stair to the dormitory, the chapter house (with central column) and a room thought to have been the treasury. Above these was the dormitory.

At the end, turn right along the S walk and look down into the undercroft of the refectory. The room just before the steps at the SW corner was the kitchen. These steps, following the natural steep slope, lead to the infirmary, an almost separate building added in the 14th c.; what is seen now is part of the vaulted undercroft.

Back at the top of the steps it is worth pausing to look at the whole S side of the nave, dramatically exposed by the disappearance of the S aisle, at the central tower, completed in 1508 and originally capped with a low spire, and at what is left of the S transept. The present stumpy pinnacles and openwork parapet of the tower are not ancient.

Go now along the W walk, with a well and the remains of storerooms on the left, through the imitation Norman S doorway of the nave (1876), across the S aisle, and back to the W end. Inside the stair turret doorway at the end of the N aisle a Roman inscribed stone has been reused as a lintel.

The small museum on the left outside the W doorway houses numerous stone fragments including memorials and relics of the earlier buildings.

Instead of returning into Abbey Close, it is better to go out through the northern churchyard, with its wealth of headstones, so as to see the N side of the nave as well as the restored N transept. Continue under the mock-medieval bridewell arch (1823) to the main road, turn right, and take the upper walkway, which gives a fresh view of the length of the interior across the site of the high altar and leads down to the bottom end of the lane. Here a chain link fence enables the infirmary and other lower buildings to be seen again; another well will also be noticed at the extreme SE corner of the enclosure.

Kelso Abbey, Borders   NT 729338
in town centre

Tironensian abbey of the Blessed Virgin and St John, founded 1113
   by Earl David (later David I) at Selkirk; moved to Kelso 1128;
   became mitred 1165. Suppressed 1560. Secularised 1607 to
   Robert, Earl of Roxburghe.

In guardianship of Secretary of State for Scotland. Open during
   standard hours without charge.

Destruction of the E parts of the church in the English invasions of
1542 and 1545 was so thorough that until quite recent years there
was a basic misconception of its plan. Discovery of a description in
the Vatican library brought to light the fact that it had a grand E
transept and tower balancing the W ones, so that the double cross
form of the complete Romanesque church was much more like a
Rhineland building than the majority of survivors of its date in
Britain. The abbots of Kelso for many years claimed seniority in
Scotland but finally conceded the honour to St Andrews.
   The abbey's virtual end in 1545 at the hands of Spanish
mercenaries under the Earl of Hertford was a dramatic one; yet it
survived fifteen years more till Knox's reformers ousted the last
monks. A parish kirk was formed in the surviving W transept in
1649, with a thatched roofed burgh prison on top! The remains of
these were removed in 1805 and the Duke of Roxburghe carried out
some repairs in 1866. His successor ceded the ruins to the nation in
1919 and built a memorial 'cloister'.

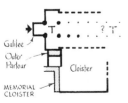

The turreted fortress-like appearance of the church seems to echo
its turbulent history. What is called the W **galilee** is in fact a
three-storeyed 12th-c. structure integral in design with the transepts

and nave. Of its unusually rich outer doorway of six orders only the N jamb remains. Inside, the intersecting wall-arcading at the base should be noted, as well as the wall passages at triforium and clerestory levels, weakening a structure that otherwise gives every impression of strength. A medieval stone coffin is on the floor.

Beyond the galilee is the **tower** space or W crossing. Its NE pier has gone, and all its main arches except the W, which is pointed and which suggests a late 12th-c. date. Here and in the transepts (which are curiously dissimilar in detail) the system is not unlike that of the galilee, with surprising disregard for the structural prudence of placing arch above arch, solid above solid. The SW transept is railed off as the burial place of the Dukes of Roxburghe, but also has three 14th-c. coffin lids on the floor of the W side; one is inscribed to Joanna Bulloc, d.1371. In the S wall is an arched recess with piscina and aumbry.

Of the **nave**, also late 12th-c., only the first two bays on the S side survive. Its original length is unknown, but it has to be imagined as having N and S arcades of, perhaps, five bays, beyond which was a second crossing with its own tower and transepts, and then an E presbytery matching the W galilee. The main arcade columns are short and round with scalloped capitals and with attached semicircular shafts each side to carry the arches. The continuous triforium and clerestory (the latter once more 'out of step') have a modern stopping-off to protect their broken end. The lines of the aisle walls are marked in the grass.

On the S side, the churchyard probably represents the **cloister** in general shape; the furthest wall is quite likely to be on the outer line of the S walk, i.e. the N side of the refectory. Several 17th-c. memorials are too weather-worn to be of much interest. The W wall of the cloister is comparatively modern but the opening towards its N end is 18th-c. (it once had gates) and leads to another burial enclosure with a small tablet to Robert Smith, d.1791.

Back now to the main doorway, and turn left. The next, round-headed doorway on the left leads to the outer parlour, used as a store and therefore normally locked. It is barrel-vaulted and has more, very worn, intersecting wall-arcading. Then comes the memorial cloister, sited in the belief that the tower was central and that the galilee formed all there had ever been of a nave; in it has been reset a 13th-c. trefoil-headed doorway of uncertain origin.

Kelso Abbey Church: W doorway: 12th c.

Finally the N side, and the imposing turreted façade of the NW transept; the gabled portal, seeming to endorse the church's Rhenish character, was somewhat altered in 1649. On the far side of the well-treed main churchyard is the octagonal parish kirk of 1771.

Kilmaurs Collegiate Church, Strathclyde   NJ 415407
½ mile SE of town and 3 miles NW of Kilmarnock on Stewarton road A735

College founded, probably in 1413, by William Cunningham in existing parish church.

Church of Scotland. Key available at the Manse, 9 Standalane.

Of the medieval church the 15th-c. chancel alone remains, in an altered form, as a mausoleum of the Cunninghams, Earls of Glencairn. The remainder underwent various rebuildings, apparently unrecorded, and the present graceful Gothic tower and traditionally T-shaped church are of 1888.

Because the chancel is walled off from the remainder, the building has to be visited in two parts, entry to the newer **parish church** being beneath the W tower, which has a plaster vault and contains a bell of 1618. High open timber roofs, galleries in the three arms, and varnished pitch-pine pews make this a typical building of its time, though better cared for than many. The organ, behind the holy table, occupies the short fourth arm of the cruciform plan, and backs on to the separated chancel. The windows are undistinguished, with two exceptions: on the E side of the N transept a memorial to Margaret Bahn by Stanley Scott (1971) and on the W side of the S transept one to Hugh Strathern by Roland Milton (1984). A tablet to a former minister, Hugh Thomson, preserved from the previous building, is on the S wall of the nave.

The old **chancel**, known as the Glencairn aisle, is entered through a small lobby in its SW corner. It has a tunnel vault and no side windows, the only light coming from a four-light E window of very reduced height. It is dominated by a memorial of 1600 on the N side to James, the 7th Earl of Glencairn and his Countess, an extraordinary assemblage of architectural motifs. The central inscription, now virtually illegible, separates two portrait busts. On the shelf below, supported by four console brackets, are eight 'kneelers' representing the family of the departed in the fashion of the time. At either end are versions of Classical columns of different orders as the mason may have seen them in a textbook but embellished to his own whim and standing side by side – Corinthian on the inside with a curious flame-like ornament, Tuscan on the outside, and between them an octagonal variant on the Doric order! All this was repaired in 1870, but is sadly in need of it again. Also in the chancel are two medieval cross-ornamented coffin lids, while the churchyard contains a good number of interesting headstones of later years.

Kilmun: St Munn's Church from W, looking across Holy Loch

Kilmun Collegiate Church, Strathclyde   NS 166821
on NE shore of Holy Loch, on A880

College founded 1441 in existing parish church of St Munn by Sir
   Duncan Campbell.

Church of Scotland. Open during normal hours (mausolea and
   ancient tower not open).

The original church here was traditionally founded in the 6th c. by
St Munn, a friend of St Columba. Its successor, which became
collegiate under the auspices of the Campbells, went to ruin in the
18th c. The tower of that building, which still stands, may have been
used by their descendants the Argylls as a residence, and certainly
many later marquises and dukes were buried here. Their
mausoleum, attached to the N side of the church, is of 1794, but the
church itself was rebuilt in 1841 under Thomas Burns.

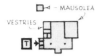

The 15th-c. **tower**, jagged-topped, has something of a fortified
appearance. The vault of the bottom stage survives, as well as
marks of the nave roof and traces of the start of its wall. On its N
face are two iron coffin covers.

The 1841 **church**, which is differently orientated, has its own
much less solid-looking tower over the E end, a landmark from the
loch. The spacious interior has a wide flat ceiling on shallow trusses,
tall four-centred arcades and a small sanctuary arch – all typical of
its date, following the usual Scots T plan but in Gothic style. The
laird's enclosed pew is at the end of the N transept. That and the
nave abut two sides of the domed Argyll mausoleum. Blind
windows and a heavy iron door entirely conceal the interior, which
contains the remains of fourteen dukes and duchesses, including
those of the marquis beheaded in 1661 and of his son executed in
1685.

A second mausoleum, smaller and detached, is the burial place of
Douglases. Gravestones in the churchyard date back in some cases
to the 17th c. A group (NE of the church) to the Clark family bear
their motto 'Free for a Blast', a reference to an ancestor who blew a
horn blast to allow James IV to kill a stag.

Kilwinning Abbey, Strathclyde   NS 303433
in town centre

Tironensian abbey of St Mary and St Wynnyn founded by 1162 by
    Hugh de Morville. Secularised 1592 to William Melville.

Owned by Church of Scotland and Secretary of State for Scotland.
    Accessible to the public at all times (except parish church)
    without charge.

Tradition says a church was founded here in 715 by St Wynnyn, and
that the abbey occupies its site. What survives suggests a late 12th-c.
and early 13th-c. building history and a layout whose only slight

peculiarity (in Scotland that is) was the open treatment of the space beneath twin W towers as part of the nave. The southern of these towers seems to have been destroyed in the 14th-c. English invasion, after which the W front was rebuilt in line with their E face.

Severe damage was done by reformers in 1561. Part of the church was used by the parish till 1775 when it was mostly demolished and the present church erected. The NW tower was struck by lightning in 1809 and collapsed in 1814, the present one being immediately built on its site. Excavations in 1878 revealed the general plan; subsequent demolitions around the cloister have uncovered more.

The S transept gable is a prominent landmark – in surroundings as unattractive as any abbey in Scotland. Coming from the main street, one passes the present so-called Abbey Church of 1775 on the left. It stands on the presbytery site; the nave lay in the churchyard to the right, and the wall with 14th-c. doorway and broken window marks its final W end. The 13th-c. arch beyond, on clustered piers, was that of the SW tower. The S aisle wall with three doorways still stands high; to its left is the transept gable with a walkway at the base of its three big lancet windows and under that the clear remains of the southernmost chapel – a dog-toothed arch and evidence of vaulting. A pier base of the left-hand chapel is embedded in the church wall but nothing shows of the other old wall-bases on which the 18th-c. church was partly built.

Round the end of the transept wall the low ruins of the chapter house and slype can be seen. Now go through the doorway into the NE corner of the cloister – a once fine one of c.1200 with dog-tooth

Kilwinning Abbey: NE doorway of cloister: 13th c.

and 'bobbin' ornament. Down the E walk are the slype opening and
the doorway and windows of the chapter house, all round-headed.
On the S transept gable is the line of the high dorter roof, cutting
into two of the lancets and thus evidently later.

The cloister garth being fenced off, one has to return to the S
aisle. At its W end are the remains of the SW tower with the arch
already seen – unusual in being of horseshoe form, curving inwards
again over the capitals. Finally the outside of the W range, three
compartments each once barrel-vaulted and now cleared of
post-Dissolution accretions. The garth can here be entered, but
there is no more to see.

Kinloss Abbey, Grampian   NH 965615
in village, 3 miles NE of Forres

Cistercian abbey of the Blessed Virgin Mary founded 1150 by David
    I, a daughter house of Melrose; became mitred 1395. Secularised
    1601 to Edward Bruce, Lord Kinloss.

Owned by Moray District Council. Open to the public (except
    sacristy and abbot's house) at all times without charge.

Little is known of the building history; what is left suggests a
construction period extending into the 13th c. For Scotland the
church plan is unusual in having aisles up to the E end. The central
tower is said to have been late 15th-c.; it fell in 1574. The early
16th-c. abbot's house later became the commendator's house and
was altered by him; its ruin is prominent.

Most of the stone still remaining was taken in 1650 to build a fort
at Inverness for the Parliamentarians. The ground continued to be a
cemetery, with various areas reserved for individual families, and is
still so used.

First to catch the eye at the gateway is the sacristy/library ruin
against the S transept wall. They are seen diagonally across the nave
and cloister. The path straight ahead leads along the N side of the
nave: on the right the outlines of the N aisle, transept, N chapel and
presbytery are clear. The gatehouse-like archway was in fact an E

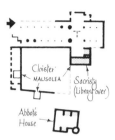

chapel to the S transept, its E wall removed. Through it and across the transept the cloister can be reached. Its quite large square form is fairly clear, and the base of the shafted doorway into the S aisle can also be found easily. The sacristy, the one building still enclosed (now a locked mausoleum), had an early 16th-c. library over its E part, though no doubt there was also an upper-level passage from the vanished dorter to a night stair in the transept. Its present doorway is of 1910. The chapter house has gone but two stone coffins lie on its site.

The still substantial abbot's house ruin to the S stands on overgrown private ground and access is discouraged. It is early 16th-c. and has a round but now empty stair turret. Next, the S side of the cloister, where 13th-c. dog-toothed jamb stones from the refectory entrance support an archway to lead into the Dunbar-Dunbar family mausoleum. A recess alongside indicates the monks' washplace, the square stone frame in the ground nearby being probably connected with its water supply. Some corbels of the cloister walk roof are still visible.

Of the W range the general layout is still clear, though little survives beyond the cloister wall. Its outer wall-base leads one back to the W end of the church, and then the column bases of the main arcades can be searched out – two at the near end of the S arcade and two at the further end of the N.

The stone barn a short distance to the W has been thought to have had some connection with the abbey, though what is now visible looks much less old.

Kinloss Abbey Church: S transept, looking SW

Kirkcudbright: Greyfriars, Dumfries & Galloway   NX 683511
in town centre

Franciscan friary founded 1455 by James II. Site given to Sir
    Thomas MacClellan 1569, and then to town, the church becoming
    parochial.

Episcopal Church of Scotland. Key available at shop 'Castle
    Corner' opposite in St Cuthbert Street.

Opinions on the circumstances of foundation vary, some ascribing it
to Roger de Quincy, Lord of Galloway, in 1239. Certainly some
surviving parts of the church appear to be earlier than the 15th c.
But later changes have rather obscured the evidence. Having
become 'unserviceable' it was rebuilt – but obviously only in part –
in 1730. In 1836–8 a new church was built in another part of the
town, and this one fell into disuse. It then became a school, a main

schoolroom and porch being built on the site of the N transept, and
the S transept or MacClellan aisle kept unaltered. But in 1922 it was
bought and handed over to the Episcopal Church by Sir Shadforth
and Lady Watts as a memorial to her son, and restored under the
architect P. McGregor Chalmers. He changed the orientation
through 90 degrees, what was the S transept becoming the present
chancel, and the newer 'north' transept occupying the site of the
friars' chancel; this made the best use of the form the building had
by then assumed, but is at first confusing to the visitor.

The present nave which is really the 19th-c. schoolroom extends
over and beyond the area of the former N transept. Contrasting
with the remainder, it retains its plastered walls, matchboarded
dado and sloping ceiling, and the lack of alignment with the present
chancel is very noticeable. The former chancel, now a transept, has
bare walls and a flat ceiling. Possibly it is 13th-c., but the two
two-light windows with simple centre mullions are more likely to be
16th-c. insertions. One contains glass of 1959 by Gordon Webster in
memory of Robert Milburn. Nearby are a small octagonal pillar
stoup, an early 17th-c. chest, and a chair of similar date.
    The present chancel, with a low semicircular arch typical of
transept arches in smaller Scottish churches, became the
MacClellan aisle after the Reformation. Sir Thomas built himself a
house out of the remains of the friary and gave the rest of the church
to the burgh, and on his death in 1597 his monument was erected in
what had been the S transept. His effigy as a knight in armour rests
under a large semicircular arch flanked by Classical columns of an
order unknown in antiquity. Above are perched a memorial
inscription with obelisks and heraldry. The window behind the
altar, similar to those of the transept, is of three lights with vertical
mullions, apparently a 16th-c. insertion into earlier walling, but the
open timber roof is much more recent. Below it, serving a former
altar where the MacClellan tomb now is, is a piscina. The lectern,
probably 19th-c., is unusual in having a little cupboard in its stem,

while the brass cross and candlesticks of the 1920s are by a local craftswoman, Mabel Brunton. A pulpit at one time in the church is now in the Stewartry Museum in the town.

Lanark: Greyfriars, Strathclyde   NT 880436
in town centre on A73

Franciscan friary founded 1326 or 1329 by Robert I; dissolved
  before 1566.

In multiple ownership.

The Clydesdale Hotel in the main street (formerly the New Inn) and its yard occupy much of the site, but there are no visible remains. There is a plaque on the front of the hotel; Friars Lane alongside, as well as the more modern Friarsfield Road, perpetuates the name.

Lesmahagow Priory, Strathclyde   NS 814398
in town, 22 miles SE of Glasgow and ¼ mile W of Carlisle road A74

Tironensian priory founded 1144 by David I, a dependency of
  Kelso. Secularised to Robert Earl of Roxburghe 1607 and to
  Marquis of Hamilton 1623.

Church of Scotland parish church; key available as advertised on
  notice-board. Excavated part of site owned by Clydesdale
  District Council and accessible at all times.

Evidence of Benedictines on this site a few decades before King David's foundation seems to be unsubstantiated. The Tironensians pioneered the extensive fruit orchards of the Clyde valley. English soldiery under John of Eltham, Earl of Cornwall did extensive damage to their priory buildings in 1335, and they were burned again at the Reformation in 1560. The church survived in parish use, and the monastic buildings were destroyed in the middle of the 17th c. Traces have been found at different times but in 1978 the site was cleared and excavated to reveal a large part of the plan. Meanwhile the church was demolished in 1803 and replaced by the present one.

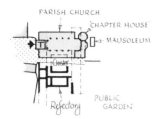

The **parish church**, entered under the tower from an attractive little square, has an open timber roof of exceptionally wide span and a brown-painted gallery on three sides on slender Doric columns. More ornate is the coloured plaster ceiling of the E apse, framed by Ionic columns and with a main window of 1871 by John Greenshields. The pulpit, in scale with the size of the church, is a fine octagonal structure on four legs; the Classical font is of *c*.1930.

Additions at the E end, not open to visitors but readily seen from the churchyard, include a suite of vestries and a so-called chapter house. On the path to the S a descriptive board provides information and at the same time a good view of the excavations. These comprise little more than wall-bases and include the further half of the cloister and its walks, together with the W range, the kitchen and refectory to the S, and sketchy evidence of the E or dorter range. This last does however retain a substantial portion of sloping plinth at its SW corner. A worked stone plinth also survives along the whole S side of the refectory, terminating at the clear base of a doorway near its SW corner.

Lincluden Collegiate Church, Dumfries & Galloway   NX 965779
1¼ miles N of Dumfries and ½ mile E of Kilmarnock road A76

Benedictine nunnery (priory) founded by 1174 by Uchtred, son of Fergus, Lord of Galloway; seized 1389 by Archibald the Grim, 3rd Earl of Douglas and converted to college of priests; annexed to Chapel Royal, Stirling, 1508 to *c*.1529.

In care of Secretary of State for Scotland. Open during standard
hours (admission charge).

The nunnery was set up beside an earlier castle. Of the latter only
the well-defined artificial motte remains; of the original monastic
buildings very little, for they were superseded early in the 15th c. by
a much more ornate church and domestic range, thanks largely to
the 3rd Earl's son and the son's wife Margaret, daughter of Robert
III. Their craftsmen are thought to have been brought from
Touraine, under the leadership of Jean Moreau who worked also at
Melrose and Paisley.

The college continued in being till very late in the 16th c., the
provost being recorded as saying mass till at least 1585. The
buildings were then turned to domestic uses, but unfortunately
much of their fine stone was quarried away in the 18th c. The
chancel and S transept however were spared, and much of the N
range survived through farm use. Some repairs were done in 1882,
and forty years later the ruin passed into State guardianship.

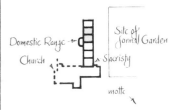

Little survives to hinder entry into the W parts of the church, which
was asymmetrical, having an aisle and transept on the S side only.
The arcade has gone (except for its easternmost pier), and the **aisle**
wall has two bays only of its original three still standing. Clearly the
aisle and the transept were both vaulted. The latter, with its walls
relatively complete to eaves height, has the sadly damaged remains
of once-fine French-style tracery, as well as a piscina and elaborate
but mutilated sedilia.

The **quire**, entered from the nave through a solid rood screen
capped by two wide bands of very worn sculpture and pierced only
by a basket-arched doorway, is one of the finest middle-Gothic

Lincluden Collegiate Church from SW

buildings in Scotland. A pointed arch of three orders towers above the screen, and at the opposite end is another big window whose fretted edge gives a tantalising hint of the tracery it once contained. The springer stones of the vaults can be seen, also the corbels which supported the actual roof (during the 18th c. it was thatched, as can be seen on an old engraving). In the E wall, some of the supports of the altar survive, and on the S side a piscina and canopied triple sedilia. The principal feature is the arched tomb of Princess Margaret (d.1456), wife of the college founder, so big that it restricts the shape of the adjoining window. Effigy and plinth are badly worn, but the crocketed arch in its panelled frame is surprisingly well preserved.

Next to the tomb is a doorway to the **sacristy**, ornamented with deep foliage carving finishing at the bottom with two monkey-like creatures. The room itself had two bays of quadripartite vaulting. The wing extending north from it presumably stands on the site of the E range of the nunnery cloister – of which there is now no other sign – and thus may still contain 12th-c. masonry. The remaining five compartments are or were barrel-vaulted storerooms – except for the end one which formed the base of the provost's house or a guest house and probably stood higher than the remainder. The projecting bay half-way along contains a stair that led to the upper domestic rooms.

From here one should walk around the domestic wing, first in order to view the powerfully buttressed quire from outside, and then perhaps to climb the motte to the SE and look down on to the square flat area to the E of the domestic wing where a 16th-c. knot garden existed – almost forgotten until its pattern was revealed one morning to the custodian by frost. The motte itself was the nucleus of a fortification of unknown date which preceded the nunnery.

Two choir stalls from the church, complete with misericord seats, are preserved in the National Museum of Antiquities of Scotland.

Lindores Abbey, Fife   NO 244185
½ mile E of Newburgh, on Logie road A913

Tironensian abbey of St Mary, St Andrew and All Saints founded
    1191 by David, Earl of Huntingdon, a daughter house of Kelso;
    became mitred 1395. Secularised 1600 to Patrick Leslie, Lord
    Lindores.

Owned by Mackenzie Smith family. Accessible at all times without
    charge, subject to permission from adjoining house.

What little architectural detail is left shows the buildings to have been as originally erected, i.e. Transitional from Romanesque to Gothic, which accords with the foundation date. A tower was quickly added to the church, in an unusual NW position, and soon followed by a N aisle. Raids by 'wild' Scots caused damage in the 15th c.; reformers sacked the abbey in 1543 and again more thoroughly in 1559.

The abbey site is used for horse grazing and exercise. The house adjoining to the W gives the impression of containing abbey materials and undoubtedly this is true of other buildings in the neighbourhood; so what remains is in a poor state.

The arch still entire by the road was part of a gatehouse. From it one looks diagonally across the cloister to the church slype and

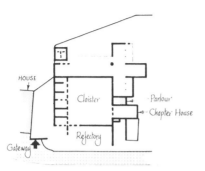

chapter house, with the W range in the foreground. The latter can be crossed half-way along to reach the cloister, and the **church nave** entered on its S. Left is the W doorway, and half left the tower base, distinguished by thicker walls. Moving now E, nothing can be seen of the N aisle or arcade, but the crossing piers are distinct, and the short presbytery with earth now piled up to its E wall. On its left, the N transept had three chapels; an aumbry and double piscina survive in the innermost. In this transept is a stone coffin; in the presbytery two more tiny ones thought to be of the founder's children.

The S transept is rather formless but parts of the S and W walls stand, and a fragment of the outer chapel vault. To its S, the E range comprises first the slype (with a bay of vault), then the **chapter house** walls to a moderate height, then the day stair, and lastly a continuation of the dorter undercroft. Of the refectory only the N wall can now be traced, with a doorway base at the dorter end. Some more fragments stand on the other side of the road, chief of them being the remains of a barn 30 yards or so to the S.

A font base from the abbey, as well as some 16th-c. carved panels incorporated into a cabinet, are in the Episcopal cathedral at Dundee.

Linlithgow: Whitefriars, Lothian   NT 006767 approx.
¼ mile SE of town centre

Carmelite friary of St Mary founded *c.*1401 by Sir James Douglas.
   Demolished by reformers 1559.

Exact site unknown. In multiple ownership.

The site was on the sloping ground to the S of the town, probably in
the vicinity of the modern Clarendon Road and Crescent, but
further E than the roads called Friars' Way, Friars' Brae and Priory
Road.

Loch Leven Priory, Tayside   NO 162003
on island in loch, 3 miles SE of Kinross

Augustinian priory of St Serf founded in 8th c. by St Serf or his
   followers; given to Culdees by King Brude of Picts, and to Bishop
   and Canons of St Andrews *c.*1150 by King David. Granted to St
   Leonard's College, St Andrews, 1580.

Owned by Kinross Estate Co. Not accessible to the public.

Also called Portmoak or St Serf's. The surviving stonework, close
to the SE corner of the island, is of a small rectangular building that
may be assumed to have been the nave of the church. A holy water
stoup is built into its outer S wall. Adjoining it have been found
traces of the presumed chancel, only 9 feet wide, and of a small W
tower. Excavations in 1877 produced bodies which were
pronounced to be those of St Ronan and of Graham, first Bishop of
St Andrews. Foundations of a much larger structure to the W were
uncovered too. At that time the building was used as a fishing hut.

□.

The island is now part of the Loch Leven Nature Reserve, and visits
by the public are prohibited.

Luffness: Whitefriars, Lothian   NT 471802
200 yards S of A198 between Aberlady and Luffness

Carmelite friary founded by 1336, probably by an Earl of Dunbar.
   Granted to Robert Hepburn junior 1609.

Owned by Luffness Ltd. Accessible at all times.

Apart from the evidence on site only a very few records exist. A
13th-c. date (rather than 1336) is suggested by what may be the
founder's effigy. The ruin, little more in fact than the foundations of
a simple church, lies on its own within the estate of Luffness House.

The site, in a small wood about midway between Luffness House
and Aberlady village, can be reached by footpath from either end.
The only wall standing to any height is on the N side of the chancel,
with a late 13th-c. knight's effigy still in an arched recess, and beside
it a fairly complete doorway. The two stone steps to the altar
platform, as well as the paving of the sanctuary itself, are also *in
situ*, with a late 15th-c. ledger stone to Kentigern Hepburn in the
centre. About half-way along the length of the church stand the
foundations of the stone pulpitum, and at the SW corner another
piece of wall a few courses high. Another S wall parallel to the main
one is difficult to explain if, as is suggested, the cloister lay to the N.
Various stone fragments can be seen piled under a nearby yew,
while two stretches of water 100 yards or so to the NE were
probably monastery fishponds.

Manuel Priory, Central   NS 972764
2 miles SW of Linlithgow close to Avonbridge road B825

Cistercian nunnery of St Mary founded by 1164 by Malcolm IV.
   Passed to Alexander, Lord Livingstone after Reformation.

Owned by Caledon Estates. Accessible at all times without charge.

A small priory of which little is recorded, it was damaged by Edward III's army in 1335 and received recompense from him. An attempt to suppress it in 1506 seems to have failed, for there were still nuns and a prioress in 1552. The church, a plain rectangle, still stood entire but roofless till about 1740. The cloister was on the S, with a single doorway in the centre of the church. Being right on the bank of the Avon, it suffered from floods. By 1787 erosion had reached the S wall of the church, and it has since removed everything but the N half of the W wall.

The remaining fragment is visible from the road and can be reached along the edge of the field on the left side of the sewage works fence. It is merely the left half of the W front of the church, the half-doorway at the base having been blocked to aid stability. The upper stage, separated by a string-course, similarly has one and a half lancet windows of the original three. On the N side the start of the return wall can be seen, but the S has entirely gone.

Maryculter Preceptory, Grampian   NJ 844000
7 miles SW of Aberdeen and ½ mile N of B9077

Preceptory of Knights Templars founded 1121–36 by Walter Byset; passed to Knights of St John of Jerusalem *c*.1309.

Owned by Kincardine-Deeside District Council. Accessible during reasonable hours by permission from Maryculter Home Farm.

Land on the S bank of the Dee is said to have been granted to the Templars in 1187 by William the Lion, much earlier than the foundation of the preceptory. On the suppression of that order the Knights of St John took over its property, with the parish and the chapel of St Mary; the chapel continued as a parish church till 1782 when a new one was built a mile further S and its contents dispersed or destroyed. Since then it has progressively become more and more ruined. Medieval effigies of the Menzies have been removed to the church of St Nicholas, Aberdeen (q.v.). At the former Maryculter House are vaulted cellars which may have been part of the preceptor's house.

The high-walled and irregularly shaped churchyard can be reached (with permission) through the back garden of the farmhouse and a small paddock. A tablet over the entrance was put up by 'Knights Templars of the District Grand Priory of Aberdeen, Banff and Kincardine' in 1925. Of the church itself, the walls around the E end stand only to a height of about 3 feet; the remainder is no more than irregular humps in the grass surrounding a big yew and dotted about with tombstones – none of which seems older than 1834.

May Priory, Fife   NT 648992
on small island 6 miles SE of Anstruther

Cluniac priory founded by 1153 by David I, dependent on Reading abbey; transferred to dependence on St Andrews *c*.1275 and became Augustinian; possibly restored to Reading 1306. Entire priory later transferred to Pittenweem on mainland. Granted to Patrick Learmonth 1550.

Owned by the Commissioners of Northern Lighthouses. Accessible by day trips in summer, advertised or by private arrangement.

The island's sanctity is supposed to have been brought about by the slaughter of St Adrian and his company of Hungarian missionaries by marauding Danes *c*.875. Legend and history are intermingled and far from clear, and uncertainties exist about the rival claims made in later centuries by Reading and St Andrews. One version says that Alexander III bought the island back in order to counter English espionage, and himself conferred it on St Andrews priory. There seems little doubt however that eventually the community migrated to Pittenweem, leaving a single hermit behind.

The only building now visible is a small roofless rectangle orientated N to S. It has the remains of two lancet windows in the W wall and one in the N and could thus be 13th-c. At the SW corner was a circular stair, and at the N end are traces of a dwelling room added in the 16th c.

The whole island is part of the National Nature Reserve, but may be visited in summer by arrangement with boatmen in Anstruther or Crail; visitors are asked to make contact with a warden on landing.

Maybole Collegiate Church, Strathclyde   NS 301098
100 yards S of town centre and A77

College of St Mary founded 1384 by John Kennedy in existing parish church.

In care of Secretary of State for Scotland. Not open to the public, but key obtainable from custodian of Crossraguel abbey by prior arrangement with the Ancient Monuments section of the Scottish Development Department (3–11 Melville Street, Edinburgh).

The college of priests (the earliest in Scotland) had its beginning with a chapel founded alongside the parish church in 1371. That is believed to owe its origin to Duncan, Earl of Carrick in the 12th c. The church as it stands is considered to be 15th-c. (though many of its details are 13th- and 14th-c. in character). The last mass was sung there in 1563, and it has long been a roofless ruin. The Kennedy family took over the sacristy as a burial place and enlarged it in the 17th c. The present parish church in the NE part of the town dates from 1808.

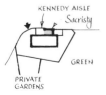

Maybole Collegiate Church: 15th c. S doorway

The ruin stands within a fairly high churchyard wall which allows partial views, the best vantage point being on the SE. The simple nave and chancel have two lancet windows and two with damaged tracery of reticulated pattern. The S doorway is also quite ambitious with three orders of arches and dog-tooth ornament of 13th-c. type, and a coat of arms above. Another coat of arms, that of the Kennedys, is over the Classical doorway leading into the N annexe, which was built as a westward extension from the sacristy, and is visible from the road alongside.

Inside, it is noticeable that burials have raised the ground level 2 to 3 feet above the original floor, so that the wall features appear far too low. These include a big trefoil-headed piscina in the S wall (probably serving a nave altar), and another near the E end, also a plain square-headed sedilia recess and in the N wall of the chancel an arched recess with three rows of dog-tooth ornament, probably the tomb of the founder. Below the blocked E window is a prominent but weather-worn plain 18th-c. tablet commemorating the Earls of Cassillis. Numbered stones projecting out of the chancel floor mark burials, while the wall-base half-way along the interior indicates the position of a screen. The original sacristy still has its primitive stone tunnel vault, but the Kennedys' westward extension is now roofless; its W wall arrogantly half blocks the N doorway of the church. Another burial enclosure E of the sacristy is also no longer roofed.

Melrose Abbey, Borders   NT 548341
in town

Cistercian abbey of the Blessed Virgin Mary founded 1136, a
     daughter house of Rievaulx. Secularised 1609 to John Ramsey,
     Viscount Haddington.

Owned by Secretary of State for Scotland. Open during standard
     hours (entrance fee).

The original buildings, of which only slight traces remain, were early 12th-c.; a Culdee church, in a sense their predecessor, stood at Old Melrose, 2½ miles to the W. Parts of the W end of the nave and most of what remains of the monastic buildings are no later than the

13th c. The remainder of the church was completely rebuilt after
extensive damage in English raids in 1322 and 1385, in a lavishly
ornamented style curiously at variance with avowed Cistercian
austerity. Though to a less extent than Jedburgh, the abbey's
position on a main N–S route led to constant attacks, particularly in
the 14th and 16th c.

After the Earl of Hertford's disastrous incursion of 1545 it never
recovered, and although a dwindling body of monks stayed on, the
buildings were pillaged or put to other uses and went to ruin. In
1618 three bays of the nave were revaulted to form a parish kirk,
and so remained until a new kirk was built elsewhere in 1810. The
Duke of Buccleuch gave the abbey church and other lands to the
nation in 1919.

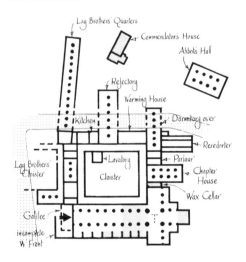

First to be noted past the ticket hut is a low wall-base which is all
that remains of the 12th-c. **W front**. Immediately below the hut can
be seen the beginnings of a new W front two bays further W, which
was never built. There are also traces of a 13th-c. galilee.

The clumsy vault and roof erected in 1618 to form a parish kirk in
the three E bays of the **nave** (the former monks' quire) are lower

Melrose Abbey Church: outer S nave arcade: 15th c.

than the original. W of that only the outer S arcade remains
standing, enclosing a series of side chapels begun in the 15th c. and
intended to continue to the line of the new W front. So at first the
nave is seen in cross-section, with the clerestory passageways
prominent on each side. At floor-level is the pulpitum that
separated the monks' quire from that of the lay brothers.

Along the S side each chapel has its piscina and some have their
vaults still complete. In the third (starting from the W) the tomb
slab is of George Halliburton (d.1538). The fourth, with St Michael
on its central vault-boss, is the burial place of the Pringle family,
whose 19th-c. arcaded memorial is on its E wall; two tomb slabs
commemorate Sir David Home (d.1589) and Cristin Lundie
(d.1602). The next chapel, also vaulted, has burials of the Scotts
and another branch of Pringles, the weathered effigy on its W side
being of Andro Pringil (d.1585).

The nave pulpitum retains its central doorway, miniature vaulting

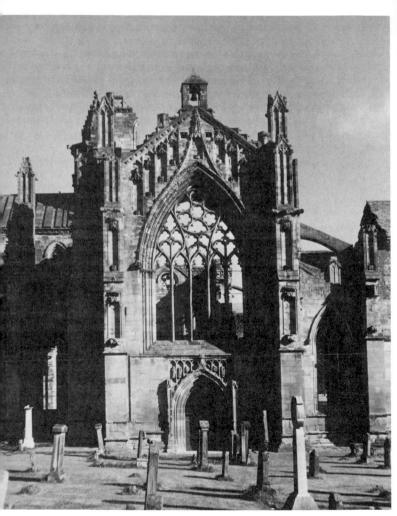

Melrose Abbey Church: S transept

and stair, and, facing W on its S side, a recess for keeping altar frontals. The E part of the nave is marred by the three massive arches put up on the N side in 1618 and by the barrel vault. Evidence of the original vault is to be seen in the springer stones on the S side, though the clerestory was also altered. It is not unlike English Decorated work, and indeed much at Melrose is an amalgam of English and French. The nave in its original form was a splendid design with subtly combined triforium and clerestory; its reasonably well-preserved sculptured detail includes cabbage-like foliage on the capitals of the main clustered piers. The N aisle, narrow because of the cloister behind, has a quadripartite vault, and the S aisle a tierceron one with foliage bosses.

The rest of the outer S chapels can now be looked at, each with a piscina and with varied window tracery akin to English Decorated. The sixth chapel (the first E of the pulpitum) has a monument inscribed 'DMF 1665'; DMF was David Fletcher, Bishop of Argyll. The eighth and last contains a 13th-c. stone prie-dieu with a Latin inscription in memory of 'Peter the Cellarer'. On its W wall is a stone with various saints' names (Ninian, Katharine etc.) which may perhaps have been a catalogue of dedications of the chapels.

From the **crossing** the design of the E end can be appreciated – very similar to the nave and with a fine E window which, more than almost anything else in Scotland, is in a mature version of English Perpendicular. Of the crossing tower only the W wall remains (towards the nave); the rest has collapsed and with it the other crossing arches.

The transepts are also much like the nave, with united clerestory and triforium, and on the S a splendid Decorated window. In the N transept are considerable remains of the night stair and upper doorway to the dorter, with a holy water stoup at the bottom. A round-arched doorway below leads to a barrel-vaulted sacristy known as the wax cellar. Above this doorway are a panel and a shelf for small statues, then three openings to the upper passage at clerestory level, and in the gable a well-preserved circular window.

The dedications of the two chapels E of the N transept are known. The left one, St Peter's, retains a credence shelf; the other was St Paul's. St Benedict's which adjoins them on the N side of the presbytery seems to have had a very unusual, nearly flat vaulted ceiling.

In the **presbytery** itself only the E bay on the N side survives more or less complete, together with the easternmost main bay and its vault and windows – E, N and S – all in Perpendicular style. The lierne vault has a central boss representing the Trinity, and others with saints or flowers and foliage. In the side walls are tomb recesses; the square-headed ones in the E wall were cupboards and on the S are a credence recess and a double-drained piscina.

Now go back across the crossing, into the E bay of the N aisle and through the 15th-c. round-headed doorway into the **cloister**. The placing of the monastic buildings N of the church was dictated by the water supply and drainage; little is left of them above foundation level. Against the N transept wall is 14th-c. wall-arcading with excellent naturalistic carving on its cornice. The church doorway, too, has well-preserved carving on this side. To its right is another ogee-headed bay, followed by a run of trefoil-headed arcading and stone benching.

Reverting to the E walk: the chapter house entrance is clear, with the bases of its doorway shafts. History tells that St Waltheof, the second abbot, was buried just inside this doorway; the remains of a tomb found here in 1921 are in the museum. Of the room itself little is left, though some original patterned tiles can be seen, rather a rarity in Scotland. Beneath the N transept gable, the doorway at the head of the night stair is again visible. After the chapter house was the parlour, then an undercroft with column bases. The dorter ran above. The reredorter stood at right angles at the end; its undercroft with latrine pit can be clearly seen.

Turn left into the N walk and pass the day stair and warming house. The original refectory was parallel to this walk but the final, much larger one stood at right angles in a N–S direction. Just before it, turn left across the lawn, up the steps, across the lane and into the garden of the **Commendator's House**. On the left is the end of the refectory, the foundations of which pass beneath the roadway; beyond it are the lay brothers' quarters. On the right is the end of the dorter and beyond that the Abbot's Hall. Running diagonally across the garden from the direction of the reredorter is the impressive 12th-c. stone-lined Great Drain, over ¼ mile long.

Commendators were by-products of the Reformation, laymen or clerics granted abbey revenues as political rewards before actual dissolution took place. The Melrose house is of the 15th and 16th c.

and was partly fortified. As a museum it now contains a wide variety of pottery, metal, carved stone etc., including the remains of St Waltheof's shrine.

Resuming the circuit of the **cloister** walk, note the remains of the washplace jutting into the garth opposite the refectory. Next along the N walk was the kitchen. Round the corner, the W range contained a series of rooms of which the one with three prominent columns was another early refectory. On the other side of that and continuing beneath the road are the foundations of the cloister of the lay brothers, a community which at the height of Melrose's prosperity numbered about 200.

Finally a circuit round the **outside** of the church, starting past the ticket hut into the S churchyard. The most noticeable features of the S aisle and transept are the window traceries, particularly those like whirling wheels. More easily missed is the shield of James IV on the extreme W buttress (1505) with beneath it that of Abbot Turnbull and a rebus of a mell or mason's mallet and a rose – 'Melrose'. The second buttress has a 'mort-lantern' on the niche-corbel, a hollowed pedestal that once contained a lamp. Further along, on the easternmost of the high buttresses, is a figure of the Virgin and Child with the heads, as usual, damaged; legend says that the man who beheaded the Child was maimed when the stone fell on him. Among the gargoyles is a pig playing bagpipes.

The transept, too, has interesting carved detail, particularly in the niches and corbels, the niche-heads being of the English Decorated 'nodding ogee' type. In the point of the door arch is another royal shield, with unicorn supporters; the rampant lion has been turned round so as not to have his back to the altar. The main E front also deserves careful study, both of general proportions and of detail – especially the topmost group representing the Coronation of the Virgin.

Near the house (now with public lavatories etc.) at the NE corner of the churchyard various interesting carved stones are lined up by the path. From there one can return along the N side and across the cloister to the W end again.

Methven Collegiate Church, Tayside   NO 026260
in village on Crieff-Perth road A85

College founded 1433 by Walter Stewart, Earl of Athole in existing
  parish church of St Marnock.

Church of Scotland. Old church not open to public. New church key
  available at the Manse, 5 Sauchob Road.

Like, for example, Bothans, Carnwath and Guthrie, this is one of
those instances where one transept of a formerly cruciform
collegiate church has survived through becoming a family burial
chapel, left behind when the church itself has been rebuilt in a
different position. In this case it is the N transept, its S end having a
comparatively modern blocking wall – probably put in when the
Smythes began to use it in 1787. The transept is attributed to Queen
Margaret, wife of James IV, and dates from 1516. The church,
rebuilt as a simple rectangle in 1783, had its own N transept, tower
and spire all added in 1825–6, to the design of William Mackenzie.
A local rhyme ran:

> In '26 the year of drought
> That frightened all the people
> Old Methven lifted up her head
> And built herself a steeple.

The crow-stepped gable and nice reticulated traceried window are
the chief features of the old 'aisle'. Parts of a niche with a
straight-headed canopy remain at one side, and there is an heraldic
lion with crown – possibly linked with Queen Margaret.
  The new church, traditionally T-shaped with pulpit and holy table
in the centre of the S side, has galleries in the three arms reached by
stairs at either end of the original rectangle. The added transept is

called the Lynedoch aisle: Thomas Graham, Lord Lynedoch and his
wife lie in the Lynedoch vault of 1792, a conspicuous feature of the
churchyard modelled on tombs in the Campagna in Rome and
standing partly on the foundation of the old chancel. A bell of 1658
is preserved from the old church, but the oak font is as recent as
1947.

Montrose: Blackfriars, Tayside   NO 714587 approx.
in town on A92

Dominican friary of the Nativity of the Blessed Virgin Mary
    founded by 1275 by Sir Alan Durward. Granted to burgh 1571.

No remains.

The site was at the N end of the town between Murray Street and
the tidal Montrose Basin. Having been destroyed by war in the 14th
c. the friary was refounded in 1517 as an amalgamation with St
Mary's hospital in the main street, but seven years later the friars
returned to their quieter abode. Parts of it still stood early in the
19th c., but the only relic today is the name Blackfriars Street. The
hospital has long disappeared.

Monymusk Priory, Grampian   NJ 685153
in village 17 miles WNW of Aberdeen, close to Alford-Inverurie
road B993

Augustinian priory of St Mary the Virgin founded by 1245 by
    Gilchrist, Earl of Mar at existing Culdee church; annexed to
    bishopric of Durham 1617.

Church of Scotland. Open during normal hours.

The parish church and Monymusk House stand half a mile apart.
Both obviously have associations with the priory, but there is no
certainty whether either formed its nucleus or whether there was a
third locality perhaps somewhere between. Though the
house,which became a castle of the Forbes family, is undoubtedly of
medieval origin, the church is the most likely monastic site, and it

seems that the Forbes family carried off much of the priory stone to it after it had become ruinous, which was by 1548 at the latest. It is also thought that the big round tower at the SE angle of the house may have started as a defensive part of the precinct wall.

The present church, parts of which are 12th-c., may thus reasonably be assumed to have been that of the priory. It was altered to a T-plan in 1822 by the addition of a N arm with a gallery, facing a pulpit and table against the main S wall. In 1929–32 it was however reinstated to something resembling its medieval arrangement.

The **tower** base, forming in effect a W porch, is obviously Norman with its small undecorated doorway and rough semicircular arch to the nave. Displayed here is the so-called Monymusk stone, about 7 feet high and carved with a Celtic cross. Brought from the roadside about a mile to the E, it had a temporary home in the billiard room of the great house. The tower is tunnel-vaulted, but the body of the church has a modern panelled and boarded ceiling. The arrangement of windows in the S wall shows that galleries formerly extended round the interior, stopping short at the two high-level ones. At that time the chancel was used partly as a coal store. Now only a small W gallery remains, and plain pine pews, simple and attractive. Wall-tablets from the 18th c. onwards commemorate the Grant family, and behind the pulpit is one of 1583 to John Forbes.

The **chancel**, probably curtailed at some stage, has a small Norman arch on scalloped capitals. The E window by Alexander Strachan depicts a Culdee preaching to the Picts; the S one, of 1975, is an abstract design by V. Thoms.

Outside, the squarer, more regular masonry of the tower indicates its greater age, though the 'galleries' pattern of nave windows can here be seen to have been superimposed on an earlier wall in which at least one blocked window and a doorway can be traced, and the tower itself has several blocked openings in its W wall, apparently post-Norman ones that have been refilled.

Newbattle Abbey, Lothian   NT 333661
1 mile SSE of Dalkeith on B703

Cistercian abbey of the Blessed Virgin Mary founded 1140 by David
I, a daughter house of Melrose. Secularised 1587 to Mark Ker.

Owned by Scottish nation. Not open to the public except by special
arrangement with college secretary.

The 12th-c. buildings seem to have been largely reconstructed
following an English raid in 1385. After the Earl of Hertford's
invasion of 1544 the abbey never recovered, and Mark Ker began to
build the present house on the site in 1580, incorporating part of the
S end of the E monastic range and using the stone of the remainder
and of the church. It was much rebuilt in the 17th and 18th c. and
altered and extended several times in the 19th c. In 1936 it was given
by the Marquis of Lothian for use as an adult education college.
Extensions built in 1968 under Sir Robert Matthew, Johnson-
Marshall & Partners occupy parts of the cloister and S transept
areas.

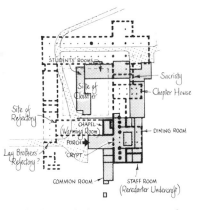

Inside the main house entrance a formal staircase of 1887 leads up
to the main rooms and down to the so-called crypt. Upstairs are a
magnificent drawing-room of c.1770 and c.1890, several 17th- and
18th-c. rooms with wood carving, plasterwork and paintings, and

over one of the administrative office doors a carved stone panel
dated 1580.

The 'crypt', actually the dorter undercroft, is divided into two by
the stairway, the positions of the removed columns being marked in
the floor. Partly 14th-, partly 15th-c., it has octagonal columns and
ribbed octopartite vaults. At the bottom of the stair are an old chest
with two enormous padlocks and two ancient tablets from Nineveh.
To the right lies the common room area, with an inserted 19th-c.
fireplace; the barrel-vaulted staff room beyond lay under the
reredorter. To the left is a smaller, somewhat similar space with a
17th-c. fireplace, and off this (to the left again) is the supposed
warming room, also barrel-vaulted, made into a chapel. The
'chancel arch', windows and elaborate marquetry floor based on
medieval tile patterns are of c.1890, but the font bowl is of c.1545; it
bears Scottish royal arms and was found in a nearby garden.

On the N side of the college extension the roadway runs along the
centre of the church site, and each of the rosebeds represents a
column; only one however has actual stonework visible. A gravel
path marks the N aisle wall and one relic of carved stone stands by
the roadway at the W end.

North Berwick Priory, Lothian   NT 546850
in Old Abbey Road close to North Berwick station and A198

Cistercian nunnery founded c.1150 by Duncan, Earl of Fife.
  Secularised 1588 to Alexander Home.

Owned by East Lothian District Council. Accessible at most times
  subject to permission from Abbey House adjoining, now an old
  people's home.

The name Abbey is misleading for this was never more than a
priory. Its recorded history is fairly sketchy. The church is known to
have been dedicated in 1242. Sixteen nuns were there in 1556, but
the buildings were largely destroyed in 1565. One range however
became partly domestic under the Homes in the 1580s and was
fortified and provided with a square tower. By the 19th c. only a
ruin in a field survived, but a house called The Abbey, owned by the
Speir family, was built alongside c.1910, making what was probably

the cloister garth into a garden. The church is surmised to have
stood to the S on what became a kitchen garden. A consecration
cross was found when the telephone exchange was built on the site
of Abbey Farm.

Entry alongside the modern house brings one into the cloister area,
with the surviving range on the right, and a big segmental arch in
the far wall of the garden. Access to the upper parts of the red stone
ruin is discouraged but most of it can be seen from ground level. It
can be quite logically interpreted as the refectory at upper level
standing on a series of tunnel-vaulted cells, though that
identification is by no means certain. The actual upper floor has
mostly gone but there are fireplaces at both ends, added after the
Dissolution. At the E end the gable stands high enough to show the
former roof line of the kitchen, now also a shell. At the back is a
very large fireplace with traces of a lancet window over; to the right
of that a gunloop points towards the entrance arch, added no doubt
after 1586. Another gunloop may be found in the return wall
towards the garden gate, while the entrance arch itself has a
defensive slit in one jamb. Returning through that arch and turning
left, one can then explore the outer wall of the main ruin, to which a
square tower was added, also probably in the late 16th c. A path
through the trees leads around to the W wall of the presumed
cloister, and then through the segmental arch first seen. This wall is
heavily buttressed and shows no sign of having formed part of a W
range of buildings.

A few relics are in the local museum near the sea-front.

Nunraw Abbey, Lothian   NT 593700
1½ miles SE of B6370 at Garvald, on road to Duns

Cistercian abbey of Sancta Maria founded 1946, a daughter house
of Roscrea, Ireland.

Principal parts open (except on Sundays and important Feast days)
to men only, 9.30 to 11.30 a.m. and 2 to 4.30 p.m. Guide
accompanies. Women permitted only in church and reception
areas.

Following a period of twenty-three years in the old abbey at
Nunraw House, the monks occupied the new buildings in their
present incomplete form, lacking the church and guest house. They
were designed by Peter Whiston, begun in 1953 and first occupied in
1969. The spacious plan is fairly traditional, the main rooms being
around a covered cloister walk and subsidiary ones around a 'work
cloister' and a future 'guest cloister'. The exterior is stone-faced,
largely two-storeyed, simple but not over-austere; the interior is
mostly plastered and many of the rooms command splendid views of
the Lammermuir Hills and the Firth of Forth.

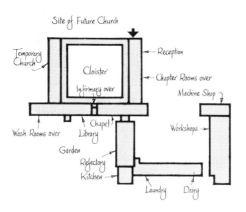

Nunraw: Old Abbey from SW

Much of the road frontage is harled (cement rendered), this being the wall against which the church will be built. At the left end a door marked 'Reception' leads to a big parlour where a model is on view and postcards and guidebooks on sale.

The conducted tour is clockwise around the main cloister, taking in first the refectory, a fine room with pitched boarded ceiling and the customary pulpit at the entrance end. Off the S walk are a monks' private chapel, and the library with a panorama of the hills. The W walk runs alongside the low-ceilinged chapel or temporary church, which will one day become the library. The public entrance is at the further end, nearest the road – an arrangement that, with a central altar separating monks and laity, suits its elongated shape.

Outside, it is possible to look alongside the parlour entrance and the E range towards the 'work cloister', the hub of the farm which is the monks' principal practical occupation. Apart from this, only distant views of the buildings are possible, but the farm buildings about 200 yards E of the abbey are open to the public.

Nunraw Old Abbey, Lothian   NT 592705
1 mile SE of B6370 at Garvald, on road to Duns

See under Nunraw for history; ceased to be abbey 1969 and became
   retreat house.

Owned by Nunraw abbey. Principal (first-floor) parts open at
   similar hours to abbey, on request. Guide accompanies.

The nucleus of Nunraw House is a fortified peel tower that
belonged to the medieval nunnery of Haddington. In the 16th c. it
passed to the Hepburn family who added to it to make a Z shape,
with a second tower. Later it became, it is thought, the original of
'Ravenswood' in Scott's *Bride of Lammermoor* and hence also in
Donizetti's opera *Lucia di Lammermoor*. In the 19th c. it was again
enlarged in typical baronial style. Together with some wooden huts,
some of which remain, it served as the abbey from 1946 until 1969,
when it became a retreat house for lay people.

From the entrance porch one is admitted to the main stair and taken
to the guests' refectory in the Victorian wing. A small common
room is alongside, then a bigger one which is within the 16th-c.
building. The room beyond, now an oratory or small chapel, has a
remarkable wooden ceiling of *c.*1610, painted with the coats of arms
of the contemporary kingdoms of Europe. The medieval tower next
to it may not be entered but can be partially seen from outside by
turning right outside the porch; the temporary buildings still
remaining unfortunately do not enhance its appearance. Possibly
more attractive is the 450-nest 17th-c. stone dovecot on the other
side of the front lawn. On the lawn is a 17th-c. multi-dialled sundial.

Oronsay Priory, Strathclyde   NR 351889
on tidal island close to Colonsay, 40 miles SW of Oban

Augustinian priory of St Columba, of obscure origin but probably
   refounded by John I, Lord of the Isles, *c.*1340. Granted to Bishop
   of the Isles 1616.

Owned by Lord Strathcona and Mount Royal and in care of
   Secretary of State for Scotland. Open at all times without charge.

The name means 'tidal island' but is sometimes spelt Oransay
through confusion with the legendary St Oran. Traces remain of a
Celtic monastic settlement, but the walls in the existing simple
group of buildings are nowhere considered to be older than
mid-14th-c., that being the date assigned to parts of the E range and
to the prior's house. It seems probable that the church was at first N
of the cloister and that it was interchanged later in the 14th c. with
the refectory when both were rebuilt. The priory's supposed
dependence on the abbey of Holyrood is unauthenticated. In later
years it became the burial place of the McNeills.

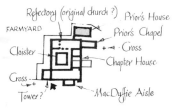

Visits to the priory have to be carefully timed to take advantage of a
period of low tide. Local advice should be sought. The walk from
high-water mark on Colonsay to the priory is about 2½ miles each
way, much of it following an ill-defined but long-used route on wet
sand.
   The walled churchyard in its farm setting is roughly circular, a
sign of Celtic origin. Prominent from the gate in the SE corner is the
E wall of the church with late 15th-c. triple lancet window. The
projection to its right is not a porch, but the 19th-c. McNeill burial
aisle, never roofed. So the way in is by a rough doorway to the

Oronsay Priory: Oronsay Cross: 1510

extreme left, through what probably was, or was intended to be, a tower, with late 15th-c. walls of fine ashlar standing to about 10 feet.

The **church** itself has quite a miscellany of openings in its S wall and some remains of original plaster. A single small window at high level suggests that there was once a gallery. The N wall is quite blank except for the doorway into the cloister and a recess at the E end. The stone altar is late 15th-c., probably repaired in 1624 when Franciscan missionaries reconverted the islanders, and containing an aumbry recess on the further side. A much bigger aumbry is in the SE corner of the sanctuary, housed in a big buttress. The S or MacDuffie aisle, entered only through a low doorway, is of the same period as the tower, with marks of a lean-to roof of no great height and of an upper floor; in its N wall is the rough round-arched tomb recess of Prior Sir Donald MacDuffie, whose effigy will be seen later. The much bigger recess in the N wall of the chancel, with a pointed arch and high flat roof, was probably used as a small sacristy. From it a 15th-c. doorway leads into what was the chapter house, divided in the 18th c. by a 6-foot cross wall and its nearer half connected into the added McNeill enclosure.

Back now to the church and through the partly reconstructed N doorway into the little **cloister**. Its S walk, alongside the church, has low round-headed arches and the upper window at its far end would have lighted the dorter. The E walk (and the N too) is represented by bases only; from it the N half of the chapter house can be reached, through a doorway altered when the dividing wall was put in. The compartment N of that was perhaps a parlour. The N range, believed to have been the first church, evidently became refectory and kitchen, with a floor level about 4 feet above the remainder; a fireplace towards the W end suggests that the kitchen was there. E of these is the prior's chapel, a fairly complete little chapel with walls standing to 10 feet or so, and a well-defined sanctuary step. The projecting masonry half-way along the N side may be the base of a pulpit, while the square-headed W doorway set within a blocked pointed arch probably indicates a change to secular use. The rebuilding of the W, N and E sides of the cloister with triangular-headed arches of the kind that in England indicate Saxon work was done early in the 16th c. The present W arcade is a reconstruction of 1883, using old materials. Two of the uprights near the middle have inscriptions in medieval characters – one giving the name of the mason and the other that of the canon in charge.

In the **churchyard** immediately SW of the church is a standing cross with a Crucifix on the head and an inscription to Prior Colin who died in 1510. From here a path leads around the W and N sides of the church and cloister to the prior's house, originally two-storeyed and re-roofed in 1927 for the purpose of housing a splendid collection of over thirty cross-slabs and other memorial stones, mostly of the 14th and 15th c. At the further end on the right is the impressive figure of a knight, possibly Sir Alexander MacDonald, *c*.1400, while third from the end lies a priest's effigy under a triple canopy, representing Prior Sir Donald MacDuffie (*c*.1554 or 1555); this was in the recess in the MacDuffie aisle. About midway on the same side is another priest in vestments with an inscription above his head to Canon Bricius MacMhuirich, also *c*.1550. Another smaller knight's effigy lies at the end on the left. The prior's house was joined on to the cloister ranges and is thought to have once included a reredorter.

Just E of the prior's chapel is a second standing cross, the head of which does not belong to the shaft; these pieces were assembled here in fairly recent times.

Paisley Abbey, Strathclyde   NS 486640
in town centre

Cluniac priory of St Mary the Virgin, St James the Greater of Compostella, St Milburga and St Mirin founded *c*.1163 by Walter, son of Alan, Steward of Scotland, a daughter house of Much Wenlock priory; became abbey 1219 and mitred 1395. Secularised 1587 to Lord Claud Hamilton, later Lord Paisley, the church becoming parochial.

Church of Scotland. Open 10 a.m. to 3 p.m. (but closed 12 noon to 1 p.m.) without charge.

Of the first church, burned in the English invasion of 1307, the lower parts of the W end and S side survive. The rest was rebuilt, but after another fire in 1498 the nave was again reconstructed along with the central tower, which late in the 16th c. collapsed and severely damaged the quire.

The nave remained in use as a parish church and the quire went to ruin. The cloister buildings, now called The Place, were adapted as a house by the Hamiltons, fell into disrepair and were restored to church use in 1930–60. The quire and tower were rebuilt under Sir Robert Rowand Anderson, P. Macgregor Chalmers and Sir Robert Lorimer, being completed in 1928.

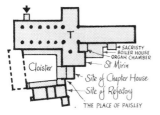

From the N porch, also rebuilt early this century, it is best to go first into the **nave**, disappointingly dark with its small coloured windows. The early 16th-c. bay design, unique in Britain, resembles that of Angers cathedral in France. There, however, it is the triforium walkway that is carried on corbels round each main support. Here the clerestory level is treated similarly, with the heavy corbels (each with a grotesque figure at its base) occupying the spandrels between the triforium arches – themselves inelegantly squat, round-arched (as is often the case in late medieval Scottish work) and with two-light tracery. The twin-windowed clerestory and the main arcades on clustered columns are more orthodox; the latter may well be largely survivals from the early 14th-c. rebuilding. The timber ceiling of the nave is of 1982, while the aisle vaults too are almost wholly modern restorations. Behind, the lower windows are early 13th-c. and the upper single one with Flamboyant tracery early 16th-c.; their curiously unbalanced glass is by Daniel Cottier, 1888 (top), Franz Fries, 1874 (bottom left), and J. Ballantine & Sons, 1888 (bottom right).

The W bays of the aisles seem originally to have been meant for twin towers. That of the **N aisle** contains a stair to the modern gallery. The first two windows E of the porch are by Sir Edward

Burne-Jones, 1870 and 1879, and specially attractive; beneath them are tablets of 1976 to John Witherspoon the theologian and Thomas Inglis (d.1559). The last two windows are by Cottier, 1880, and Charles Kempe, 1890; under the latter stands a grave slab of 1584.

The **N transept**, partly reconstructed when the quire was rebuilt, has windows (from left to right) by Louis Davis 1909, Clayton and Bell, 1907 (Te Deum), and (less attractive) a pair by Cottier, 1874. The **crossing** with its vault and piers is rebuilt too. The lectern, with St Andrew on his Cross, remembers the Rev. Dr A. M. MacLean who promoted the rebuilding, while inside the **quire** on the left is a memorial of 1928 to the Clark family, the principal donors. Old grave slabs from the 17th c. onwards throughout the floor are a relic of the centuries that the quire was a ruin. The window in the N wall in a Walter Crane style is of 1934; just beyond is an effigy traditionally that of Marjory Bruce, daughter of Robert I, but on a tomb which clearly does not belong to it. The choir stall carvings are worth close examination.

The glass of the great E window is by Douglas Strachan, 1930; so are the next two, 1932 and 1936 respectively. The dark piscina and four sedilia are relics of the 14th-c. quire, other parts of the wall-base of which can also be traced. The white cenotaph on the S side was given by Queen Victoria in 1888 to commemorate Stewarts buried in the church.

Back in the crossing, the modern pulpit is copied from that at Fotheringhay, Northamptonshire, and bears a plaque to Mary, Queen of Scots who was imprisoned there. The early 20th-c. font, actually within the very short S transept, is of inappropriate marble and onyx.

The whitened **St Mirin's chapel**, approached through iron gates of 1957, was founded in 1499 and has a barrel vault with false stone ribs. Its former reputation as the 'Sounding aisle', owed to its being walled off from the rest of the church, was lost when the two-bay arcade was reopened in 1907. The E window is by Francis Stephens and John Hayward, 1945; beneath is a series of 12th-c. carvings of the life of St Mirin (some of them are lost). On the N wall is a sad late 16th-c. memorial to Lord Claud Hamilton's children, on the S a 19th-c. Dutch painting *The Death of the First Born*, and at the W end another, smaller marble font and two more interesting grave slabs.

Paisley Abbey Church: nave triforium, N side: early 16th c.

The first window of the S aisle is another by Burne-Jones, 1877. The remainder are much less attractive. The round-arched doorway to the **cloister** is a reminder that this wall is late 12th-c. The N and E cloister walks were reconstructed in 1914 with pretty arcades while along the N side is the second processional doorway into the church, trefoil-headed with richly moulded arches. The W range no longer exists; so from the street one can look back and see St Mirin's chapel with its intersecting tracery, to its right a building on the chapter house site, and on the far right another on the refectory site: this is the Place of Paisley, the 16th-c. Hamilton mansion now restored for church and social use.

Next the **W front**. Its splendid doorway has no fewer than fifteen shafts each side; its little flanking arches pick up the dog-tooth of the outermost order. Above are the Geometric and Flamboyant windows already noted inside. Round on the N side are the two-storeyed porch and a good view of Lorimer's dignified tower. The transept E wall and the whole quire are effectively 20th-c. and so (on the S side) are the sacristy and the organ chamber with the 'Cathcart aisle' below it. Beside the latter is St Mirin's chapel again, and The Place, with a well in front of what was once the refectory range.

Peebles Collegiate Church, Borders NT 246405
¼ mile W of town centre close to Glasgow road A72

College founded 1543 in parish church of St Andrew by magistrates and John Hay; abandoned 1560 following burning by English.

Owned by Tweeddale District Council. Accessible at all times without charge.

The church is said to have been founded in 1195 by Jocelyn, Bishop of Glasgow, but seems to have been rebuilt in the 13th c. Largely destroyed in the English invasion of 1548, it was eventually given up in favour of the Cross Kirk. Only the tower was allowed to remain; it was restored in 1883.

The tower with its 19th-c. saddleback roof stands prominently in the middle of a large graveyard. Its arch to the nave has been blocked and a small doorway substituted. Of the nave itself, a stretch of the N wall survives, covered with ivy and with a rugged doorway opening. A tablet on the W face of the tower commemorates William Chambers who restored it and who as Lord Provost of Edinburgh also promoted the restoration of St Giles'. Of the innumerable tombstones most are 19th-c., but there are some older ones against the S wall of the tower, and towards the SE where many bear the favourite skull and cross-bones emblem of mortality.

Peebles: Red Friars, Borders   NT 250407
¼ mile N of town centre, close to A72.

Trinitarian friary founded or refounded 1474. Church taken over by
   parish 1561 and friars dispersed; lands granted to John Hay 1624.

In care of Secretary of State for Scotland. Open at standard times
   without charge.

Usually known as Cross Kirk, it is said to have originated with the discovery of a large cross and an inscribed stone on the site in 1261. They were believed to be relics of St Nicholas. Alexander III thereupon built a church dedicated to the Holy Cross, much of which survives. The date and manner of arrival of the friars seem to be matters of doubt. Some were expelled in 1463 after a tenure of perhaps fifteen years, for alleged frauds, but a new establishment was set up in 1474 and the church tower was built about that time. In the English invasions of the 1540s this and the parish church were both burned – the latter apparently faring much the worse, for the parish used the Cross Kirk from 1561 and continued to do so until a new parish church was erected in 1784.

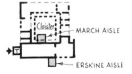

Peebles: Cross Kirk from W

Entry is through the tunnel-vaulted base of the 15th-c. tower, where a plan is displayed. The outer arch is rather decayed but the inner, facing the **nave**, has remains of moulded work. The 13th-c. nave walls stand mostly to around eaves level, except at the W end of the S side where a large gap is filled with more modern masonry. Opposite is a plain round-arched opening to the cloister, then a blocked segmental arched opening to the cloister, then a blocked segmental arched opening which led to the March 'aisle' or mausoleum.

The **chancel** arch is extremely small with no sign of ever having been bigger. The large window opening above it does not mean that the chancel roof was low; probably there was a screen at this point. Little more than foundations remain of the E end, including the sacristy on the N side. On the S side but out of sight and inaccessible is another burial aisle, that of the Erskines.

Rather than returning to the nave, it is best to go out at the E end, skirt the sacristy and then go into the **cloister** area. Few actual walls remain except close to the church, but enough foundations have been identified for the layout to be established, and the missing wall lines have been marked out in the turf, following the normal arrangement with refectory on the further (N) side and the chapter house in the middle of the E range. The flat-roofed March aisle intrudes over the cloister walk next to the church, and into the area of the garth.

Finally another look at the strong square tower with its jagged top. More of the E side is broken away than is at first evident, and no architectural detail is left.

Perth: Blackfriars, Tayside   NO 118239
in town, near SE corner of North Inch

Dominican friary founded 1231 by Alexander II; granted to burgh
   1569.

Site in multiple ownership.

A place of some historical importance, it was a frequent resort of kings, and several parliaments were held in its church. From the gardens Robert III saw the battle of the Clans on the North Inch in

1396, and in 1437 the buildings were the scene of James I's murder and of the legendary heroism of Catherine Douglas who thrust her arm through the staples of a door lock to try to prevent it. They were destroyed by the rabble in 1559 and all that can be seen today is a plaque on a building on the corner of Blackfriars Street and Charlotte Street.

Perth: Charterhouse, Tayside   NO 115234 approx.
in town centre

Carthusian priory founded 1429 by James I; granted to burgh 1569.

Site in multiple ownership.

The splendid set of buildings in what was known as the Vallis Virtutis was annihilated by the mob in 1559. The church contained the tomb of James I and his Queen (later removed to St John's church), as well as that of Margaret Tudor, wife of James IV. The James VI hospital was founded on the site in 1569, but was destroyed by Cromwell for material for his fort and not rebuilt till 1750. Only the name Charterhouse Lane survives.

Perth: Greyfriars, Tayside   NO 120233
in town centre

Franciscan friary founded 1460 by Lord Oliphant; destroyed by mob 1559; grounds became town cemetery 1580.

Site owned by Perth and Kinross District Council. Open to the public at all times.

Lying between Princes Street and Tay Street, the burial ground contains mostly 19th-c. memorials and headstones in profusion. The oldest, including some more interesting ones of the 17th and 18th c., may be found in the SW corner. Nothing of the actual friary survives.

Pittenweem Priory, Fife   NO 549025
in town on A917, 9 miles SSE of St Andrews

Augustinian priory founded 1318, or possibly much earlier;
buildings granted to burgh 1592, and lands to Frederick Stewart
1606.

Church of Scotland, but parts of site owned by Episcopal Church
and others. Key to parish church available at chemist's shop in
town square during shop hours. Key to cave similarly available at
tea shop in main street (small fee). Domestic buildings not open
to public.

The priory evolved around the cave of St Fillan, a roughly Y-shaped
natural opening into the rock, from one of the arms of which in
monastic times or later an access stair was formed to the flatter
ground above. Sometimes confused with that on the Isle of May,
the priory was indeed closely associated with it, and it is thought
that the monks of May moved here when their own house passed
from the control of Reading abbey to that of St Andrews priory in
1318. In later centuries the cave became a haunt of smugglers.

The present parish church occupies part at least of the priory
church site and contains a trace of medieval work, but is mostly of
the 17th c. and 1882. The N gatehouse was removed in 1805 for the
building of the Episcopal church. The E one still exists in somewhat
mutilated form, as does an L-shaped block comprising the so-called
Priory and a wing partly rebuilt in 1821–2 as a town hall but since
converted to domestic use and called the Great House. The latter is
said to be on the site of the refectory, dorter and chapter house,
though it is difficult to see on what evidence.

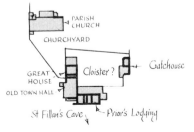

The parish church presents a picturesque **tower** to close the view along the main street, capped by a balustraded parapet and spire. It is mostly of 1588, but the upper part is 17th-c. It contains two bells, one of them made in Stockholm in 1663. The bottom stage, which is vaulted and has been used as a town prison, is a reminder that Pittenweem was at one time plagued with so-called witches, victims of the incredibly cruel treatment meted out around 1700 by the superstitious. The **church** itself is rather muddled, and not improved by the remodelling of its N side in somewhat florid Gothic in 1882. That gave it a stumpy stem to a conventional T plan in which the galleries on three sides face a pulpit and table in the centre of the S wall. Four noteworthy windows in this wall were the work of William Wilson, 1958–63. Near the NE corner of the church a fragmentary shaft is possibly 14th-c., older than anything else on the priory site except the cave, and almost certainly part of the priory church. There are one or two 17th-c. memorial slabs nearby.

The rest has to be seen piecemeal. First, in the W wall of the Episcopal church and presumably preserved from the gatehouse that occupied its site, is a stone with the arms of Bishop Kennedy, d.1465. S from there along Abbey Walk Road is the **E gatehouse**, a somewhat forbidding affair with a small round-headed entry and an upper floor with heavy machicolation – 15th-c. but rather altered. Behind this is the so-called **cloister**, a W and a S range forming an L. The left or S range is three-storeyed with the lowest floor vaulted, and will be seen better from the other side; much of it is 15th-c. The other, with nothing visibly older than the 16th or 17th c., is three-storeyed only at the N end.

Now it is necessary to go back past the churches to the main street where, a few doors along on the right, is the tea and gift shop where the cave key may be borrowed. Below the tower a lane called Cove Wynd leads past the Priory buildings, disguised here by the town hall built, it is said, on the site of the refectory. Further down however the seaward face of the Priory with its oriel windows can be seen with advantage. Further still is the **cave** entrance.

Just inside the iron gate are light switches, so the two-branched interior can be seen quite well. Its history and legends are intermingled, and various versions exist of the story of St Fillan who is reputed to have lived in it and preached from it in the 7th c. His spring and well are at the inner end in the left branch. In the right one an altar was set up in 1935 close to the saint's traditional living-place. Shortly before that, the rock-cut steps leading upwards from the side of the cave into what is now a private garden had been dug clean and made usable again; they may be climbed but normally the top exit is locked.

Pluscarden Abbey, Grampian   NJ 142576
6 miles SW of Elgin and 3 miles S of Inverness road A96

Valliscaulian priory of Our Lady, St John the Baptist and St Andrew founded 1230 by Alexander II, a daughter house of Val des Choux, Burgundy. United in 1454 with Urquhart priory to become a Benedictine cell to Dunfermline abbey. Secularised 1560 to Alexander Seton, Lord Urquhart. Became cell to Prinknash abbey 1948; Benedictine priory again 1966; abbey 1974.

Church open during normal hours.

One of only three Valliscaulian houses in Britain. The old local name Kail Glen, 'cabbage valley', is a translation of Vallis Caulium or Val des Choux. The buildings, largely 13th-c., were probably damaged in 1390 in the course of raids by Alexander Stewart, the 'Wolf of Badenoch'; some work is clearly subsequent to that date and some, later in the 15th c., shows the influence of Dunfermline. Monks remained till about 1596.

The buildings fell gradually to ruin, disused except for burials. In 1821 the vaulted day room was repaired for parish use, and in 1898 the 3rd Marquis of Bute began repairing the church. His son gave it to Benedictines from Prinknash, who re-established a monastic community in 1948. Re-roofing of the buildings commenced – the tower by 1955, the domestic buildings and transepts by 1960, and the presbytery by 1983 – and in 1974 abbey status, which had never been enjoyed before, was granted.

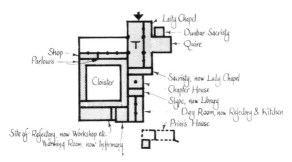

The approach is towards the newly re-roofed E end and **transepts**. From inside the N transept entrance one looks across to the S transept through the base of the tower, with the severe new pulpitum wall occupying the big blocked nave arch on the right, and on the left the quire arch which was rebuilt *c.*1500 on new piers; the little gallery is modern, but around the arch can be seen faint traces of 16th-c. wall paintings. The Rood is of 1909, from Oberammergau, and was in an Anglican convent at Haywards Heath.

The E aisles of both transepts, with columns of quatrefoil section, are screened off for the laity, facing the principal altar which is at the W end of the quire. The broken weather-worn masonry bears witness to four centuries of neglect – but the aisle vaults remain complete. The N window, by Br Gilbert (1962), was made in the abbey workshop; so was the E one, depicting the Agnus Dei (1985). Flanking the altar are two bronze standard candlesticks from Pavia Charterhouse in Italy, and beyond are the N transept and Lady chapel (one-time sacristy/library) visible through a skew arch. The **quire** is notable for the modern stalls by Thompson of Kilburn and the E window (1983) also by Br Gilbert, with rich reds in the four lower lancets and blues in the three-light window above. The present roof is wholly of the 1980s.

Back now to the main **crossing**. The splendid N transept windows are by Sadie McLellan, the great circular one being on a Revelation theme. Numerous old grave-slabs have been assembled round the walls. On the right are two showcases with various relics, then the weather-worn arch that led to the S aisle, then the reconstructed

Pluscarden Abbey from SE

night stair and – ahead – a private doorway to the Lady chapel.
From this end it is interesting to examine the clerestory of the
transepts, much higher on the E side than the W, and incorporating
a walkway with a probably unique series of narrow openings
punctuating the wall between the main ones. The S transept is more
elaborate than the N, and evidently later.

The S transept chapel can be entered at the far left corner of the
transept. From it can be seen the little vaulted Lady chapel and,
looking again into the quire, the sacrament house of *c*.1500 in its N
wall and an elaborately traceried Gothic chest.

The rest of the interior is private. Of the medieval parts the
chapter house has reverted to its proper use and the day room is
used as refectory and kitchen. Both are still vaulted. Access to the
outside too is limited. The nave, now believed to have been
completed in the Middle Ages, has no more than its N and W
wall-bases and the start of its W doorway. Part of the S aisle site is

occupied by a temporary building (including the abbey shop), and there are others on the further side of the enclosing cloister wall. Dominating all these is the high slated roof (1960) of the monastery wing which extends from the S transept and which was adapted from the 'hunting lodge' formed in the 19th c. by the Duke of Fife. The S walk of the cloister has recently been rebuilt in stone and there are plans to rebuild the other three, as well as a W range to serve as a guest house.

Near the E end of the church is the vaulted Dunbar sacristy of c.1540, built by the last medieval prior. The quire has smallish windows within ambitiously big arches, in a way that suggests belated caution over storm damage. Round on its S side the restored monastic wing can be seen again, with a glimpse of the ruin of the medieval prior's house at the far end. This again is not accessible to the public.

The ancient precinct wall is the most extensive in Scotland after St Andrews, a particularly fine stretch being on the left as one returns to the eastern entrance. The N gatehouse retains traces of a prison cell, and further along are recesses that were used for beehives.

Queensferry: Whitefriars, Lothian   NT 128785
in village on B924, between Forth road bridge and rail bridge

Carmelite friary of St Mary founded by Sir George Dundas c.1330; refounded by James Dundas 1441; granted back to Dundas family 1560. Used as parish church 1610–35; passed to secular use but restored for worship 1890.

Scottish Episcopal Church. Key available from churchwardens as advertised on notice-board.

The Carmelite settlement in Queensferry was probably associated from the start with the crossing of the Forth, named after Queen Margaret who journeyed this way to Dunfermline. The more permanent buildings, of which only the church remains, probably included a hospice for travellers, but excavations have revealed no trace of other structures. The nearby Forth road bridge (1964) made the ferry obsolete.

Though in many respects more 13th-c. in character, the church cannot be earlier than mid-15th-c. It was evidently intended to be cruciform, but probably never had a N transept. The nave, shown roofless in surviving pictures, was pulled down early in the 19th c. In 1890 the remainder was leased in perpetuity to the Episcopal Church and restored under John Kinross, a small porch-vestry being added against the W side of the tower. It is the only ancient Carmelite church in Britain still used for regular worship.

Site of Nave

The porch leads directly into the quite spacious **crossing** space, with a tunnel vault running N to S. Above that but not normally open to visitors are two rooms with fireplaces, and over them a one-time doocot now containing a bell of 1635. The arches to both chancel and S transept are semicircular. The **chancel** has a plain unplastered vault and – rather unusually – a big E window with two smaller ones over. Plain corbels along both walls probably indicate where an upper floor was supported during the period of secular use. At the E end are an aumbry and 'basket-arched' piscina and sedilia. The altar rail and pulpit are by Ian Lindsay, 1963. The E window glass (Ascension) is by Mayer of Munich, 1904; that in the westernmost window of the S wall (St James and St John) is by Ballantine & Son.

The **S transept**, five steps up, has a timber barrel roof and is now St Joseph's chapel. Here the main window is by Lavers and Westlake, 1891. The font is of 1905. Memorials to the Dundas family (descendants of the friary founders) include a fine 17th-c. heraldic ledger stone.

Outside, the low tower is the principal feature. It was once higher but now has a comfortable low pyramidal tiled roof. The lines of the former nave roof are visible on its W face. That of the chancel has traditional stone slabs. A round-headed niche is over the E window, while along the whole N side (including the tower) is a line of corbels which prove that a cloister or other building, possibly of timber, adjoined.

Queensferry: Whitefriars Church from SE

Restalrig Collegiate Church, Lothian NT 283745
2 miles ENE of Edinburgh city centre

Collegiate church of the Holy Trinity and St Mary. College founded
   1487 by James III.

Church of Scotland, but chapel in care of Secretary of State for
   Scotland. Key of church at 126 Restalrig Avenue: key of St
   Triduana's chapel at Village Pharmacy, 50 Restalrig Road South,
   weekdays 9.30 a.m. to 5.30 p.m.; both within short distance of
   church.

This small parish church about half-way between Edinburgh and the
coast, now swallowed up in suburbs, was created a Chapel Royal by
James III about 1460 in association with his house at Leith. He
added a two-storeyed hexagonal chapel apparently in honour of the
legendary St Triduana, and endowed a chaplaincy in it in 1477. The
reason for this very unusual form of construction is unknown; it was
too grand to have been a chapter house for an establishment so

comparatively small, and on the other hand there is no obvious place where a spring or well could have been – a feature sometimes linked with an unusual plan. A separate hexagonal well-house did however exist nearby, but it was transplanted to Holyrood Park in 1859. The king died at Sauchieburn only a few months after his chapel had become collegiate, and his son James IV was killed at Flodden in 1513. The latter had increased the number of prebendaries, and so did James V again in 1515.

In 1552 the prebendaries' houses were destroyed by the English. Eight years later the General Assembly, probably spurred on by John Knox, ordered the church itself to be 'raysit and utterly casten downe and destroyed'. Only parts of the outer walls survived, and the lower part of St Tirduana's chapel. Another church of St Mary was chosen as the church of Leith parish and Restalrig churchyard later became a burial place for Episcopalians. The ruin remained till 1836 when it was restored under William Burn as a plain nave and chancel (there is evidence that aisles existed or were at any rate planned). The W porch is of 1884. St Triduana's chapel was restored in 1908 (without its upper storey) by the gift of the Earl of Moray, and four years later the church itself was given parish status again. The vestry on its N side was added in 1963.

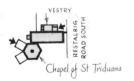

comparatively small, and on the other hand there is no obvious

A visit has to be in two parts, for there is no physical connection between church and chapel. Weekday entry to the **church** will probably be through the comparatively new vestry porch on the N side, where the medieval sacristy stood. The structure is a straightforward one with plastered walls and a boarded barrel roof with applied ribs. The glass is of varying quality, the three best being the W window with three saints by William Wilson (1966), the second on the N side commemorating the beneficent medieval Logan family with emblems of the Evangelists, by Sadie McLellan (1982), and the one opposite in praise of music by Sax Shaw (1980).

Next to the latter is a large 18th/19th-c. tablet to the Wood family.

Outside the church, all is now so blackened that it is hard to distinguish genuine medieval walling from that of the 1836 reconstruction, though the E and side walls are mostly original and there is a short stub of masonry at the NE corner where an eastward extension for a new chancel is thought to have been begun. Excavations have also revealed slight traces of intended enlargements to form N and S nave aisles. The churchyard has many interesting memorials from the Episcopalian period, and a search will reveal headstones of quite a number of masons and others, depicting the tools of their trades.

The approach to **St Triduana's chapel**, with its high slated modern pyramidal roof surmounted by the saint's statue, is through one of the burial compounds built against its W sides, where an 18th-c. inscription refers to Robert Grant who 'repaired this ISLE'. Of the fifteen steps down to lower level, those within the wall thickness are medieval. The fascinating interior is just like the undercroft of a chapter house, with a regular star-shaped vault supported on a central clustered column with foliage capital, and on smaller shafts at the angles. As well as the foliage bosses in the vault itself, numerous others have been collected on the floor; these are relics from the destroyed main chapel above. A fine heraldic memorial slab has also been set up on the stone wall bench that runs right round the chapel.

Restennet Priory, Tayside   NO 481516
1½ miles E of Forfar and ½ mile N of Friockheim road A932

Augustinian priory of St Peter founded *c*.1153 by Malcolm IV, at church probably founded 710 by King Nectan of Picts; secularised to Viscount Fenton 1606.

In care of secretary of State for Scotland. Accessible at all times without charge.

Or Restenneth. At this spot St Boniface is said to have baptised King Nectan, who proceeded to build a church with the aid of masons from Monkwearmouth in Northumbria. The lower part of the existing tower is thought to be his and could thus be the oldest church building in Scotland. Even the upper part is pre-Norman, and on that stands a 15th-c. broach spire. Round it in the 12th and 13th c. the Augustinians built their priory, which stood at that time on an island or peninsula in a small lake. This was drained in the 18th c.

Till 1591 the church served as the parish church of Forfar. It then became merely a burial place for the Dempster and Hunter families. Some 'repairs' were done in 1863–66.

The steeple is quite a landmark, of a form more familiar in parts of England than in Scotland. The approach, an open field path, leads to the W doorway of the nave. Only the bases of the jambs and of the flanking shafts remain, and indeed of the whole nave only the base of the walls with, on the W, another doorway base towards the cloister. All this is 13th-c. The line of its former high-pitched roof on the W face of the tower stands out clearly; apart from being quite a barrier between the nave and quire it is very much off-centre as a result of the widening of the building taking place towards the N only; its retention must have been influenced by age and historical associations, though whether the lower parts really are a survival from the church built in the 8th c. by King Nectan cannot be conclusively proved.

Beneath the tower a plan is displayed, as well as various stone fragments including a rather amusing but incomplete incised effigy; beside this is a holy water stoup, and in the narrow space N of the tower a stone coffin.

In the N wall of the quire are a tomb recess and remains of two wall tablets, all very badly damaged; a large section of this wall has been rebuilt on the old base, probably in the 1860s, but the E wall has the lower parts of three 13th-c. lancet windows with some remains of their shafted jambs, and along the S side are five more that are virtually complete. There are an aumbry and piscina too, rather formless stepped sedilia under a single arch, and a tomb

Restenneth Priory from NW

recess. In the centre of the quire lie two primitively carved medieval slabs.

On this side of the tower the high roof line just misses the belfry window. The spire is not a true broach one because the cardinal faces splay out to meet the eaves; nevertheless it is remarkably similar to those of the English limestone belt.

Near the W end of the S wall is another damaged tablet – but more importantly a blocked Norman arch showing that a short length of masonry is a relic of the first church of the Augustinians. An even earlier arch in the S wall of the tower leads into the cloister, an area now rather featureless following the rebuilding of its S and W walls, higher than the original and plain except for a peppering of pigeon-holes. On this side the tower face contains the chases for roof abutments at two levels, the upper (together with a line on the S wall of the quire) being that of the dorter. A few low walls show where the chapter house and other buildings stood. The opening at the SE corner of the cloister is not ancient, nor that in the centre of the W side.

From the cloister it is worth while skirting right round the church, noting the sacristy wall base on the N side, and the rebuilt section of quire wall which incorporates the stonework of two lancets.

Rosslyn Collegiate Chapel, Lothian   NT 275631
in Roslin village 8½ miles S of Edinburgh and 1½ miles E of Penicuik road A701

Collegiate chapel of St Matthew. College founded 1450 by Sir
  William St Clair.

Episcopalian, but owned by Earl of Rosslyn. Open from April to
  October, 10 a.m. to 5 p.m. (weekdays) and 2 to 4.30 p.m.
  (Sundays) (admission charge). Admission during rest of year on
  application to curator at College Hill House nearby.

'Unique' is a word that can be applied in some sense to any building. For all its modest size, the architecture of Rosslyn chapel merits the description more than any in Scotland, as much for some unusual features of its construction as for the famous exuberance of its stone carving.

The spelling Rosslyn applies to the earldom, to the chapel and to the ruined castle which was probably begun about 1304. The form Roslin is only used for the village and for the battle of 1302 in which the Scots defeated an English army nearly four times as numerous and so asserted their independence. By the time the chapel was built, Roslin had, it is said, become the third most important place in Scotland.

The founder died in 1484, leaving only the eastern parts approaching completion: an aisled quire with four E chapels, a sacristy or lower chapel at a much lower level, and the beginnings of transepts. Foundations for the remainder had been laid too. Had the transepts and nave been actually built the total length would have more than doubled. As it is, the aisles have blocking walls at their W end and a vestry of 1880, by Andrew Kerr, stands where the crossing would have been.

Many explanations of the architecture and its decoration have been put forward. On the one hand it is argued that individual features, however unusual, can in fact be traced back to historical Scottish precedents, even if their derivations and original purposes were at the time not fully understood. The contrary theory, that much must be owed to similar buildings in Spain and Portugal (such as the Jeronimos church near Lisbon), rests partly on knowledge that craftsmen did come from those countries and elsewhere in Europe, but is seriously weakened by the fact that the 'similar buildings' are a good deal later in date than Roslin.

Building commenced in 1446, i.e. four years before the college was created, the date 1450 being taken from a decoding of an inscription in the clerestory. The high vault of the quire was put on after the founder's death, and instances of poorer workmanship here and there suggest a last-minute tidying up rather than any earnest desire to go forward to completion.

Some damage to the carvings was done at the Reformation, the altars were removed, and decay set in. After the battle of Dunbar in 1650 the chapel was used as a stable by General Monk's troops, and in 1688 both it and the castle suffered damage from a mob. During the 18th c. the windows and stonework received a certain amount of attention, but no proper restoration was done till 1861–2 when David Bryce directed an over-enthusiastic renewal of decayed stone and some wholesale recarving and re-tooling which evoked severe criticism. From that time it has been used for Episcopalian services. The last, less violent restoration was done in 1957–60.

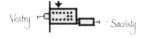

As with many far bigger churches, there are several 'levels' at which a visit may be made. A brief one will attempt no more than a general impression of its impact and associations, with a glimpse at a few details of particular popular interest. At the other extreme – in the case of Rosslyn likely to involve the best part of a day – will be a studious attempt to seek out every technicality of construction and to locate and identify every carving of any significance; that approach is fully provided for by the excellent little book on sale at the chapel. The middle course taken here is in many ways less

Rosslyn: St Matthew's Chapel from SW

satisfactory, being neither one thing nor the other, for it has to involve a conscious attempt to be selective and will inevitably omit, for lack of time or space, things that another visitor might notice and ask about.

The weekday approach through the roadside souvenir and refreshment shop is not exactly uplifting. From there the path leads to an ordinary-sized doorway in the complex N wall of the chapel. The exterior will be looked at later. Inside, it is best to go straight into the centre and first to absorb and marvel at the extraordinary elaboration. Every single surface seems to be encrusted with ornament in profuse and unending variety, making up by sheer quantity what the chapel lacks in size.

The **quire** – which is what the main structure really is, though used for congregational seating because the nave was never built – is of five bays but has an ambulatory of two more bays across the E end, giving access to four small chapels as though it were a miniature cathedral.

The proportions of the main arcades and their piers are normal for a Gothic church, though in other countries by the latter half of the 15th c. there would have been a marked lightening of weight, a subtler interpretation of thrust and counter-thrust in the mouldings, and a more logical relationship of ornament to purpose. At Rosslyn the clustering of the columns and the rather lumpy foliage capitals only seem to make them heavier, an effect accentuated by the two separate bands of foliage forming continuous hood moulds, and the broader bands of even more foliage around the soffits of the arches. Added to all that are four individual carvings on each capital, facing in the cardinal directions.

The clerestory is a series of windows without tracery, alternating with projecting canopies and empty brackets which once held figures of the Apostles. The reveals are each encrusted with lumpy rows of rosettes and other carving, curiously out of scale with the size of the openings, while below them runs a rather more delicate string course of flowers. The E window arch and its tracery are even more lavishly ornamented; the tracery itself is apparently a 19th-c. insertion, and so are the Virgin and Child in the niche below. This window, by far the biggest in the chapel, reaches right up into the crown of the pointed stone tunnel-vault. Its Resurrection glass of 1869 is in memory of Harriet, daughter of the 3rd Earl.

This is believed to be the only stone tunnel vault supported on a clerestory. Other medieval vaults in such a position are at least quadripartite and mostly ribbed, so as to concentrate the pressures away from the windows. Other tunnel vaults (and there are plenty in this part of Scotland) rest on the thick walls of a single storey – walls that were readily made massive enough to carry their great weight and outward thrusts. To construct such a wall at high level and to pierce it with a normal series of windows was extremely unscientific and, as will be seen outside, the system of buttressing seems to rely on sheer weight rather than considered analysis of lines of force. As for the vault itself, the attempt to lighten an unavoidably heavy appearance has been rather self-defeating, every bay being marked by a patterned arch and every compartment by monotonously repeated motifs which have been likened to the products of a pastrycook set out for the oven.

A further peculiarity of construction should next be examined

from one of the aisles. Here the roof consists of a series of short
tunnel vaults across its quite narrow width. These appear to rest on
flat stone beams, mostly carved with big and small leaf patterns in
repeating units, quite contrary to any expression of structural
significance. But examination shows that each of these 'beams' is in
fact a flat arch, its stones slightly wedge-shaped so that it does
behave as an arch, but supporting no more than its own weight
because above it is another more recognisable arch. Every window
is flanked by niches with carved corbels beneath – almost all of
angels in a variety of poses.

Looking again from the centre of the chapel but this time
westwards, the arch into the intended crossing is prominent; it now
frames a 19th-c. organ gallery, with the baptistry below and beyond.
In the latter are memorial windows by William Wilson to two
airmen (1950) and by Carrick Whalen to Princess Dimitri (1970).
Most of the other glass is by Clayton and Bell, put in during the last
decades of the 19th c.; it includes the Majestas W window. The
scheme of the clerestory windows was to have comprised Old
Testament warriors on the N side and Christian ones on the S, but it
was never completed.

In the **N aisle** the arched memorial on the W wall is to George,
Earl of Caithness (d.1582); the wall capital at the end of the arcade
portrays a dragon and an angel with scroll. Bay 1, the westernmost,
has no window. In bay 2 the window has an Annunciation and
Nativity, while the next wall capital (to the left of the entrance) has
a Crucifixion at which three figures on the corresponding arcade
capital seem to be looking. The next arcade capital has what
appears to be an angel rolling away a stone from the Tomb, and on
the wall opposite is a Crown of Thorns. In the glass of bay 4 are
scenes of the Presentation in the Temple and Baptism and on the
next wall capital a lamb and pennant with possibly David and his
harp above. On the further side of the 'beam' joining this to the
main arcade is a dog leading a blind man.

Bay 5 has in its window the Sermon on the Mount, and in the
floor beneath the arcade the 15th-c. tomb slab of a knight in
armour. The wall capital beyond, in line with the E arcade, is
heraldic; the 'beam' running from it has on its E side carvings
interpreted as Christ and seven kings, a sort of condensed version of
a Jesse tree. At the back of the central column capital behind the

Rosslyn: St Matthew's Chapel: interior, looking NW

altar are, on the N the Expulsion from Eden, and on the S palms representing the victory of good over evil.

Each of the six windows around the E end portrays two saints. These, forming the first part of the Clayton and Bell series, are a memorial to the 3rd Earl of Rosslyn and date from 1867. While the vaults of the ambulatory itself follow the same pattern as those of the aisles, the four chapels have the wildest and most extreme of all, with carvings of fantastic illogicality. They are in fact rib vaults, the only ones in the chapel, but with the most complex and intricate ornamentation it is possible to imagine. Every rib is festooned in a series of multiple cusps, and on either side of these run band upon band of foliage carvings in endless variety. Openwork pendants fall from the central bosses of every compartment, and others of equal luxuriance sprout from the rib ends in diagonal stances as though attracted, not by gravity but by some unseen magnetic forces.

Besides all this, plenty of figure carving can be found in these chapels (which together are often called the Lady chapel); there are also brass memorials in the floors to the first three earls of Rosslyn.

In the first, the diagonal ribs from the outer corner back to the first free-standing column have sixteen figures each with a skeleton, representing the Dance of Death; this medieval allegory of the supremacy of death is met with elsewhere but Rosslyn's may be the earliest in stone. In the second chapel all the capitals have figures of angels with musical instruments and the central pendant has an eight-pointed Star of Bethlehem with eight figures or groups, e.g. the Virgin and Child, the manger, and three Wise Men. The free-standing columns of these chapels are particularly ornate. The southernmost is the famous 'apprentice column' which gave rise to the (fairly modern) story of the apprentice who in his master's absence carved and completed the design the master had planned to do himself, and was thereupon killed in a fit of jealous rage. At the base of the column lie eight intertwined dragons, from whose mouths issue bands of most delicate foliage, carved as though bound by ropes in spirals round the column. On the S side of the capital are Isaac bound to the altar, and a ram in a thicket, and on the 'beam' connecting it to the main outer wall is a Latin inscription comparing in order the strengths of wine, kings, women and truth. Two of the vault ribs of this bay have more figures with skeletons, near the top facing E.

Beneath, twenty-four stone steps lead down into the sacristy, thought to have been a chapel not only because it contains an aumbry and piscina but also because traditionally the princes of Orkney and barons of Rosslyn used it as a burial place before the main chapel was even begun. The corbels of the vault are varied and interesting and the ribs are ornamented – but very modestly by comparison with the chapel itself. There are an altar (with medieval stone top), fragmentary statues of two priests, and incised drawings on the walls suggesting that the room was used as a design shop during the building operations. The E window is by Patrick Pollen (1954), a memorial to the 5th Earl of Rosslyn.

Returning to the main chapel, one of the most fascinating viewpoints is from the top of the stair, two or three steps down.

The **S aisle** bays are here numbered as on the N side, beginning with bay 7 at the E end. The 'beam' between bays 6 and 5 has scenes of the Seven Acts of Mercy on the E side and Seven Deadly Sins on the W. However one stone has somehow been reversed so that giving drink to the thirsty appears as a sin and gluttony as a virtue! The window of bay 5 shows the Crucifixion and Resurrection; over it are carvings of the seven orders of angelic hierarchy, while one of the niche corbels portrays Moses instead of the usual angel. The next window has Christ blessing little children, and the Last Supper, and the wall capital beyond (to the left of the door) the Conception or the Annunciation. On the corresponding capital of the main arcade are various human beings and animals – of unknown significance like so much of the sculpture. The next has a lion and a horse on the N side, while on the aisle side is the prophetess Anna looking across to the Presentation of Jesus in the Temple on the wall capital. In bay 2, to the right of the door, the glass represents the Marriage Feast of Cana and the Raising of Jairus's daughter. The last full capital of the arcade is specially elaborate, with a group of carpenters on the E, Samson or David with a lion on the W, and over them groups of figures comprising twelve Apostles and four martyrs.

Finally the **exterior**, starting again at the N doorway with its arched hood flanked by giant gargoyles. The general forms can readily be related to the internal construction, and indeed much of the detail is similar to the interior. The clerestory window arches, for instance, are encrusted with the same kind of ornament inside

Rosslyn: St Matthew's Chapel: E column of S arcade, the 'Prentice Pillar'

and out. Slender flying buttresses come down to massive pinnacles on the aisle walls, and on to a second, rather meaningless, series of less tall ones perched on the outer edges of the buttresses. To the left of the doorway can be seen a carving of a fox and a goose and the farmer's wife in pursuit; to its right, a man with pointed ears bound with ropes, another with a stick and another on a horse. The lower window jambs have more niches and so have the faces of the buttresses; it is doubtful whether statues were ever made for them. The actual tracery of the windows is unusual not only in being encrusted with more carving (including ornament of dog-tooth type which was current two centuries before) but also in some cases – at the E end – by being based on the saltire or St Andrew's cross. From the E end one can look down on the roof of the sacristy, and across the wooded valley of the North Esk.

On the S side all the details are similar and need no further description except that the doorway is more ornate, with an arched head instead of flat. Further round are the beginnings of the transepts, their E walls built to the height of the aisles and containing piscinae for the intended chapels along their further sides. In the churchyard to the SW is a big monument to the 4th Earl of Rosslyn (d.1890), who was responsible for adding the baptistry at the W end of the chapel.

Roxburgh: Greyfriars, Borders   NT 720335
½ mile SW of Kelso, beside St Boswells road A699

Franciscan friary founded 1232, probably by Alexander II.
    Destroyed 1545.

Owned by Roxburghe Estates. No remains.

The important medieval burgh of Roxburgh stood on the peninsula between Tweed and Teviot, its isthmus straddled by the great castle of which impressive earthworks and fragmentary walls remain. The friary is supposed to have stood at the place still called Friars, marked now by a low white-walled cottage, on the left just past the Teviot bridge on the westward road from Kelso. Records show that the cemetery was dedicated in 1235. Along with the rest of the town, the friary was burned by the English under the Earl of

Hertford in 1545 and never recovered; the buildings were however
partly re-roofed for English military use two years later.

Saddell Abbey, Strathclyde   NR 785321
8 miles NNE of Campbeltown, close to Carradale road

Cistercian abbey of the Blessed Virgin Mary founded *c*.1160 by
   Somerled, Lord of the Isles, or later by his son Reginald, a
   daughter house of Mellifont, Armagh. United with bishopric of
   Lismore 1508.

Owned by Argyll and Bute District Council. Open to the public at
   all times without charge.

Evidence of the abbey's building history is meagre. It was never of
any size, was probably little altered after *c*.1200, and died out in the
15th c. In 1770 most of the stone still remaining was used to extend
Saddell castle. The broken ruins amongst rhododendrons are more
picturesque than informative.

Inside the entrance gate eleven medieval grave slabs stand beneath
an ugly modern shelter, uncommonly like a petrified bus queue.
Three are men in armour of the 14th and 15th c., one a priest, and
one (headless) a monk. The others portray a fascinating range of
emblems: swords, galleys, deer, caskets, shears etc. In the centre is
a reconstructed 15th-c. standing cross with interlaced patterns. All
came from the **church** ruin, which lies up the path, the approach
being towards the N transept with the presbytery on one's left. The
transept can be entered through a broken opening; the presbytery
entrance is narrowed by a modern wall. The position of the altar is
evident; the wall recesses however may not be authentic. High on

Saddell Abbey: monumental effigies

the S wall is a modern but worn tablet to Somerled and Reginald.

The roughly square cleared area with two railed-in graves represents the **cloister**. Some further ruins beyond are of the S range, while irregularities on the N and E sides show respectively where the nave and chapter house stood. A large memorial to Col. Donald Campbell (d.1784) dominates the top end of the churchyard, but other graves and monuments abound, some of them obviously much older.

Some carved stones are now in the Campbeltown Museum.

St Andrews: Blackfriars, Fife   NO 508165
in South Street in city centre

Dominican friary of the Assumption and Coronation of the Blessed Virgin founded c.1274 by William Wishart, Bishop of St Andrews; united with friaries of Cupar and St Monans 1519 but afterwards revived; destroyed 1559 and site granted to municipality 1567 for grammar school.

Owned by North-East Fife District Council. Accessible at all times without charge.

.ɲ..

A general rebuilding of the church was promoted by Bishop Elphinstone of Aberdeen in 1514. It was burned in 1547 but the reformers did not finally eject the friars till twelve years later. What survives today is a chapel which projected from its N side, standing next to the public pavement and in the forecourt of Madras College. Though railed against entry, the interior with its sexpartite vault and piscina can be adequately seen. The three- and four-light windows have uncusped flowing tracery, not too badly damaged.

St Andrews: Greyfriars, Fife   NO 506167
in city centre

Franciscan friary founded 1458 by Bishop James Kennedy;
    destroyed 1560 and granted to municipality 1567.

Site in multiple ownership; no remains.

The site was at the W end of Market Street immediately N of West Port, and is marked today by the street name Greyfriars Garden. The open area beside the street probably represents the eastern end of the precinct. Like the Blackfriars' establishment, it was burned in 1547 by followers of Norman Lesley. Nothing remains above ground.

St Andrews Priory, Fife   NO 514166
at E end of city

Augustinian priory founded 1144 by Robert, Bishop of St Andrews;
    granted to Ludovic, Duke of Lennox 1592.

In guardianship of Secretary of State for Scotland; open during
    standard hours (admission charge to St Rule's church and to
    museum).

St Regulus or Rule is said to have founded a monastery, probably in the 8th c., around the relic of St Andrew he had brought from Greece. The bishopric was transferred from Abernethy in 908, but its actual relationship with the priory seems never to have been very clearly defined. During the 12th c. the Augustinian order gradually displaced the Celtic, and the little church of St Regulus (most of which still stands) was enlarged to serve as cathedral.

The great new cathedral, which was also the church of the priory, was begun about 1160. It was the largest church in Scotland and at one time the longest in Britain except Norwich. The quire was completed by 1238 and the whole building was consecrated in 1318. A serious fire about 1380 occasioned extensive rebuilding, which was not completed till 1440. The prior became mitred in 1418. There is no record of the bishop being regarded as abbot of the monastery, but the see became an archbishopric in 1472.

After the Reformation the usual desecration, pillaging and theft of materials occurred. The cathedral ruins were taken over by the Barons of the Exchequer in 1826 and the priory buildings by the Ministry of Works in 1946.

From the NW gate to the churchyard the general layout is easily grasped. On the left the E gable is prominent, and on the right, close to the road, the W front. In between stands the whole S nave aisle wall, curiously intact; behind that were the monastic buildings. The **W front** should be examined first. Following storm damage this was rebuilt two bays inwards about 1275 and a galilee porch built outside; parts of its side walls and vault corbels are clearly visible. After the fire a century later it was removed and the upper part of the front, above the wall-arcading, rebuilt.

Within the **nave** it is just possible to imagine the former grandeur, though so little is left but marked-out column bases. In the S wall, however, even the windows are fairly complete; the change from round-arched late 12th-c. work to two-light 13th-c. windows is misleading, for all but the two W bays are really 12th-c. and the later windows indicate a partial rebuilding which probably included the vaults also. Their springers and wall-shafts can be seen. Further E in the nave is a deep well believed to have been originally put in for the masons' use.

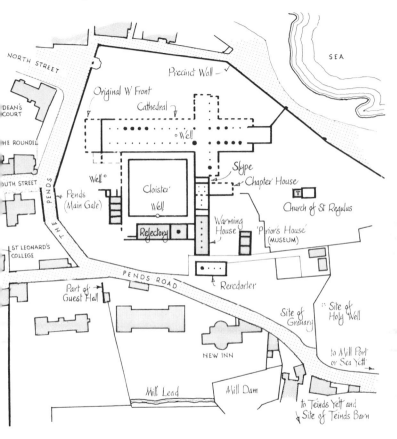

Continuing E, the **N transept** has little left but foundations, but its
three E chapels are clear enough. In the **S transept** the 12th-c. W
wall is nearly complete, with intersecting wall-arcading at its base;
much of the remainder is early 15th-c., again with three chapels. In
its SW corner is the night stair that led down from the dormitory. Of

St Andrews Cathedral looking E

several floor-slabs one has been identified as that of Canon Cathall (d.1380).

Next the **quire**, where the bases of several clustered piers remain (late 12th-c.). Tomb slabs here include the great Tournai marble one set up on medieval stone coffins at the top of the sanctuary steps, roughly where the high altar once stood. The W wall can now be clearly seen to be almost entirely 12th-c., but with a 15th-c. window inserted. Originally there were three rows of round-headed windows: the second is clearly delineated, the third less obvious.

Now the monastic buildings, commencing to the SE of the S transept with the clearly defined **chapter house**. It has several medieval coffins in the floor and on its S wall retains the wall-arcading that backed the seating. This and what is left of a splendid doorway are clearly 13th-c. Going next towards the cloister, there is a vestibule which was the original chapter house; this has a triple doorway to the cloister, with nail-head ornament.

Another arch, closer to the transept, led to the slype. Above all this range was the dormitory.

The **cloister** walks have gone but the layout is clear enough, with doorways at the NW (13th-c.) and NE (12th-c.) into the S aisle. The well in the centre of the S side served the washplace. The S range, the undercroft of the refectory, was virtually rebuilt in the 19th c. The W range, standing to the full height of its lower storey, was used for storage. It is a good idea to pass round to the back of this, thus seeing the inside of the priory's outer wall, and then to go along the outside of the S range: the bulbous projection, preserved in the restoration, was the support for the refectory pulpit. A doorway at the end leads back into the cloister, but beyond is a projecting wing, the end of the dormitory range with the (restored) vaulted warming house in its undercroft, now the museum. To the right of the roadway the room with a single standing column was the reredorter; the main priory drain passes along its further side.

On the left of the road is another building, called the Prior's House and now a store for post-Reformation tombstones. The graveyard wall here has a re-entrant angle, and it is best to follow it to the N and then to turn W, back into the E walk of the cloister; the **museum** entrance will be found in the SE corner passage. Displayed here are numerous carved memorial stones, many being of the 8th, 9th and 10th c., as well as some medieval fragments. The last include a beautiful 13th-c. head of Christ and two pieces of the same effigy of a bishop, one of which was found used as a lintel in a house in South Street. Many of the little cross-slabs were discovered when the church of St Mary of the Rock (q.v.) was excavated; some show in their designs of plaits and animals the influence of Northumbrian art. A particular treasure is a sarcophagus thought to show David as a warrior and variously attributed to the 8th or 10th c.

The **church of St Regulus** is remarkable for its 108-foot tower and is thought to date from the 1070s and to have been extended E and W c.1130 to serve as a cathedral. The roofless walls E of the tower represent the quire; beyond that was a 12th-c. sanctuary which has disappeared. The nave, the 12th-c. addition W of the tower, has also gone; the stair was put in in 1789. Remarkable resemblances have been found between this church and those of Wharram-le-Street in Yorkshire and Aubazine in Aquitaine. In the churchyard are countless post-Reformation gravestones and memorials of great historical and artistic interest.

The 14th-c. priory wall was strengthened about 1516 and was about a mile long. It starts with the 14th-c. main gatehouse called the Pends, SW of the cathedral. This is now a shell, through which the road passes, but in the vault springers and end walls has ample evidence of a former upper storey which was no doubt a porter's lodging. Continuing S and then turning left towards St Leonard's College (q.v.), a smaller gatehouse can be seen at the entrance to what is now a girls' school. From there the wall runs through private ground, but its line can be picked up again by going along South Street and down Abbey Street and Abbey Walk. The latter follows immediately outside the wall almost to its SE angle passing on the way the gatehouse known as Teinds Yett (Tithe Gate). This had a large entrance and a smaller pedestrian one, and over it another porter's quarters with small windows; just within stood the Teinds Barn. The longest and most impressive part of the wall is that facing the sea – stretching first beside the road called The Shore, past the Mill Port or Sea Yett, getting nearer and nearer the cliff top beside the exposed foundations of St Mary of the Rock, and finally running back past the W front of the great church.

St Andrews: St Leonard's College, Fife   NO 513166
E of city centre and immediately SW of cathedral

Augustinian secular college of Poor Clerks of the Kirk of St Andrew
    founded 1512 by Archbishop Alexander Stewart and Prior John
    Hepburn in existing hospital and parish church of St Leonard.

Owned by University of St Andrews. Chapel open Mondays to
    Fridays 10 a.m. to 4 p.m. without charge.

The hospital existed before 1144 when it passed from the Culdees into the control of the cathedral priory. Its chapel was being used as a parish church by 1413, and possibly as early as c.1200 which is about the date of the earliest masonry. The college, though part of the University, was semi-monastic until the Reformation. It became for a while the residence of John Knox, so that the saying 'to drink at St Leonard's well' meant to listen to Protestant teachings.

Subjected to the changing currents of church opinion, it

maintained till 1747 a more or less independent existence as St
Leonard's College. Then it was united with St Salvator's College
(q.v.), the buildings went into private ownership, the church was
abandoned, the tower demolished, and some of the contents
transferred to St Salvator's church. In 1838 and again in 1853 some
attempt was made to arrest decay, but the church was not re-roofed
and made weathertight again till 1910 and had to wait until 1948
before a proper restoration began. St Leonard's School, a girls'
boarding school founded in 1877, occupies the site and incorporates
some parts of the original buildings of the college.

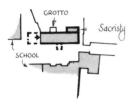

The **interior** as reopened in 1952 is arranged as it would have been
in the Middle Ages, divided midway by a screen so that the E end
has a more academic character. The structural features run right
through: traditional pale blue boarded ceiling, white plastered walls
and new stone floor dotted about with ledger stones (two in the
ante-chapel are medieval, that on the N to John Archibald (d.1534)
and his wife, and the other to Mariota Graeme (d.1502)). The
'Dutch' chandeliers and brackets, and the big square late 16th-c.
style pulpit and the screen are all of 1948–52.

The chancel has some interesting memorials on the N side. First is
a rather crude tablet with very large gilt lettering and an aedicule
over, to college principal Robert Vilich (Wilkie) (d.1611). Next, a
much restored large tablet flanked by pairs of Corinthian columns,
to his successor Peter Bruss (Bruce) (d.1630), and finally in the NE
corner the canopied tomb, without figures, of Robert Stewart, Earl
of March (d.1586); the superstructure is in two stages, with a Latin
verse around the lower frieze. The painting in the grey Classical
altarpiece, *The Legend of St Leonard*, is by Walter Pritchard, 1956.

Outside, the W front is a curious patchwork with its two windows
and a doorway made in 1853 out of bits of old moulded stones

recovered from various sources. The top part is of 1910. The position of the W bay, which contained the tower, is marked on the ground. In the S wall, parts of which may be of *c*.1200, windows at two levels in the W half result from the introduction of a gallery in 1578, while the easternmost in the chancel is unusual for its quatrefoil heads. There is no E window, for the church was extended in the 16th c. right up to the precinct wall, a short length of which became the church gable and contains passages with defensive openings originally intended to command the gatehouse; that was rebuilt in its present more easterly position *c*.1600. The sacristy on the N side of the chancel is of the same date as the extension and although at first two-storeyed it was soon reduced to a single barrel-vaulted room.

St Andrews: St Mary on the Rock, Fife   NO 515166
on Kirk Heugh, W of harbour

Chapel of St Mary of the Rock, probably founded in 9th c. and made collegiate in 13th c.; demolished 1559.

Owned by North-East Fife District Council. Accessible at all times.

Variously known as the Church of the Blessed Mary of the City of St Andrews or the Chapel of the King of Scotland on the Hill, it stood just outside the priory on a low cliff top overlooking the harbour. It developed from a Culdee foundation, and assumed the dignity of a Chapel Royal. From 1501 to 1504 the provostry was united with that of the Chapel Royal in Stirling Castle. Following its destruction at the Reformation all trace was lost till the foundations were discovered in 1860.

Apart from the foundation of the principal altar, it is only the bases of walls that are visible above the turf and these are 13th-c.: most of the nave and chancel and a large part of the N transept. So the actual appearance of the church can only be guessed.

St Andrews: St Salvator's College, Fife   NO 510168
in North Street in city centre

Secular college of St Salvator founded 1450 by James Kennedy,
   Bishop of St Andrews.

Owned by University of St Andrews. Open during normal hours
   without charge.

Though the University had been founded forty years before, St
Salvator's was the first full college in the proper sense. Its chapel
was also used by the public, though it did not become a parish
church until the amalgamation with St Leonard's in 1748. The
college itself was totally rebuilt, except for the chapel and the
building immediately to its SW, in 1829–49.

The chapel dates from the earliest years of the college and was
consecrated in 1460. Building of the tall tower probably continued
for a few more years, but a spire did not appear till c.1530. As it was
of lead on a wooden frame it suffered in 1547 when Catholics
besieging the castle removed it to make space for a gun. A few years
later it was replaced in stone. The heavy mock-Jacobean cloister
added on the N side c.1840 was by the government architect
William Nixon. In 1861–2 a full 'restoration' was done under
Robert Matheson (the window tracery, roof and much of the
seating are his) and in 1929–31 a reversion to a collegiate internal
arrangement was undertaken under the direction of Reginald
Fairlie. Meanwhile the parish congregation of St Leonard's had
moved elsewhere and so the chapel became solely the University's.

The usual entry is not direct from the street but through the pend
beneath the tower, past the janitor's office and by the N door within
the 'cloister'. This leads into the low **ante-chapel** under a deep
gallery. The stone screen dividing it from the main chapel is of
1929–31. Of the memorials here the most interesting is the tomb
slab on the W wall with incised effigy and inscription to provost

Hew Spens (d.1534). Close to it are two consecration crosses; others may be noticed elsewhere in the building, though some are concealed behind panelling. In the S wall is a tomb recess used for the display of some carved stone fragments; the tablet beside it is to John Home (d.1754).

The main **chapel** had a stone vault, which was taken down as unsafe in 1773. The present boarded roof on arched wooden trusses and with a gilded vine frieze and stone corbels is of 1861–2, and so is the stonework of the big windows to the E and S; the N wall is bare because a covered way always abutted it. The medieval screen stood one bay further E than the present one, which bears modern arms of the University and college founders on the gallery front. The oak stalls, arranged 'chapelwise', are of 1930 by Reginald Fairlie and terminate on the N side in a series of fine pinnacled canopies marking the professors' seats. Beyond these is the sadly mutilated tomb of the founder Bishop Kennedy, believed to have been intended for the cathedral. Its plain Tournai marble slab rests on a restored bronze-faced base ornamented with standing figures in niches. Round the back of the deep recess are broken empty stone niches, and on top a remarkable storeyed superstructure with broken pinnacles. When the tomb was opened in 1683 it was found to contain six silver maces. One of them, a magnificent piece made in Paris in 1461, may be viewed by arrangement with the janitor. To the right of the tomb is a 15th-c. sacrament house or aumbry, ogee-arched and finely carved.

The glass is a special feature of St Salvator's, though its styles are somewhat assorted. The heraldic NE and SE windows of the apse are by William Wilson, 1960, and the central one, a Crucifixion, by Gordon Webster, c.1930. On the S side, the two easternmost are also by Wilson and the third, a memorial to Jessie Playfair, by John Hardman, c.1890. Then comes one by Alexander Ballantine in memory of Duncan, Lord Colonsay (d.1870). The next, the one with deep rich colours, is the work of Henry Holliday and James Powell and commemorates John Sharp (d.1835). The big U-shaped pulpit (which has lost its canopy) is late 16th-c. and was brought from Holy Trinity church in 1798. Two further windows on the S side, neither of them readily visible because of the gallery, are by Herbert Hendrie.

The cloister or covered way on the N is 19th-c., but part of the return wall at the far end may mark the extent of the original sacristy, the present one being on the further side of it. The **tower** with its oddly proportioned 16th-c. spire, is best appreciated from a distance and is indeed a principal landmark of the city. It contains the college's great bell Kate Kennedy, originally of 1460 but three times recast, as well as that of St Leonard's College (also recast). The arms over the main archway, flanked by empty niches, are those of Bishop Kennedy.

The S side of the chapel is remarkable for its heavy buttresses, necessary when there was a stone vaulted roof, and deep enough for a porch to be formed between two of them. On the eastern pair their ornamental niches are turned inwards in an unusual way, and one has a sundial. The boundary wall to the street incorporates, opposite the porch, a weather-worn old arch from the original cloister.

St Evoca Priory, Dumfries & Galloway   NX 6548 approx.
2½ miles SW of Kirkcudbright close to Borgue road B727

Cistercian nunnery of St Evoca founded by 1423 (but already
    abandoncd by that date).

Exact site unknown.

Accounts of this priory are sketchy in the extreme. It has left the names Nunton and Nun Mill attached to lands on the right bank of the Dee estuary opposite St Mary's Isle, and its supposed site was to the S of the bridge at Nun Mill.

St Mary's Isle Priory, Dumfries & Galloway   NX 675493
1½ miles SW of Kirkcudbright, off Dundrennan road A711

Augustinian priory of St Mary possibly founded *c.*1129 by Fergus,
    Lord of Galloway, a dependency of Holyrood. Granted to James
    Lidderdale 1608.

Owned by Dunbar family. Presumed site accessible at all times.

The island, really only a peninsula, was originally called Trahil or Trayl. An extensive precinct wall existed, with an outer gate half a mile away at a place called Great Cross and an inner one at Little Cross. All this was demolished late in the 17th c. by the Earl of Selkirk, and the actual priory buildings are known to have been in a bad state by 1711. The Earl's mansion on their site was the scene of a famous robbery of silver plate by Paul Jones at the time of the War of American Independence. It was returned at the instigation of Benjamin Franklin. The successor to that house, set in the wood that occupies most of the 'island', has itself been burned down in recent years and the remains are reduced to rubble. They can be reached by following the drive marked 'Private Road' just S of the town. This starts as a metalled road and eventually becomes a rough track leading to the ruin. Nothing older than the 19th c. is evident.

St Monans: Blackfriars, Fife   NO 523014
on coast 11 miles S of St Andrews and 600 yards S of Leven-Crail road A917

Dominican friary founded by 1477 at existing church; became parochial 1646.

Church of Scotland. Open during normal hours.

On a dramatic cliff-top site beside the sea, the church was founded in honour of an Irish saint said to have been killed by the Danes c.875. It was rebuilt in 1265–7 and largely again in 1362–70. The nave was never built, nor apparently was a cloister; before long the friary was incorporated into that of St Andrews and in 1544 the church was burned in an English raid. The transepts later fell to ruin, but repairs were done in 1826–8 under William Burn, and a more sensitive restoration in 1955 under Ian Lindsay.

The orientation is reversed, so that the holy table stands now under the tower at the intersection of the arms of a traditional T plan, and what was the chancel has become the congregational nave. The original points of the compass are used here. Entry then is into the E side of the **S transept** by a doorway inserted in 1828, and the first view of the bright lime-washed interior includes both of the well-proportioned transept arches – of three orders with moulded caps. The boarded barrel ceilings are not ancient. Windows generally are Early English in character, but it is not known for certain which parts of the building are 13th-c. and which represent a survival of the style into the 14th c. They are of two lights except for the three-light Y-traceried one at the further end. The two at the S end have plate tracery of even earlier type. Beneath them a piscina marks a former side altar site, and another can be seen beside the entrance door.

The **crossing** contains the stone font of 1933 as well as the pulpit and table. Masonry blocks the narrow arch which once formed the main entrance. The N transept contains the only monument of particular note, a tablet to Henry Anstruther, killed in the Crimea in 1854.

The former **chancel**, wonderfully light thanks to big windows of Decorated or Flamboyant type, is embellished with a tierceron vault with little coloured shields and bosses. The transverse ridge ribs finish in an unusual manner and the wall-shafts have unfortunately had their lower parts cut off. At one time twin doorways were inserted in the E wall and the floor was lowered about 3½ feet, so as to allow the insertion of a loft or gallery. All round are prominent consecration crosses, and a pictorial badge from the gallery front has been framed and mounted on the E wall. That this was the chancel is emphasised by the double aumbry on the N wall and opposite it a large piscina and fine triple sedilia, the arch supports of which sweep back gracefully into the wall behind.

The **exterior** is as capable and well-proportioned as the interior, and little different from its 14th-c. appearance despite intervening changes. The tower, however, was raised in the 16th c., parts of the broaches of the earlier spire being visible in the second storey; its circular stair is 16th-c. too, though the external doorway replaces an inside one. The windows on the S side of the chancel, of three and four lights, are particularly fine. The vestry on the other side, though modern, stands on the site of the medieval sacristy.

Scone Abbey, Tayside   NO 115267
in grounds of Scone Palace 2 miles N of Perth on A93

Augustinian priory of Holy Trinity and St Michael (later also St
    Mary, St John, St Lawrence and St Augustine) founded 1114 by
    Alexander I and colonised from Nostall priory, Yorkshire.
    Became abbey *c.*1164, mitred 1395. Secularised to Earl of Gowrie
    1581.

Owned by the Trust for the Viscount Stormont. Abbey site and
    chapel open during opening hours of house 10 a.m. to 5.30 p.m.,
    Easter to mid-October (Sundays 2 to 5.30 p.m.).

The monastery succeeded a Culdee cell founded in the 6th c., and
achieved great importance. On Moot Hill, a probably prehistoric
artificial mound within its precincts, was placed the chair of state for
coronations of Scottish kings, with the Stone of Scone which in 1296
in the course of a series of raids was carried off by Edward I to
Westminster.
    The abbey buildings were destroyed by reformers in 1559 and the
Earl of Gowrie built a house of the stone, probably using the
abbot's house as a nucleus; parts are said to be traceable in the base
of the E wing of the present Palace, most of which dates from
1803–8 and which since the late 16th c. has been the home of the
Earls of Mansfield. A parish church built on Moot Hill in 1624 was
later moved to a different site, and in 1804–5 was removed (with the
entire village) to New Scone by order of Viscount Stormont. A
private chapel still on the mound is a rebuilt relic of the 1624
church, of which an aisle was left.

The E avenue to the house brings one (on foot) to an inner gateway
of *c.*1620; just before this on the left is a 13-foot high standing cross
(medieval with a modern head) left behind when the village was
moved away. Past the gateway, also on the left but lying further
back, is a cemetery on the abbey site. A few foundations have been
found here.
    The chapel is on the other side of the drive nearer the house. A
single-cell structure with a crypt, now all essentially 19th-c., it is
dominated by the giant memorial of David, Viscount Stormont

(d.1631), whose kneeling armoured effigy under an arch on the E wall is flanked by figures of Earls Marischal and Tullibardine. A chaste white marble memorial with urn is to Henrica, Viscountess Stormont (d.1761); near it on the S wall are two 17th-c. plaques and a coat of arms from the earlier building.

There is no definite evidence for the position of the main abbey buildings.

Semple Collegiate Church, Strathclyde   NS 376601
2 miles NE of Lochwinnoch and ½ mile N of Glasgow-Irvine road A737, close to N shore of Castle Semple Loch

Collegiate church founded 1504 by John, 1st Lord Sempill.

In care of Secretary of State for Scotland. Open at all times without charge.

Wholly early 16th-c., this is a noteworthy (but little-known) example of the final period of Scottish Gothic, on a miniature scale and, although roofless, well-preserved. The founder, whose tomb is in the N wall of the chancel, was killed at Flodden.

The building stands beside a lane almost impassable with farm mud after wet weather. Its small tower, sturdily built with large stones, has lost its extreme top. The remainder, a simple nave and polygonal-ended chancel, is virtually complete to wall-head except for a small gap on the N side. Its former roof line can be seen on the E wall of the tower. Corbels all along both sides about 7 feet up would have supported an upper floor during the long period of farm use, from which the church has only been rescued in recent years.

Most of the openings are square-headed, and some of the windows have quite odd details. Those of the apse have unusual pierced heads and curiously moulded mullions, all different, while the three main two-light S windows have a kind of clumsily beheaded reticulated tracery; their internal sills have been partly renewed. Inside, the facets of the apse are lined with round-headed

Semple Collegiate Church: tomb of first Lord Semple (d.1513)

arches and capped with a plain cornice, while outside each is framed with a simple roll moulding.

The principal feature is the canopied tomb recess of the founder (d.1513), a cusped arch with inscription above, surmounted by an ogee hood in very low relief. The actual tomb chest has shallow arcading, and the appearance of the back of the tomb on the external wall confirms that the doorway alongside led to a sacristy which has disappeared. To the left of that doorway is an inscribed stone to Gabriel Sempel (d.1587).

Seton Collegiate Church, Lothian   NT 418751
10 miles E of Edinburgh and 200 yards N of North Berwick road
A198

Collegiate church of St Mary and the Holy Cross. College founded
1492 by George, 4th Lord Seton.

In care of Secretary of State for Scotland. Open during standard
hours, but closed Tuesday afternoons and all day Wednesdays.

Though the plan is now a simple T shape, with tower at the crossing, the building history is more complex. The earliest recorded date is 1242. A short S aisle added to the nave early in the 15th c. was demolished about a hundred years later. The chancel was rebuilt about the middle of the 15th c., its sacristy being added by the college's founder c.1500. He was killed at Flodden, and his widow subsequently built the transepts and tower. The rebuilt nave may never have been finished, for the building was ransacked by the English in 1544. In 1580 the parish was joined with Tranent, and when it was reconstituted in the 17th c. a new church was built elsewhere and the old one put to farm uses. It was restored in 1878 by the Earl of Wemyss and apart from the nave is remarkably complete though so long disused. A history of the Seton family written by George Maitland c.1560 provides interesting and often-quoted information on the building.

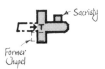

Sacristy

Former Chapel

The situation close to Robert Adam's Seton House (successor to the big medieval 'palace' of the Seton family) is usually picturesque and well screened by trees from the main road. The nave having gone, entry is through the W arch of the crossing-tower. This matches the N and S arches (*c.*1540) but the E arch into the quire (*c.*1460) has noticeably more delicate mouldings and foliage carving, and at its base on the N side can be seen the start of the original nave, taken down from that point when the transept was built. The quadripartite vault of the tower survives complete and so indeed do the pointed tunnel vaults of the other parts. On the floor is a bell of 1577, and at the SW corner a holy water stoup.

At the end of the **N transept** is a tomb recess, and on the right a very worn tablet to James Ogilvie (d.1617). There are also five very worn ledger stones. Two old font bowls have been set on wooden stands, one round and the other octagonal.

The **S transept** has a similar tomb recess, as well as a damaged monument to James, Earl of Perth (d.1611). Parts of two figures from the latter are set on a wooden stand nearby. There is also a piscina. The row of holes above were housings for beams for an upper floor put in perhaps in the 17th c.

The E end of the **quire**, being polygonal, has a ribbed vault. Amongst the bosses are the Scottish royal arms on the easternmost. The statue brackets flanking the E window have coats of arms too. Also close to the altar position are a fine piscina (practically complete excepting its pinnacle), and a single sedilia recess set uncomfortably near the floor. Another tomb recess on the N side contains effigies of a knight and lady, not positively identified but probably a Lord and Lady Seton, and in the centre of the floor are two incised medieval cross-slabs.

Another cross-slab has been re-used to form the door threshold to the **sacristy**, which was originally two-storeyed, with a barrel vault on top. That survives, but the upper floor has gone. On the side wall is a big plain marble-bordered slab in memory of the 7th

Seton Collegiate Church from SW

Lord Seton (d.1585). A squint or hagioscope provided a view of the altar, and there is a piscina.

Outside, the principal feature is the tower with its truncated stone spire. Enough was built to show that the Scottish way of forming broaches, the triangular corner pieces where octagonal merges into square, was quite different from the English. On its unfinished state, Maitland commented that the founder's widow 'biggit up the steeple as ye see it now to ane grit hight swa that it wants little of compleiting'. By building the transepts she had achieved 'ane perfyt and proportionat croce church'. Her nave has since gone, but its roof line is prominent on the tower – rather off-centre because the original chancel and nave were not in a straight line. The transept roofs have interlocking stone slabs of the locally traditional kind, but that of the chancel has been renewed in ordinary slate. The blank areas at the tops of the walls (unavoidable with tunnel vaults) are relieved by bands of grotesques and flowers. The end windows of the transepts have big thick centre mullions like those at Haddington, and the buttresses throughout have empty image brackets with little canopies. Round on the N side, the almost windowless sacristy retains its stone roof. Against the churchyard wall opposite some fine 17th-c. heraldic panels from Seton Palace have been set up.

The exposed foundations to the SW of the church, once thought to be of priests' houses, are now believed to date only from the 17th c.

Soulseat Abbey, Dumfries & Galloway   NX 101586
3 miles ESE of Stranraer

Premonstratensian abbey, possibly at first Cistercian and founded in 1148 by Fergus, Lord of Galloway; said to have been a daughter house of Prémontré. Annexed to Portpatrick parsonage 1630.

Owned by Church of Scotland. No remains, but site accessible with permission from the Manse.

Though claimed to be the premier Premonstratensian house in Scotland, the appointment of its abbot being one of the few under royal, not papal control, its founding and history are very obscure. The parish was merged with that of Inch in the middle of the 17th c.

and the abbey buildings were ruined at least by 1684.

The picturesque peninsular site by Soulseat Loch now contains only the manse of 1838 and a few outbuildings. Behind them lies an indeterminate graveyard with a few headstones: three robust ones of the 17th c., the most recent as late as 1911. The exact position and layout of the abbey buildings are quite unknown.

Stirling: Blackfriars, Central   NS 796935
in town centre

Dominican friary of St Lawrence or St Kentigern founded 1233 by
    Alexander II; destroyed 1559.

No remains.

The only trace of this monastic house is the name Friars' Street. The Bank of Scotland building is said to stand on the site.

Stirling: Chapel Royal, Central   NS 789942
within castle

Collegiate chapel of St Mary and St Michael founded 1501 by James
    IV.

In guardianship of Secretary of State for Scotland. Open during
    castle opening hours, 10 a.m. to 8 p.m. (June to August), to 6.45
    p.m. (April, May and September) or to 4 p.m. (October to
    March) (but Sunday opening 11 a.m. April to September and
    1 p.m. October to March, and closing 6 p.m. April, May and
    September): admission charge.

The first recorded chapel, dedicated to St Michael only, was founded by Alexander I early in the 12th c. and in the 14th c. was served from Dunfermline abbey. Late in the 15th c. it was rebuilt by James III and constituted a Chapel Royal, but it was his son James IV who founded the college of priests – largely, it is thought, by way of penance for abetting the downfall and death of his father. The Bishop of Whithorn became first dean. That building however was replaced by a bigger one in 1594 under James VI, which still stands.

It was debased to use as a store and an armoury and until quite recent times housed a substantial display of arms and armour. Now it is a memorial hall for the Argyll and Sutherland Highlanders.

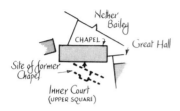

Parts of the wall lines of the former chapel, the actual collegiate one, are marked out in the setts of the inner court or upper square. The present building has a simple semi-Classical façade with twin round-headed windows beneath round arches. Only its considerably more ornate centre doorway echoes the luxuriance of the Palace opposite.

Inside, the highly polished boarded floor and whitened walls provide an excessively hygienic background for the regimental colours and pennants. The rather weak open timber roof is ingeniously strengthened by steel girders; below is a much restored frieze of rather unconvincingly painted shields and military emblems, dating from 1628. In place of a real W window is a *trompe-l'oeil* painting; the principal regimental memorial is on the daïs below. Portraits of James I and of the 5th and 6th Earls of Mar by Sir Godfrey Kneller hang on the side wall.

Stirling: Holy Rude, Central   NS 792937
¼ mile SE of castle

College founded 1546 by the magistrates and community in existing parish church of the Holy Rude.

Church of Scotland. Open 10 a.m. to 5 p.m. May to September.

As it now stands, the church represents a rebuilding which probably began after a great fire destroyed much of the town in 1406, though some authorities believe it was not started till after the middle of that century. Much earlier foundations have been found beneath the present floor. The chancel was certainly commenced in 1507 and not finished till 1555.

James VI was crowned here in 1567 at the age of one, with John Knox preaching the sermon. Thereafter the building endured the usual treatment from reformers, the insertion in later years of numerous galleries, and eventually in 1656 a division into two to serve the sects into which the reformers themselves had divided. But the so-called West Church was abandoned during most of the 18th c.; in 1818–20 it was brought back into some kind of repair by James Gillespie Graham, who demolished the medieval S porch, the outer N chapel called St Mary's aisle, and another called Bowye's aisle at the E end of the S aisle. The East Church in its turn was 'restored' in 1868–9 under James Collie; he rebuilt the S transept and made other extensive and not altogether necessary changes. St Andrew's chapel, in the corner between the N aisle and transept, was properly restored in 1899 under Sir Rowand Anderson, and the West Church in 1911–14 under Thomas Ross. Only in 1935 were the East and West congregations united, and in the following five years, with James Miller as architect, the division was torn down and the building unified and brought back to a condition closely resembling its medieval state.

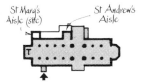

The massive piers of the **nave**, with thin bands of foliage round the capitals, at first suggest a quite early medieval date. Some experts however assign them to the start of the 15th c. and others to a period as late as 1455–70. More certainly, the building process as a whole was continuous and prolonged, and the clustered design of the easternmost column on each side could have resulted from a shortage of available worked stone (perhaps salvaged from the previous building) or merely the advance of architectural fashion.

Stirling: Holy Rude Church from S

The clerestory of very small lancet windows, on the S side only,
gives an unusual lack of balance. The sturdy open main roof, late
medieval in origin, has trusses of alternating kinds; in the final one
at the W end a carefully chosen timber neatly clears the tall wide
tower arch. The aisles have quadripartite vaults with ridge ribs and
central bosses with plain shields, probably once painted. An
interesting feature of these vaults is that the infilling of the panels is
brought up parallel with the ridge. Like numerous other details of
Scottish medieval building this follows French practice rather than
English.

Turning back to the **tower**, the W window has rather poor glass of
1854, but above is an original vault with central bell-hole (three
bells are of 1657, 1781 and 1853, and a fourth will be seen on the
church floor). The marble panels on the W wall perpetuate the
names of civic benefactors, and nearby stands the small font.
Consecration crosses will be noticed on the westernmost responds
of both arcades, and elsewhere in the church.

Memorial tablets in some profusion line the walls, but few are of
particular aesthetic or historical merit. Similarly there is 19th-c.

coloured glass in some windows, pleasing in a general way but unremarkable individually. In the **N aisle** is the bell already mentioned, a 15th-c. one bearing an 'AVE MARIA' inscription. St Andrew's chapel, leading off the aisle further along, has a pretty tierceron vault with leafy bosses, as well as an aumbry and a credence recess. The worn bowl standing on a pedestal was a pillar piscina from Cambuskenneth abbey. A fine ledger stone in the floor bears an inscription to Alexander Foster (d.1598), a member of the Forrester or Forestar family who built the chapel and whose family tree is displayed in it.

The N transept (now almost wholly modern) is largely occupied by the organ introduced in 1940. It faces the crossing, which has great clustered piers evidently meant to carry a central tower that was never built. They do however support a vault, a plain one with central boss. The pulpit, made about 1914 for the West Church, contains parts of a 17th-c. predecessor.

Next the N chancel aisle, vaulted like the nave aisles. Two more consecration crosses can be found on the side wall, as well as a big tablet bearing a eulogy to Janet Reger (d.1776); the empty recess just beyond is believed to have been an Easter sepulchre, while at the far end are steps leading down to the suite of vestries etc. formed in the crypt.

The **chancel** has equilateral arched arcades with a modest amount of foliage carving on the capitals, two-light clerestory windows, and a boarded roof of 1867 which does nevertheless contain old oak beams. A tiny window high in the W wall indicates how much loftier this part of the church is than the nave. Much of its dignity however is owed to the polygonal E apse, wider and altogether more spacious than the centre part of the chancel, and generously lit by tall windows of almost Perpendicular character. The glass of the big six-light central one is by James Ballantyne. The roof of this apse is curiously contrived. The builder, being for some reason determined on having a barrel vault of rectangular plan, carried it on side arches which, in a manner more ingenious than logical, spring from the crowns of the diagonally placed window openings. The enriched oak choir stalls date from 1965; the oak communion table was in St Giles', Edinburgh, from 1879 till 1911.

The S chancel aisle, similar to the N in its design, has the best windows in the church, all three with a preponderance of brown colouring and all of *c*. 1880. The easternmost is by Adam and Small, and the centre one (Christ in the house of Zacchaeus) by Sir Edward Burne-Jones. Finally, in the S transept, there is a fine example of Douglas Strachan's glass, a Benedicite of 1946 in memory of John and Margaret Risk.

Now the **exterior**, starting with the porch, which is a fairly modern reconstruction. So is most of the window tracery, though the stonework generally is old and extremely weather-worn. Prominent features are the water spouts all along the clerestory and aisle parapets – though, rather oddly, the clerestory does not have them on the blind N side. The tower, much less equal-sided than it at first appears, was not given its top stage till the 16th c., as has been proved by the existence of masons' marks corresponding with those on stones in the chancel. The W window was lengthened in Gillespie Graham's alterations, so more or less obliterating the former W doorway. On the N side of the church, the position of the former St Mary's aisle is clear from the arch over what is now the westernmost window in the main aisle wall. This 'aisle' occupied the walled sunken area and was only one bay long, and its roof line can be seen on the clerestory wall. Beyond the little St Andrew's chapel and the rebuilt N transept the ground slopes steeply to the roadway, with glimpses of Mar's Wark, the ruin of the town house put up late in the 16th c. by the Earl of Mar.

The powerfully tall apse set on a crypt is extraordinarily reminiscent of French churches and its appearance from the street beyond has been described as 'the most striking medieval scene left us to be enjoyed in burghal Scotland'. Not surprisingly, its niched buttresses and noble traceried windows were an inspiration to the Aberdeen-born Sir Ninian Comper early in his career as a church architect.

Nothing has been said of the whitewashed 17th-c. Guildhall or Cowane's hospital to the S (where in contrast the ground is so flat as to allow a bowling green), or of the churchyard tombs and monuments which as usual around town churches are rich in history and associations. Along the N side, for example, is a typical array of burial enclosures.

Strathmiglo Collegiate Church, Fife   NO 216103
in village, 8 miles NE of Kinross and ¼ mile S of Cupar road A91

College founded 1528 in existing parish church by Sir William Scott.

Church of Scotland.

The burgh was divided into two parts: Templelands which belonged
anciently to the Knights Templars and then to the Knights of St
John, and Kirklands which belonged to the church. Of the
collegiate church nothing whatever remains. It, or more likely its
successor, was rebuilt in 1785 and added to at the SW in 1890–91.

Parts of the churchyard wall against the street may be medieval or at
least built with medieval stone. A text of 1647 has been re-sited over
the porch: 'JESVS CHRIST IS THE DOORE AND HE THAT ENTERES IN BE HIM
SHAL BE SAVED JOHN 10 9'. But by far the oldest stone is a Pictish one
of c.700 found to the W of the village in 1969 and placed near the
churchyard gate facing the street. Like many others it depicts a
deer's head and a device like a tuning fork. The little upturned
volutes on the 18th-c. gable ends seem to have something strangely
in common with it.

As a blocked doorway shows, the church entrance was in the
centre of the street side before the new porch was built. The pulpit
stands there now, with war memorial windows on either side, and
galleries on the other three sides – all plain and trim.

Sweetheart Abbey, Dumfries & Galloway   NX 964663
in village of New Abbey on A710

Cistercian abbey of the Blessed Virgin Mary founded 1273 by
    Devorgilla de Balliol, a daughter house of Dundrennan. Became
    mitred 1398. Secularised 1624 and granted to Sir Robert
    Spottiswoode.

In guardianship of Secretary of State for Scotland. Open during
  standard hours (entrance fee).

Named in honour of the heart of the foundress's husband John,
which was carried with her in a casket till her death and buried here
with her in 1289. Balliol College, Oxford was founded by him. The
abbey is almost wholly late 13th- and early 14th-c., but some
alterations were necessitated by a great storm in 1381. The last
abbot was ejected more than once and died in exile in Paris in 1612.
    The refectory is thought to have been adapted as a parish church.
In 1731 it was demolished, and a new church built alongside the S
aisle wall stood till 1877. The abbey church appears to have been
burned out at some time, but of this no record exists; its stonework
has been little interfered with but the other buildings were taken
down in the 17th and 18th c. The site passed to State ownership in
1928.

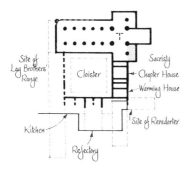

The isolated doorway encountered first is one from the cloister into
the otherwise vanished W range that ran parallel to the street. But it
is the red church ruin that dominates, and it is best to look first at its
small but once fine W doorway and then to stand just inside the
nave facing the central tower with its clear high-pitched roof line.
Only the aisles were vaulted – as can be seen at the W end of the S
aisle. Little remains of the N aisle. The clustered arcades, still
complete, support a combined clerestory-gallery with groups of
three lancets, which in the two eastern bays differ in detail. So far

Sweetheart Abbey Church: interior, looking W

all is of *c*.1300, but the big W window was strengthened with a band of masonry below the topmost 'wheel' after collapsing in the 1381 storm.

Moving further E: all the **crossing** arches, on rich clustered columns, are complete, and so are the walls and E arcade of the N transept. The main N window has lost its tracery; across its base is a continuation of the upper walkway, and above it a smaller three-light window. The two chapels retain their vault springers, and one has its piscina. Amongst the grave slabs, mostly 18th- and 19th-c., are one of 1613 with bold lettering and a broken medieval one with shield and sword.

The **presbytery** is remarkable for Scotland in having so much complete window tracery, of Geometric type – the E window and two each to N and S. The top window of the E gable has lost its tracery and there is little detail left of either the double piscina or the triple sedilia. The upper walkway continues over the great E window. It goes on round the **S transept** too. This is like the N transept but quite different in its end wall where the dorter roof came so high that it cut into the wheel window. Towards the bottom right a high doorway marks the head of the dorter night stair. This side the two E chapels are more complete and contain some interesting stones; in the northern the grave slab of the first abbot in the centre and half that of a later one by the NW pier, and in the second the tomb chest of the foundress Devorgilla, made over 200 years after her death in 1289 and rebuilt from fragments in 1933.

The S doorway leads to the sacristy and thence into the **cloister**. The chapter house, at a much lower level, has an E window arch complete. Beyond this, much less survives. The treasury, parlour and warming house are represented by low walls: above them ran the dorter. Of the S range hardly anything is left, and of the W only the one doorway; this and the chapter house window have been incorporated into the 18th-c. church.

From the N side there is a good view of the gabled tower, and of the nave clerestory which has semicircles enclosing groups of five lights – though, as inside, the two E bays are different. There is no way right round the E end. The precinct wall, built of granite boulders about 4 feet in diameter, survives on the N side (80 yards or so N of the church), and on the W where it crosses the village street and part of a gatehouse pier can be seen. About ¾ mile to the

NE is the ruined Abbot's Tower, a small L-shaped castle thought to be no earlier than the late 16th c.

Tain Collegiate Church, Highland   NH 780822
in town, 20 miles NE of Dingwall and ½ mile E of Wick road A9

College founded 1487 in existing church of St Duthus by Thomas, Bishop of Ross; continued as parish church till 1815; now called St Duthus Memorial Church.

Owned by Tain Guildry Trust. Open during normal hours without charge.

Remains of earlier churches include an 11th- or 12th-c. ruined chapel outside the town to the NE (said to be on the site of St Duthus' birthplace) and the roofless so-called 'chapter house' in the churchyard which has been attributed to the Culdees. The present building is mid-14th-c., English Decorated in style, and was restored in 1849–82 after falling into disuse when the new parish church was built in another part of the town. Though used by the Presbyterians till then, it no longer owes allegiance to any one church community and is occasionally used for exhibitions and other purposes. In the Middle Ages it seems to have been much resorted to by pilgrims to the shrine of St Duthus, born in Tain c.1000.

A simple four-bay nave and chancel, it is unusual for its well-proportioned large windows and gabled buttresses. The lofty **interior**, with 19th-c. timber roof on thin trusses, now has few seats and a somewhat random arrangement of furnishings. Beginning at the W end, there are a 17th-c. table, in the NW corner a headless bust from a monument, and a font bowl from the former church of Suddie on the Black Isle. Next on the N side is a tomb recess containing a mutilated stone with a priest's effigy and edge inscription. The wooden structure above is the front of a former gallery, bearing trade guild shields and the dates 1680 and 1776. The memorial with mourning figures, to Arabella Rose (d.1806), the most distinguished of many on this wall, is signed 'Williams of London'.

The comparatively small windows on the N side are of no special interest, but the big Geometrical E window (its tracery said to be an exact reproduction of the original) contains fine glass of 1854 depicting in its five main lights the vine, rose, lily, pomegranate and apple. The two big marble tablets below, also 19th-c., commemorate Thomas Hog (d.1692), a noted preacher, and Patrick Hamilton, Abbot of Fearn, burnt at the stake 1528 for preaching the Reformation and thus its first martyr.

On the S side are three pictorial windows of 1876–7, the first of which depicts King Malcolm Canmore conferring a charter on Tain. Below it are stepped triple sedilia. The great square canopied pulpit was a product of the Reformation, having been given to the church by the Regent Murray, a friend of John Knox; its elaborate traceried and linenfold panelling have been extensively restored. A piscina just W of it evidently served a subsidiary altar.

The glass in the W window is of 1892. It commemorates the church's restoration by John McLeod and portrays the adoption of Knox's Confession of Faith by Parliament in 1560. Below is a blocked doorway. **Outside**, lines over the S doorway indicate that there was once a porch.

The little so-called chapter house to the SE, which probably formed part or even the whole of the previous church and may have contained the shrine of the Culdee St Duthus, has been much altered. A date 1743 suggests that its N wall was rebuilt then, or possibly refaced, for affixed to the inner face are the remnants of a 17th-c. memorial. The ground level inside and out has risen, so that a semicircular arch (probably 12th-c.) under the three-light E window is partly buried. The churchyard gates, robust examples of Victorian ornamental ironwork, date from 1885.

Temple Preceptory, Lothian   NT 315587
close to Penicuik-Gorebridge road B6372, 5½ miles S of Dalkeith

Preceptory of the Knights Templars founded by 1175 by David I.
  Passed to Knights of St John 1312, and church later became
  parochial. Abandoned in favour of new church 1832.

Owned by Midlothian District Council. Open at all times without
  charge.

Formerly known as Balantrodoch, and the chief seat of the Knights
Templars in Scotland. Though there is little doubt that the existing
roofless shell is on the site of their church, recent informed opinion
suggests that it may be of the mid-14th c. at the earliest. The
principal basis for later dating is merely the absence of cusps from
the Geometrical tracery which would otherwise be late 13th-c.;
however local precedent was perhaps less likely to have been
followed by a 'foreign' order. Against that, an authentic Templars
church might be expected to have a circular nave, as in several
English examples, but no trace has ever been found. The building
remained in use after the Reformation, and the western third was
rebuilt, possibly using stone from a demolished W tower. The
present bellcote is 17th- or 18th-c. and is over the E gable. The
church of 1832 on the other side of the road is itself now used for
other purposes.

Picturesquely situated below a very steep wooded bank, the ruin
gives an immediate impression of a purely 13th-c. building, with a
tall three-light E window of intersecting tracery with two circles in
the head and shafted jambs inside. If one enters by the
trefoil-headed N doorway of the chancel there is a tomb recess to
the left (possibly an Easter sepulchre) and in the opposite wall a
badly damaged double sedilia and a piscina; the doorway beside the
latter is not medieval. Two other three-light windows in this S wall
have a large circle in the head, and moulded rear arches, and it is
chiefly these that raise doubts about the dating. Towards the W end
of the N side one jamb of a former doorway can be identified; it

Temple: Old church from E

marks the point where the post-Reformation W end commences.
This change can also be readily seen on the outside of the S wall
where, apart from the differences in the masonry, the plinth
becomes much simpler. Some beam holes 6 feet or so above the
floor are probably relics of a gallery.

Opposite the W doorway is a delightful headstone to a local
farmer, John Craig (d.1742), with uninhibited portrait figure.

The other possible remains of the preceptory are in private
grounds.

Tongland Abbey, Dumfries & Galloway   NX 698539
1¾ miles NNE of Kirkcudbright close to A711

Premonstratensian abbey founded 1218 by Alan of Galloway, a
daughter house of Cockersand; annexed to bishopric of Galloway
1530.

Church of Scotland. Site accessible at all times.

The little Romanesque church ruin antedates the abbey's likely foundation date of 1216. Alternatively its founder may have been Fergus of Galloway (d.1161) and the 12th-c. doorway ('excavated and restored in 1851') could then have belonged to it. Little else is known of its building history; it was 'ruinous' by 1509, though still occupied. The last abbot was an Italian alchemist who tried to fly to France from Stirling castle, landed in a dunghill and broke his thigh. The present parish church of 1813, now abandoned alongside its predecessor, may occupy part of the site.

The bigger red blocks of stone in the church and churchyard wall probably came from the abbey, which is thought to have stood to the E of the present church, its precinct extending down to the river and up to the road. The long embankment alongside the main road is nothing to do with it; it covers a 20-foot diameter water pipeline to the nearby power station. On the other side of the road the nursery name Meikle Yett commemorates the 'Great Gate' of the monastery. Further up, opposite the petrol station, is a lane to several houses; a left fork leads to some private garages into the front of which has been built part of an insignificant carving of a man with kilt and club said to have come from the abbey; permission to see it should of course be sought at the house.

Torphichen Preceptory, Lothian   NS 969725
in village 2½ miles N of Bathgate on A792

Preceptory of Knights of St John of Jerusalem, founded by 1153,
    probably by David I. Surrendered to Crown 1560 by last
    preceptor Sir James Sandilands and bought back by him as Lord
    Torphichen.

Church of Scotland parish church open during daylight hours except
    after 5 p.m. on Saturdays. Remainder in care of Secretary of
    State for Scotland and open during standard hours (admission
    charge).

The Knights Hospitallers, or Knights of St John, inherited the
Templars' property when that order was suppressed in Scotland in
1312. Torphichen was the principal Scottish residence of the Order
of St John, which was reconstituted in Scotland in 1827 and raised
into the British Orders of Chivalry in 1888. The Priory of Scotland
was revived in 1947 and has the care of a hospice at Turnberry and
hospitals in Aberdeen and Glasgow.

The cruciform church, partly late 12th-c. but much altered in the
15th c., retains its central tower and transepts but has lost the quire,
nave and S nave aisle. A new parish church was built on the site of
the nave in 1756, and fitted with galleries and new seating in 1803.

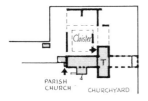

A visit has to be in two parts: the parish church with its graveyard to
the S, and the ruin with excavated foundations and the remainder of
the churchyard fenced off to the N. Here the **parish church** will be
taken first. The plan is a T as was normal in 18th-c. churches, the
cross-bar in this case on the site of the knights' nave, and the stem
projecting S into the churchyard. Very pale grey paint throughout
and rich red carpet however mark the interior as something more
than a parish church, and the front stalls labelled Prior of Scotland,
Cross Bearer, Genealogist etc. confirm its status as the Priory
Church of the Order of St John, the equivalent in Scotland of the
Grand Priory Church at Clerkenwell in London. Slender iron
columns support galleries in all three arms, with heraldic panels on
each front, and plain flat coved ceilings contrast with high brass
chandeliers.

The **exterior** walls are plain stone and the roofs slated, with a little
square bellcote. Lines on the W walls of the medieval tower and S
transept indicate the roof levels of the original nave and aisle. It is
then worth going round the transept as far as the boundary fence to
see the fine four-light window with Geometric tracery, and the

massive saddleback-roofed tower of *c*.1200. The quire has totally disappeared and its original length is uncertain – if indeed it was ever built. The unusual height of the transepts (now slate-roofed) is accounted for by the sizeable rooms added on top in the 15th c., giving something of the air of a castle.

To reach them means going back to the road and taking a different entrance. In the N wall of the parish church are parts of the jambs and shafts of the 13th-c. doorway that led from the S walk of the cloister. The four **cloister** walks have been clearly laid out as paths; a few bits of stonework survive alongside them and on the site of the refectory and other buildings beyond.

The **transepts** and crossing all have quadripartite vaults with ridge ribs; the S transept is noticeably bigger than the N, and slightly later in date. The E and W arches of the crossing are both blocked, that of the nave having pieces of a monument of 1538 in the infill. On the wall above can be detected a pattern of painted lines to resemble ashlar joints. The Geometric window already noted dominates the S transept; below it is a tomb recess with a little window through the back, and nearby a piscina. Below the lancet window in the E wall are traces of a painted diaper pattern, while in the W wall is a blocked arch that led to the former S aisle; incised into the plaster here is a mason's working detail of the setting out of vault voussoirs.

The N transept is interesting for carved inscriptions on the vault: 'IHS' and 'MARIA' on the central boss, 'TRINITAS' where the ribs meet it, and on the ridge running S a reference to the early 15th-c. preceptor Sir Andrew Meldrum. A circular stone stair in the NW pier of the tower leads to the bell chamber, which has a collection of stone fragments, and to the rooms on either side over the transepts, where an exhibition is mounted.

A stone like a milestone with a cross on top near the W end of the church is thought to mark the centre of a sanctuary area. This extended a mile in all directions, and other stones have been found that probably indicate its limits. Several buildings in the vicinity seem to contain stone from the many preceptory buildings which have disappeared.

Tullibardine Collegiate Church, Tayside NN 910134
3 miles W of Auchterarder and ½ mile N of Crieff road A823

Collegiate chapel of the Holy Trinity intended to be founded 1446
by Sir David Murray.

Owned by Earl of Perth and in care of Secretary of State for
Scotland. Accessible at all times: key at farmhouse opposite.

It seems fairly certain that the projected college of priests was never
actually established. Although therefore technically disqualified
from inclusion here, it is architecturally one of the most perfect and
unaltered examples of the private type of foundation. Even if the
college did not materialise, building appears to have continued: the
nave and transepts and the tower must have been added to the
mid-15th-c. chancel somewhere around 1500, judging from
architectural detail and from a coat of arms which refers to a
marriage of that time. The Murrays had a castle nearby, and
continued to use the chapel as a burial place after the Reformation.
Described as a ruin about 1900, it has since been sensitively
restored.

Set almost on its own in rolling countryside, the slate-roofed chapel
has a diminutive tower but is otherwise an almost exact Greek cross
in plan. The S doorway, round-headed with imposts rather than
capitals, leads into a curiously dark empty **interior** with partly
ancient timber collared roofs. There is a holy water stoup just
inside. The transept arches are segmental, and the crossing is
reached down two steps that would have coincided with the position
of a transverse screen. In the N transept a small explanatory
exhibition is mounted; a piscina marks the site of an altar nearby,
and there is another in the chancel. There is no E window except a
very small one high up. In the S transept an original consecration
cross can be faintly seen on the wall plaster, and in the arch jamb is
a small niche.
  Outside, another empty niche is half-way up the W face of the

tower; its parapet is modern. A complete circuit within the churchyard is prevented by the boundary wall being built right up to the N transept – no doubt enabling the founder's family to enter that part of the chapel direct from the lane.

From the S side the crow-stepped gables are conspicuous and attractive, and so is the very late flowing tracery of the S transept window. On the adjoining gable is the heraldry referred to above, which dates it to *c*.1500, while round on the N side of the chancel can be seen a shield combining the arms of Murray and Stewart, commemorating the founder's parents and thus about a century earlier. The window here is ogee-headed, with a curious imitation 'hood mould' merely incised on its lintel. The N transept gable (seen from outside the churchyard) has a two-light window of Decorated type and two more shields of rather later date than those on the chancel.

Whithorn Priory, Dumfries & Galloway   NX 444403
in town on A746

Premonstratensian cathedral priory probably founded *c*.1175 as
    daughter house of Soulseat abbey, on site of monastery originally
    established *c*.400.

In guardianship of Secretary of State for Scotland. Open during
    standard hours (admission charge).

Tradition says that the original monastery was founded by St Ninian, that he was born in the middle of the 4th c., and that he was buried in his own cathedral here in 432. About 727 a Northumbrian bishopric was established, and some time in the 12th c., after a period of Norse rule, the monastery was refounded as a Premonstratensian priory with the church as cathedral. This 12th-c. cathedral was cruciform: it was rebuilt much bigger in the 13th c. with aisled transepts and probably an aisled quire, and a cloister N of the nave. The nave, which never had aisles, was also extended westwards. A big chapel S of the E end was added about 1500. After the whole had fallen to ruin in the 16th c. the nave was repaired about 1635 to serve as a Protestant cathedral. It later became a Presbyterian parish church, but was again abandoned after a new church was built in 1822.

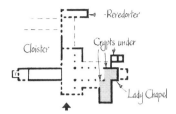

The approach to the **nave** is from the S, and the entrance,
confusingly, is in the E wall. This with its window is 17th-c. and the
actual doorway 18th-c. Inside, the present grass floor is 2 feet or so
above the original, as can be seen from the two empty 14th-c.
cinquefoil-headed tomb recesses on the right. Remains of a third
one are on the left, i.e. S of the doorway, and a fourth is near the
middle of the N wall. The prominent W gable is 18th-c., rebuilt (E
of its original position) after the tower had collapsed. The N wall,
on the right, has no windows because the cloister adjoined it; the
three big windows in the S wall were 15th-c. but have lost their
tracery. The many 19th- and 20th-c. memorials are of little interest.

Now the **outside**, taken clockwise. The shafted doorway at the E
end of the S wall was made up of the 13th- and 15th-c. work in the
1630s. The unusually rich Norman doorway near the W end may
have been re-set there when the nave was repaired c.1610. The ruined
walls beyond belonged to an early 17th-c. tower. Near it are a
number of interesting tombs, including a 'table' of 1790 on Ionic legs.

Looking along the N side: the church of 1822 is on the left.
Straight ahead, the terrace and reconstructed low wall represent the
E end of the cathedral, probably the Lady chapel. Further on and
below more masonry can be seen: this is a modern marking-out of
foundations that exist below the surface, possibly of St Ninian's
original church. It can be reached by turning towards the
churchyard gate and then taking the path on the left. On the left
first, however, is a long low vaulted chamber, the crypt of the SE
chapel. Further on, under the terrace, is another crypt and beyond
that a small re-roofed 14th-c. building which may have been a
sacristy. The key to these crypts, which contain many carved stone
fragments, can be got from the museum, which is on the left of the
lane leading back to the burgh. In the museum, too, are numerous
interesting crosses and carved stones from this and other sites.

Appendix

Authenticated monasteries and collegiate churches which have left no traces though in some instances the site is known more or less accurately. Those which only existed up to about the twelfth century are omitted.

Aberdeen	Grampian	Red Friars
Aberdour	Fife	Franciscan nunnery
Ayr	Strathclyde	Blackfriars
Dalmilling	Strathclyde	Gilbertine priory
Dirleton	Lothian	Red Friars
Dundee	Tayside	Blackfriars
Dundee	Tayside	Franciscan nunnery
Dunrossness	Zetland	Collegiate church
Edinburgh	Lothian	Dominican nunnery (Sciennes)
Edinburgh	Lothian	St Mary in the Fields (Collegiate)
Edinburgh	Lothian	Whitefriars
Elcho	Tayside	Benedictine nunnery
Fogo	Borders	Tironensian priory
Glasgow	Strathclyde	Greyfriars
Haddington	Lothian	Blackfriars
Houston	Lothian	Red Friars
Inverbervie	Grampian	Whitefriars
Irvine	Strathclyde	Whitefriars
Jedburgh	Borders	Greyfriars
Kingussie	Highland	Whitefriars
Markle	Lothian	Collegiate church
Perth	Tayside	Augustinian nunnery
Renfrew	Strathclyde	Cluniac priory
Rhynd or Rindalgros	Tayside	Benedictine (priory?)
Scotlandwell	Tayside	Red Friars
Selkirk	Borders	Tironensian abbey (moved to Kelso)
Stirling	Central	Greyfriars
Strathfillan	Tayside	Augustinian priory
Tullilum	Tayside	Whitefriars
Urquhart	Grampian	Benedictine priory
Wigtown	Dumfries & Galloway	Blackfriars

Glossary

Abbess The head of an abbey of nuns.

Abbey A monastery having an abbot or abbess at its head. The traditional definition requires there to be at least twelve monks or nuns.

Abbot The head of an abbey of monks or canons.

Aisle An outer part of the body of a church, separated by an arcade and usually less tall. The colloquial meaning, a walkway between pews, is misleading. In Scotland the use is extended to transepts and similar projecting parts, particularly those preserved for use for family burials.

Almonry A building where alms were given to the sick and needy.

Altarpiece An ornamental panel, particularly one containing a painting, behind an altar.

Ambulatory A passageway, especially for processions, particularly one leading from one side of a church to the other behind the high altar.

Anchorite A solitary religious person (female sometimes Anchoress).

Apse A semicircular or polygonal (usually semi-octagonal) termination to a church or chapel, particularly common in Norman work. In Scotland polygonal apses continued to be built, under French influence, up to the close of the Gothic period. Adjective = apsidal.

Arcade A row of arches, either free-standing to separate an aisle or walkway, or attached to a wall as ornament or strengthening.

Ashlar Finely squared stonework.

Aumbry A cupboard or recess for sacred vessels, often in the wall to the N of an altar.

Ball-flower A common ornament of the Decorated style.

Barrel *See Tunnel vault and Waggon roof.*

Basket arch A flat arch with rounded ends of small radius.

Battlements Interruptions in the line of a parapet, originally for defensive purposes (e.g. arrow-shooting) but later usually for ornament.

Bay A unit of building, consisting for example of one arch of an arcade, one window or set of windows at each level, and one set of vault ribs.

Belfry A part of a tower where bells are hung (not where they are rung from, which is the ringing chamber).

Bishop The chief church dignitary of a diocese.

Boss A piece of wood or stone, often carved, covering an intersection of vault ribs or roof timbers.

Brass A flat metal memorial plaque with incised effigy, heraldry, inscription, etc., usually originally filled with enamel and let into a stone. Hardly any survive in Scotland.

Buttress A projection from a wall to stiffen it and to help support particular loads, especially side-thrusts from roofs.

Cadaver An effigy in the form of an emaciated corpse.

Calefactory The warming house, the only room in early monasteries to be heated.

Campanile   A bell-tower: usually a detached one, as at Cambuskenneth.

Candelabrum   A multiple candle-holder.

Canon   A member of a priestly order (in the Middle Ages the Augustinians and Premonstratensians in particular) with headquarters at an abbey. The same word also means a cathedral dignitary entitled to a stall in the quire, a church decree, a metal loop on a bell, or a piece of music in which one subject is repeated by different parts.

Canopy   A covering or hood, used to add dignity to seats, pulpits, memorials, etc.

Capital, Cap   The uppermost part of a column; in classical architecture carved in one of a number of set patterns (Tuscan, Greek or Roman Doric, Ionic, Corinthian, Composite) and in Romanesque and Gothic more freely.

Cartouche   An imitation rolled-up scroll: used particularly to describe wall-monuments of similar informal shapes.

Cell   A small dependent community.

Cellarium   The cellarer's or storekeeper's building, usually the range W of the cloister.

Chancel   The eastern part of a church (not usually applied to monasteries).

Chantry   A very small chapel endowed for a priest to say masses for a dead person.

Chapter house   The meeting room for business of a monastic chapter, consisting of the abbot (in the case of an abbey) and monks or canons.

Choir   See Quire.

Cinquefoil   A cusped decoration, dividing an arch or a circle into five lobes.

Classical   Descriptive of ancient Greek and Roman architecture in general and the styles derived from them.

Clerestory   Upper windows letting light in over the roof of an aisle.

Cloister   A covered passage around a quadrangle or garth at the side of a (usually) monastic church, linking the principal rooms. Adjective = claustral.

Collegiate church   One with a college of priests or chapter but no bishop.

Commendator   The grantee of monastic revenues at the Reformation, successor to the abbots and often himself an ecclesiastic.

Communion rail   The low rail or wall in front of an altar at which communion is taken.

Conversi   See Lay brothers.

Corbel   A projection from a wall, usually of stone, supporting a roof member or a jutting wall.

Corinthian   An order of Classical architecture, with bell-shaped capitals decked with acanthus leaves.

Cornice   The projecting upper part of a wall, particularly on a Classical building. See Entablature.

Corrodiar   A person granted a life pension and accommodation (in the case of laymen, on payment of a lump sum or corrody).

Credence   A shelf for sacramental vessels.

Cresting   An ornamental, often openwork, band along the top of a wall or fitting.

Crocket   A small repetitive leafy ornament, particularly on the side of a pinnacle or spire.

Crossing   The part of the church where the nave and chancel (or presbytery or quire) and the transepts intersect, often crowned with a tower.

Crow-stepped   Of a gable: rising in squared steps instead of being sloped. Also called corbie-stepped.

Cruciform   Cross-shaped: particularly applied to a church plan. Haddington and, on a smaller scale, Dunglass, are good examples.

Crypt   A substructure, often vaulted and sometimes used for burials.

Cupola   A little ornamental dome, usually Classical in detail.

Cusp   A pointed projection in Gothic tracery.

Day stair   To the dorter from the cloisters, usually near the SE corner.

Decorated   The second principal style of English Gothic, *c.*1250–1360. Tracery is either Geometric or Curvilinear. Columns and arches are richly moulded. Carving is luxuriant and often naturalistic. Vaults have tiercerons and sometime lierne ribs. Smaller arches are often ogee-shaped.

Diocese   The territory served by one cathedral and its bishop.

Dissolution   Of monasteries, the act of dissolving or breaking up, with particular reference to that of the mid-sixteenth century. *See Reformation.*

Dog-tooth   A little repetitive pyramidal ornament common in Early English work.

Dome   A part-spherical dome or roof.

Doocot   Dovecot.

Doric   An order of Classical architecture (differing somewhat between Greek and Roman) with plain capitals.

Dorter or Dormitory   A monastic sleeping-hall.

Early English   The first principal style of English Gothic, *c.*1140–1260. Windows are mostly simple lancets or combinations of them with, sometimes, elementary tracery. Columns and openings often have attached shafts of darker stone such as Purbeck marble, and capitals of springing or 'stiff-leaf' foliage. Dog-tooth was the favourite ornamental moulding, but naturalistic or figure carving is common. Vaults are usually quadripartite.

Effigy   A statue, usually of stone and often horizontal on a tomb.

Embattled   With battlements.

Entablature   The element of Classical design above the columns, consisting of cornice, frieze and architrave.

Façade A principal front of a building.

Fan vault A type of vault invented in England in the fourteenth century, in the form of inverted concave half-cones.

Farmery A corruption of 'infirmary'.

Feretory The setting of the principal shrine of a church, usually behind the high altar.

Flamboyant The final phase of French Gothic, contemporary with English Perpendicular and found in less ornate form in Scotland (Melrose). It makes play with flowing curves in the tracery.

Flèche A small spire mounted on a roof.

Flying buttress A buttress in the form of a part-arch, especially one transferring the thrust from a high vault across the roof of an aisle.

Font A ceremonial basin for baptism.

Four-centred arch A shallow, pointed arch based on arcs of circles described from four centres, the end ones having a smaller radius than the middle ones.

Frater A monastic refectory or dining hall. In this book the word Refectory is used.

Fretted Pierced with a pattern.

Friars Religious men of various orders bound by vows like monks, but wandering instead of being confined to monasteries.

Galilee A large porch (usually W), sometimes enlarged into a chapel. St Andrews had one.

Gallery An upper floor overlooking the main one, for congregational use, for organ or musicians, or for maintenance: *see Loft*.

Gargoyle A fancifully carved water spout.

Garth A garden, especially inside a cloister.

Geometric A kind of tracery; *see Decorated*.

Gothic The pointed-arched style of architecture.

Grange An outlying dependency of a monastery, in the form of a farm establishment.

Groin The intersection between planes of a vault. A groin vault (typical of early Norman work) has no ribs.

Grotesque Fanciful carving, e.g. of dragons and monsters.

Guest house An often separate building used for visitors' accommodation.

Habit A monk's dress. That of Cistercians and Premonstratensians is white: that of Benedictines, Augustinians and Cluniacs black.

Hagioscope An opening in a wall or pier to give a view of an altar (also called a squint).

Hammer-beam A projecting bracket giving support clear of the side walls to the main trusses of a timber roof.

Indent The hollow in a stone to receive a memorial brass.

Infirmary Sick quarters, looked after by the Infirmarer.

Ionic An order of Classical architecture with twin-volute (spiral) capitals.

Italianate Italian in character, particularly in imitation of medieval styles.

Jamb The vertical side of an opening.

Jesse tree A family tree showing the descent of Jesus from Jesse: a favourite subject for glass.

Kirk Synonymous with the English 'church'.

Lady chapel A chapel dedicated to the Virgin Mary.

Lancet A single tall pointed window of the Early English style.

Lane In Cistercian monasteries, an open area between the W cloister walk and the W range, for use by the lay brothers.

Lantern tower A tower with clerestory or similar windows above the surrounding roofs.

Lavatory or Laver A washplace, usually just outside the refectory.

Lay brothers or Conversi A community of workers, separate from fully professed monks, in a Cistercian monastery.

Lean-to A single-sloping roof, as over an aisle.

Leat A small stream, often an artificial branch for drainage purposes.

Lectern A reading desk on a stand, often in the form of a brass eagle. A fine one from Holyrood is now at St Albans (St Stephen's church).

Ledger-stone A flat grave slab in a floor, usually with deeply incised lettering.

Lierne A linking rib in a vault, not a tierceron or ridge rib. Lierne vaults were first built late in the thirteenth century.

Light A subdivision of a multiple window.

Locutorium *See Parlour.*

Loft A gallery. In England the word survives in the terms organ loft and rood loft, but in Scotland it embraces all church galleries, particularly those of trades and guilds.

Loops Arrow slits or other wall openings for defence.

Manse Minister's house.

Matrix The hollow or indent in which a memorial brass is fixed.

Minster An inexact term implying a one-time monastery.

Misericord A ledge on the tip-up seat of a stall, intended to provide rest for infirm clergy during long periods of standing. The undersides often have fanciful and humorous carvings. Also a name for a room where meat eating was allowed.

Mitre The ceremonial headgear of a bishop or of an abbot of the same rank. Also a junction between mouldings running in different directions.

Monastery A group of buildings housing a community of monks, canons or nuns.

Mouldings The continuous contours of arches and other parts of buildings and furniture.

Mullions The vertical posts separating the lights of a window.

Narthex   A western compartment of a church, bigger than a porch.

Nave   The main congregational part of a church, in abbeys often used by lay brothers or others of the community.

Necessarium   *See Reredorter.*

Niche   A recess for a statue.

Night stair   To the dorter from the church (usually from a transept).

Norman   The Romanesque, round-arched style of 1066–*c*.1190. Window, doorway and other arches are usually semicircular (or sometimes semi-elliptical) and, especially in later work, ornamented with zigzag and other repetitive patterns. Vaults are quadripartite, groined in early work and ribbed in later. Ornamental sculpture contains a high proportion of grotesque and often semi-barbaric elements.

Ogee   A wave-like shape formed by alternate concave and convex curves, either in small arches (with two such curves meeting at the apex), frequent in Decorated work, or in mouldings.

Order   One of several arches round a doorway. Also used to describe a standard unit of Classical design, consisting of entablature, column and base (*see Capital*).

Orientation   The placing of a building in relation to points of the compass. Traditionally a church altar is at the E end.

Parlour   A room where talking is permitted, sometimes called the Locutorium.

Pediment   A triangular gable-end or features over an opening in Classical architecture.

Pend   A covered way, for example under a part-ruined gatehouse.

Pendentive   One of the triangular spandrels below a dome when it is supported on a square base.

Pentise   Covered porch or way.

Perpendicular   The last principal phase of English Gothic, *c*.1340 onwards, characterised by vertical patterns in tracery and wall-panelling and a general impression of height and light. Windows are large. Arches are often four-centred. Ornament is often conventionalised: foliage, flowers and heraldry. Vaulting is usually complex, either broken into small compartments by liernes or of fan type. Timber roofs are often almost flat.

Pier   A mass of masonry supporting part of a building and not necessarily joined to a wall.

Pilaster   A projection from a wall in the form of a flattened 'column'.

Pinnacle   A common Gothic upward termination, sometimes provided to add weight and stability.

Piscina   A stone basin for washing consecrated vessels.

Poppyhead   An ornamental top to a seat-end, usually carved with foliage (not with poppies, the word being a corruption of *poupée*).

Precinct   The immediate surrounds enclosed by a boundary wall.

Presbytery   Either the E part of a church containing the altar, or a priest's residence.

Priory   A monastery having a prior as its head. Many monastic cathedrals had priors (e.g. St Andrews) and ranked as abbeys.

Pulpit   An enclosed platform for preaching or reading.

Pulpitum   A heavy stone screen to the W of a quire, sometimes containing small chapels or other rooms.

Quadripartite   The simplest type of vault over a rectangular or square bay, divided into four segments.

Quatrefoil   A cusped decoration dividing a circle into four lobes.

Quire or Choir   Architecturally the part of a greater church intended to contain the stalls of dignitaries and singers and usually E of the crossing. In this book the spelling 'choir' is reserved for those who sing. In Scotland, however, the version 'quire' is regarded as archaic. In many abbeys the ritual quire has been extended beyond the architectural one.

Range   A long building, especially one bounding a cloister.

Refectory   Monastic dining hall, also called a Frater.

Reformation   The change in Church doctrines and organisation in Britain and elsewhere early in the sixteenth century, when the authority of Rome was increasingly rejected by the so-called Protestants. The Dissolution of the Monasteries was part of this process.

Renaissance   Rebirth; particularly applied to Classical architecture as revived in Britain in the sixteenth to nineteenth centuries.

Reredorter   An annexe to a monastic dormitory containing garderobes and therefore built over a drain or stream; sometimes called the Necessarium.

Reredos   A screen or panelling behind an altar.

Respond   A corbel at the end of an arcade instead of a pilaster or half-column.

Retro-quire   The part of a large church immediately behind the quire.

Rib   One unit of the main framework of a vault.

Ridge   The apex-line of a double-sloping roof or ceiling.

Romanesque   One of the round-arched styles derived from Classical Roman architecture, in Britain principally Norman.

Rood   Crucifix, especially one hanging at a chancel or quire entrance or set on a rood screen.

Rusticated   Cut into strongly marked blocks to give an effect of strength, especially around openings and at corners.

Sacrament house   Aumbry or cupboard for safe keeping of reserved sacrament close to altar.

Sacristy   Room close to an altar, where sacramental vessels are kept.

Sanctuary   The part of a church within a communion rail and containing an altar.

Sedilia   Priests' seats within a sanctuary, usually of stone.

Sexpartite   A French form of vaulting in which one unit of six segments covers two bays.

Shaft   A small column, especially one attached or partially attached to a larger member.

Shrine   A housing of a saint's body or relics.

Slype   A passage out of a cloister, particularly on the E side.

Spandrel   A space between two shapes, especially between an arch and its enclosing rectangle, often used for ornament.

Spire   A pointed termination, usually on a tower, and usually either of stone or framed in wood. A broach spire is an octagonal one with broaches or part-pyramidal corner supports where it rises from a square base.

Springer   The lowest stone of an arch or vault.

Stalls   Dignitaries' or singers' seats in a quire.

Steeple   A tower and/or spire.

Stews   Fishponds.

Stoup   A basin for holy water at a church entrance.

String course   Horizontal projecting stone band.

Teinds   Tithes or tenths given to the church in kind, i.e. in the form of goods.

Tester   A suspended canopy, especially over an altar or pulpit.

Throne   A ceremonial seat, for example for an abbot.

Tierceron   One of a group of ribs rising from the base of a vault and reaching the ridge.

Tolbooth   Literally a tax office; a building usually containing also a council chamber and burgh prison.

Tomb-chest   A box-like structure, usually of stone, often highly ornamented and carrying an effigy of the person commemorated, and ostensibly containing his or her body.

Tracery   Patterns in the heads of Gothic windows and elsewhere.

Transept   A cross-arm of a church, projecting N and/or S from a crossing, and usually of similar height to the nave and chancel or quire.

Transitional   An architectural style between two clearly defined ones; particularly applied to that between Norman and Early English when round and pointed arches occur. In Scotland the use of round arches continued much later.

Trefoil   A cusped decoration of three lobes.

Triforium   A gallery below an aisle roof, or the arcade screening it from the nave. The gallery is also called a tribune.

Triptych   A three-panelled picture, with the outer panels often hinged to fold over the centre.

Trumeau   An ornamental column dividing the parts of a twin doorway.

Truss   A single unit of a roof frame, usually triangular in form.

Tudor   The last phrase of Perpendicular architecture in England, characterised by four-centred arches, fan and similar vaulting, and over-all panelling of surfaces. Many chantries and tombs are in this style.

Tunnel or Barrel vault   A part-cylindrical vault, usually twelfth-century or earlier.

Tympanum   A semicircular panel, especially one within a Norman door-arch.

Undercroft   Basement or crypt.

Vault   A stone roof on the arch principle, usually rectangular in plan, or an imitation in wood and plaster.

Vesica   A two-pointed shape formed by the intersecting arcs of two equal circles.

Vestry   A robing room.

Voussoir   One stone of an arch.

Waggon or Barrel roof   A framed timber roof of part-cylindrical shape.

Walk   One side of a square cloister.

Wall-arcade   A low blank arcade usually at the base of a wall, either ornamental or for strengthening or to form a series of canopies.

Warming house   *See Calefactory.*

Yett   Gate or gateway.